Competition Law and Policy in Japan and the EU

Competition Law and Policy in Japan and the EU

Etsuko Kameoka

Van Bael & Bellis, Belgium

Edward Elgar

Cheltenham, UK • Northampton, MA, USA

Published by
Edward Elgar Publishing Limited
The Lypiatts
15 Lansdown Road
Cheltenham
Glos GL50 2JA
UK

Edward Elgar Publishing, Inc.
William Pratt House
9 Dewey Court
Northampton
Massachusetts 01060
USA

A catalogue record for this book
is available from the British Library

Library of Congress Control Number: 2013944948

This book is available electronically in the ElgarOnline.com Law Subject Collection, E-ISBN 978 1 78100 056 4

MIX
Paper from responsible sources
FSC® C013056
FSC
www.fsc.org

ISBN 978 1 78100 055 7

Typeset by Columns Design XML Ltd, Reading
Printed and bound in Great Britain by T.J. International Ltd, Padstow

Contents

Preface

The last several years have been particularly challenging for the enforcement of Japanese competition law, which has faced turbulent political and economic situations. The regulation and policy implications arising from these recent changes in Japan have not yet resulted in much literature written in English. This book is intended to go some way towards filling the gap, and in doing so it takes account of an additional challenge confronting Japan: the increasing globalisation of competition law. In a global competition world, the unique developments of EU competition law and policy are drawing increasing attention, while the role of competition law and policy in Japan has never been more important than now. The growth of international competition investigations and the spread of bilateral and multilateral competition agreements have resulted in increasing convergence, affecting almost all jurisdictions of the world. This has brought about many changes in the competition law and policy of both the EU and Japan.

Against this background, I endeavour in this work to embark on a fundamental comparative analysis of competition law and policy in Japan and the EU after practising EU competition law in Brussels for around 15 years. The basic questions concern fundamental differences in the approach of these jurisdictions and the actual and potential impact of the EU approach on the current and future enforcement in Japan. This quest grew into a broader exploration that sometimes carried me into the fields of history, art and literature.

To analyse these questions, this book aims to provide a clear and well researched exposition of the differences between the relevant rules, systems and underlying ideas found in the competition laws of Japan and the EU. The book also includes reflections on the past and recent case law in the EU and Japan, and discusses current debates that suggest future directions in competition law and policy.

In my concluding observations, I note that Japan has become increasingly motivated to examine foreign models, especially that of the EU, and to incorporate desired elements into the Japanese system. At first glance this may seem like a new development, but a more accurate understanding requires a broader historical perspective. A key point advanced in the book is that not only do Japan and Europe have an even longer history of cultural and scientific exchanges than that of Japan and the US, but EU competition law also appears more to fit into the Japanese competition enforcement culture.

I am grateful to the many people who helped me with this project. In particular, I wish to thank Professor Mitsuo Matsushita and Professor Eleanor Fox for reading my drafts and giving their valuable comments and encouragement. I am also indebted to Professor Mel Marquis for his very instructive feedback and editing of my earlier draft. In addition, Mr Yves Devellennes and several other officials of the JFTC and European Commission have kindly read the manuscripts and provided me with their useful comments. I also thank the team of Edward Elgar Publishing for their precious support.

Needless to say, the opinions expressed in this book are solely the personal views of the author.

8 September 2013
Brussels

Table of cases

JAPANESE CASES

JFTC Decisions

Japanese Court Judgments

EU CASES

European Commission Decisions

Court of Justice of the European Communities/European Union

European Court of Justice

General Court

US CASE

1. Introduction

LASTING CONNECTION AND DIALOGUE BETWEEN THE EU AND JAPAN

Although Europeans colonised many Asian countries between the sixteenth and eighteenth centuries, Japan miraculously avoided European colonisation, so to speak, and maintained its traditional culture. The first contact with the Europeans occurred when Portuguese missionaries arrived in *Chipangu* (Japan) in 1543. Europeans at that time were interested in this island particularly because merchant travellers such as Marco Polo depicted Japan as a symbol of richness. The European missionaries also imagined, in the wake of the Reformation, that as first movers they could seek to develop Catholicism in Japan because it was not known as a territory targeted by other religions such as Islam or Judaism. In 1549, the Jesuit missionary Francis Xavier arrived in Kagoshima, a southern part of Japan, and was authorised by the *Daimyo* (feudal lord) to be engaged in missionary work and to communicate European culture to the local people. The missionaries stayed in Japan not only to propagate religion; they also became advisors to the *Daimyo* and his subordinate for military and commercial issues. The trade between Spain/Portugal and Japan during this period was called *nanban boeki*. The Europeans imported Western medicine, founded a hospital where the first surgery in Japan was undertaken, and established the first orphanage in the country.[1,2] One of the characteristics of *nanban boeki* was that it was closely related to the spread of Christianity. Through the

---

1 José de Freitas Ferraz, 'Looking forward to 470 years of Japan-Portugal "Kizuna" bonds', *The Japan Times* (Tokyo, 10 June 2012).

2 See, e.g., Fréderic Mantienne, 'Commerce occidental et sociétés asiatiques, XVIIe–XVIIIe siècles, les marchands européens au contact des pratiques commerciales et des sociétés locales', in Martine Raibaurd and François Souty (eds), *Europe-Asie, Echanges, Ethiques et Marchés*, XVIIe–XXIe siècles (Les Indes Savantes, 2004) pp. 60–62.

missionaries, Japan added European and Christian cultures to its own, which had already incorporated Confucian and Buddhist cultures.[3,4]

Confucianism seems to have arrived in Japan in approximately the third century AD and it became an important basis for Japanese philosophy. It has been disseminated in virtually every corner of Japan from daily life to academic work without being visibly identified. In contrast with the influence of Christianity in Europe, the influence of Confucianism is so embedded in Japanese culture and custom that it cannot be clearly distinguished from the other elements that have affected them as well.

Confucianism was developed by Confucius in China and was integrated into the fields of, among other things, culture, philosophy, politics, education, economics, history, art, literature and military science. Later, it became a central determinant of moral and ethical principles and a foundation for ideology and philosophy in other countries, including Japan. Competition is normally rooted in comparison and creates a winner and a loser. However, basic Japanese moral philosophy attached more value to social harmony, order and consensus, mainly owing to the influence of Confucianism.

More importantly for the purposes of this book, Confucius, who was a politician as well, created a political ideology of benevolent government and his philosophy contributed to the consolidation and development of Chinese culture and the economy through a wise government and a thoughtful ruler.[5] As he preached on how to govern the people in particular in difficult situations, Confucius has had an impact not only on the spirits of the people governed but also on the basic philosophy of those who govern the people such as the government and public authority. Although it is true that the traditional credibility of official bureaucracy has deep roots in Europe too, Japanese psychological

---

[3] For details see, e.g., Teizo Kitamura, 'Portugal in the Age of European Expansion and the Introduction of Boobura (Pumpkin) into Japan', *Journal of Osaka Aoyama Junior College*, **25** (1999) 229–35 (in Japanese).

[4] In addition, Japanese culture is also based on other concepts including Shintoism and Taoism. Shinto is an indigenous spiritual concept in Japan, while Taoism was essentially 'imported' from China. Neo-Confucianism, which is a mixture of Confucian and Buddhist beliefs, was considered to be introduced into Japan at the turn of the twelfth and thirteenth centuries. See, e.g., Kong Xianglin, *Confucius* (Foreign Languages Press, 2010) p. 180.

[5] Ibid. at p. 5.

reliance, to a comparable degree, on public authority and on social norms favouring hierarchy may also be observed.[6]

Confucianism was also promulgated in Europe, but much later. *The Travels of Marco Polo* was considered the first book that made Confucius known to the Western world. Italian missionary Matteo Ricci arrived in China in 1582 and was the first to translate Confucian canons into a Western language, enabling an academic exchange between Europe and China. During the seventeenth century, Europe's attention to China was focused on Confucian doctrine, and numerous scholars and philosophers were influenced by Confucianism. Voltaire, who was the leader of the eighteenth-century Enlightenment movement, advocated Confucianism in his numerous publications. François Quesnay, a French economist of the eighteenth century, admired the economic doctrine and political principles preached by Confucius, and was himself highly regarded by his contemporaries as the 'Confucius of Europe'.[7] Thus, the philosophical base of Confucianism so important in Japan was already known to Europe a long time ago and shared with Europeans. For instance, in Europe the idea of a 'benevolent government and ruler' has been incorporated through Christianity and was, to a lesser extent, influenced by Confucianism.

In 1624, Japan decided to exclude the Spaniards and then in 1639 the Portuguese from its territory and close itself to the outside world under the *sakoku* (seclusion) policy. This decision came from the fear of the wider spread of Christianity in Japan. However, trade exchanges between the Japanese and the Europeans quietly continued. Holland was the only European country that escaped this ban and was exclusively allowed to come to Japan owing to its economic prosperity and rather weak link to Christianity.[8] At that time, in the Netherlands, numerous important academic and revolutionary books were being published. For instance, the first edition of *The Discourses and Mathematical Demonstrations Relating to Two New Sciences* by Galileo Galilei as well as *Meditation on*

---

[6] See Frank Gibney, 'Introduction', in Frank Gibney, *Unlocking the Bureaucrat's Kingdom: Deregulation and the Japanese Economy* (The Brooking Institute, 1998) p. 9. Of course, trust in public institutions and governments in Europe, Japan and elsewhere is eroding significantly (without being replaced by greater trust in market-based institutions, for obvious reasons).

[7] Wei-Bin Zhang, *On Adam Smith and Confucius: The Theory of Moral Sentiments and the Analects* (Nova Publishers, 2000) pp. 22–28.

[8] In Japan and China, the European traders were under stricter control of the governors than those from Tonkin, Cochinchina, Burma and Siam. For further details, see Mantienne, supra note 2 at pp. 59–60.

the First Philosophy by René Descartes had been published in the Netherlands, partly because of the country's lenient attitude towards religion. Numerous publications were imported by the Dutch into Japan and developed *rangaku*, which at first meant 'Dutch learning' and at a later stage came to mean 'Western (European) learning of scientific and technological knowledge in Japan'. In turn, Dutch literature that depicted Japan and Japanese culture was published in the Netherlands and sold elsewhere in Europe. Furthermore, the Dutch continued to import Japanese objects such as porcelain, painting and clothes (*kimono*) and the Japanese tea ceremony, kabuki and architecture.[9] The European interest in Japanese culture reached its peak in the 1880s but it arose much earlier. The word *Japonisme* was created in 1872 by the French author and collector Philippe Burty to indicate a new area of study of artistic, historic and ethnographic borrowings from the Japanese arts.[10, 11]

Accordingly, even during the *sakoku* seclusion period (whose fundamental purpose was not economic isolation but rather, as suggested above, to remove a perceived threat to the social order posed by religious and potentially colonialist influences of Portuguese and Spanish origin), commercial trade and cultural and scientific exchanges between Europe and Japan still actively continued.[12] In the seventeenth century, despite the *sakoku*, many Europeans visited Japan and *Ieyasu Tokugawa*, the 'King of Chipangu', appointed William Adams, an Englishman, as a foreign advisor. Adams taught Tokugawa European sciences such as

---

9 Discovery of Japanese art in Europe mainly started with the universal exposition in Paris in 1867. See Yvan Daniel, 'Le baron Charles-Gustave de Chassiron et Paul Clauel au Japon: Les éventails du voyageur', in Martine Raibaurd and François Souty (eds), cited supra note 2, p. 123.

10 It is well known that Van Gogh imported Japanese prints and used them for his paintings. The numerous other artists who were influenced by *Japonisme* and gave a new direction to the arts included Renoir, Monet, Whistler, Munch, Gallé and Puccini. See, e.g., Lionel Lambourne, *Japonisme: Cultural Crossings between Japan and the West* (Phaidon, 2005).

11 For the influence of Europe, and in particular of France, on Japan during the nineteenth century, see, e.g., Robert Calvet, 'La faiblesse de la présence française dans le japon du XIXème siècle', in Martine Raibaurd and François Souty (eds), cited supra note 2, pp. 91–101.

12 Professor Oshima (a historian) has explained that the impression the Japanese word *sakoku* gives is misleading, because one of the Chinese characters used to write *sakoku* has the meaning of chains, but it is wrong to consider that Japan was completely subjugated by the Japanese rulers and completely secluded from the rest of the world during the early modern period. See Akihide Oshima, 'Name of "Sakoku Soho"', Prefectural University of Kumamoto, *Bunsai*, **6** (2010) 29, at 30 (in Japanese).

mathematics and navigation. European influence came to Japan indirectly as well, through other Asian countries such as China, and the exotic aspects of European culture understandably appealed to the public in the period of seclusion since the law prohibited Japanese people from travelling abroad.[13] Indeed, isolation under the *sakoku* regime made the people even more curious and prepared to absorb Western culture.

Japan opened its frontiers 250 years later to the industrialized nations.[14] During the Meiji era, which started in 1868 and ended in 1912, exchanges in the field of culture, science, economy and law became significantly active and this gave rise to the famous words *bunmei kaika* (civilization and enlightenment) Some studied law and economics in Europe at schools such as Leiden University in the Netherlands and published what they learned after returning to Japan.[15] Numerous *rangaku* scholars played an important role in the modernisation of the country. *Rangaku* scholars generally took a pro-Western stance, but later some of them opposed European imperialism. One such scholar was Yukichi Fukuzawa, who visited Europe and the US and published enlightening works; he believed that Europe owed its advanced developments to an education system based on the principle of equal opportunity, national and individual independence, competition and communications. Although not all the cultural and industrial evolution coming from the Western world was smoothly integrated into traditional Japan,[16] the radical change from a feudal society to a modern society inspired by *bunmei kaika* were in general appreciated by Japanese society.

As comparative legal scholars know, the Japanese legal system supporting the enforcement of the Antimonopoly Act was also based largely on European models. Although the Antimonopoly Act itself was drafted

---

13 The popularity of Chikamatsu's Kabuki play *The Battles of Coxinga* (battles that lasted over 200 years) was partly attributed to the exotic appeal of its Chinese scenes to the Japanese public during the Tokugawa period. See Donald Keene, *Four Major Plays of Chikamatsu* (Columbia University Press, 1998).

14 For the European involvement during the opening of the Japanese territories, see, e.g., Calvet, supra note 11, pp. 92–93.

15 Amane Nishi and Mamichi Tsuda, who studied public international law in the Netherlands, published *Taisei Kokuho-ron* (A Treatise on Western Public Law) and *Elements of International Law,* respectively.

16 Modern Japanese novelist Soseki Natsume mentions in his publication *The Enlightenment of Modern Japan* that Japan's development in that period was driven mainly by external forces, while European growth was the result of endogenous factors. He also considers that it is natural that Japan could not digest everything at once when it faced so many novelties at the same time.

on the basis of US sources,[17] the Constitution of 1889 was influenced by Germany while the Japanese Civil Code was enacted in 1896 under the influence of the Code Napoléon and later revised following the German Civil Code.[18] The Law of Civil Procedure was based on the German model.[19] In addition, the current Commercial Code was enacted under mixed influences of the German, American and traditional Japanese rules.[20]

After World War II, amidst reconstruction efforts on both the losing and winning sides, Europe established the European Economic Community in 1957 to develop a common market. European leaders saw the need for a unified Europe unhampered by national political interests and economic protectionism, and to achieve conciliation between France and Germany.[21] Against this background, on 1 January 1958, the Treaty of Rome, with its distinctive competition provisions, entered into force. Thus, as in Japan, competition law in Europe was created in the context of economic and social crisis, in particular, the post-traumatic difficulties following the war.

In the meantime, Japan envisaged expanding market access on various national European markets. Confronting radically reduced productivity and decimated infrastructure in Europe, in the 1970s and 1980s, the bilateral relations between Europe and Japan were marked by trade

---

[17] See, e.g., Harry First, 'Antitrust in Japan: The Original Intent', *Pacific Rim Law and Policy Journal*, **9** (2000) 67–70. See also David J. Gerber, *Global Competition: Law, Markets, and Globalization* (Oxford University Press, 2010) p. 209. Japan does follow an imported Western model but it operates on principles and cultural patterns often quite different from those found in the US or the EU.

[18] For example, Gustave Emile Boissonade Fontarabie's immense contribution to the drafting of the Civil Code of 1890 is famous in Japan. Boissonade was also involved in drafting the criminal law. For the details of his work as a legal adviser to the Meiji government, and of his role in drafting legal codes and advancing legal education, see, e.g., Harushi Kishigami, 'Analysis of Introduction of Japanese Civil Law: Boissonade and Legislative Intent', *Chukyo Hogaku*, **30** (4) (April 1996) 7–37. See also Jean-Louis Sourioux (translated by Katsuhiko Yoshida), 'Boissonade's Influence on Drafting of the Japanese Civil Code', *Horitsu Jiho*, **71** (2) (1999) 40–47 (in Japanese).

[19] For the details on the process of drafting, see, e.g., Masahiro Suzuki, *History of the Law of Modern Civil Procedure: Japan* (Yuhikaku, 2004).

[20] For further details, see, e.g., Mitsuo Matsushita, *International Trade and Competition Law in Japan* (Oxford University Press, 1993) pp. 1–4.

[21] Pascal Fontaine, *Jean Monnet l'Inspirateur* (Jacques Grancher, Paris, 1988) pp. 53, 58–66.

frictions, and both became important players in the global market.[22] In the 1980s, the main cases before the European Commission involving Japanese companies concerned antidumping, but these were later overtaken by competition cases.

The foundations of modern relations between the EU and Japan were laid down in the Joint Declaration between Japan and the European Community and its Member States, signed in The Hague in 1991.[23] The Joint Declaration confirmed the need for enhanced cooperation between the parties. Following its adoption, a number of important summits and informal 'dialogues' have taken place with a view to strengthening trade and economic ties both on the bilateral and multilateral levels. Subsequently, the EU-Japan Regulatory Reform Dialogue was launched in 1994 and formalised in 1995.[24]

Subsequently, at the 2001 EU-Japan Summit an Action Plan was adopted, which signalled a new decade of reinforced partnership.[25] Special emphasis was put on ensuring improved market access in Japan by gradually removing entry barriers to trade and foreign investment.

In 2002 the EU-Japan Mutual Recognition Agreement came into force. This agreement allows both parties to accept a conformity assessment carried out by one party in accordance with the rules of the other in certain product areas.[26] This Agreement was perceived as an important step towards effective market access. Further, in 2003 the Agreement on Co-operation on Anti-Competitive Activities between the EU and Japan was signed by both parties.[27] The purpose of this Agreement is to facilitate cooperation and coordination of the Commission and JFTC to promote effectiveness of antitrust enforcement in both jurisdictions and reduce the likelihood of conflicting decisions. Moreover, a Free Trade Agreement between the EU and Japan is currently under negotiation.

---

22 For a history of EU-Japan relations, see, e.g., Hans Dietmar Schweisgut, 'The EU and Japan: The Way Forward of Two Likeminded Strategic Partners', in Globalization and Review on EU Integration (eds), *EU Studies in Japan*, **32** (EU Studies Association in Japan, 2012) 1.

23 Available on the European Commission's website at http://eeas.europa.eu/japan/docs/joint_pol_decl_en.pdf.

24 For further details, see the European Commission's explanation on External Action, available at http://eeas.europa.eu/japan/regulatory_reform_en.htm.

25 An Action Plan for EU-Japan Cooperation, available on the European Commission's website at http://eeas.europa.eu/japan/docs/actionplan2001_en.pdf.

26 Agreement on Mutual Recognition between the European Community and Japan, OJ L284/3-26.

27 Official Journal L183, 22.7.2003, pp. 12–17, available at http://eur-lex.europa.eu/LexUriServ/LexUriServ.do?uri=CELEX:22003A0722(01):EN:NOT.

Another significant channel of EU-Japan bilateral relations has been the Regulatory Reform Dialogue. As noted above, the Dialogue has aimed at reducing unnecessary and burdensome regulations hindering the development of trade and foreign investment. For the last two decades, the EU and Japan have actively participated in each other's regulatory reforms, mainly with a view to improving the rules governing the establishment of business and facilitating investment flows into Japan.[28] For instance, in Japan, the modernisation of EU competition policy of 2003 was appreciated as an example of regulatory reform that reduced the cost of conducting business.[29]

In 2009, the Liberal Democratic Party, which had pursued the principle of a free market economy together with the ideology of cooperation as a ruling party, was replaced by the Democratic Party of Japan, which places less emphasis on free market competition. However, regulatory reform has not been neglected by the DPJ; to the contrary, it has advanced in various sectors.

Ever since the *nanban boeki* trade with Spain and Portugal developed in the mid-sixteenth century, economic relations have been always at the centre of Europe-Japan relations. Competition law is a reflection of culture, politics, industrial and economic policies, and the EU and Japan have influenced each other for approximately 470 years, that is, for much longer than the duration of US-Japan diplomatic economic relations. It would not be surprising to find that there is more in common between the EU and Japan than between Japan and the US. Although after World Word II, for political reasons, Japan adopted its first competition law on the model of US statutes, it does not necessarily mean that the constitution of the competition culture in Japan was more similar to that of the US than to that of the EU. Rather, because Japanese competition law and policy adopted the US model at the outset, Japan developed its life and economy in an American-oriented way after World War II.

In light of the foregoing, this book proceeds on the premise that a comparative analysis of Japan and the EU will yield insights regarding both jurisdictions.[30] The main aims of the book are three: to compare the

---

28 The EU has cited the revision of the AMA as one of the results of the Regulatory Reform Dialogue. For further details see the European Commission's website at http://eeas.europa.eu/japan/regulatory_reform_en.htm.

29 See, e.g., Mitsuo Matsushita, 'The New Enforcement Rule of EU/EC Competition Law', *Journal of the Japanese Institute of International Business Law*, **31** (5) (2003) 616 (in Japanese).

30 In a recent Japanese-language work, Professor Takigawa undertakes a comparative approach to three jurisdictions, i.e., the EU, Japan and the US. See

EU and Japanese approaches to competition law and policy; to examine the reasons why there are differences and similarities between them; and to explore how the future enforcement of EU competition law and of the Japanese Antimonopoly Act could be developed in a harmonious way.

Toshiaki Takigawa, *Competition Laws and Policies in Japan, the US and the EU* (4th edn, Seirin Shoin, 2010). Another notable comparative study was conducted by Haley, who focused on Japan and Germany. See John O. Haley, *Antitrust in Germany and Japan: The First Fifty Years, 1947–1998* (University of Washington Press, 2001). The present book is the only one thus far in English, to our knowledge, presenting, from a legal perspective, detailed comparisons between Japan and the EU.

2. Historical background

A BRIEF HISTORY OF JAPANESE COMPETITION LAW IN COMPARISON WITH EU COMPETITION LAW

Before and After World War II

In Europe, during the last decade of the nineteenth century, a series of ideas concerning the regulation of competition was created.[1] Subsequently, the first European competition legislation was enacted in Germany in 1923. France enacted an *Ordonnance* in 1945 with fragmentary competition provisions, and the UK Monopolies and Restrictive Practices Act was adopted in 1948, followed by the Treaty of Paris, signed in 1951, and the Treaty of Rome, signed in 1957. By the time the latter Treaty was concluded, Germany was wrapping up eight years of legislative debates, which in the summer of that year culminated in the Act against Restrictions of Competition (GWB).[2] Thus, competition law was not *completely* new to the Europeans when the Treaty of Rome entered into force in 1958, although effective enforcement in Europe was still a long way off.

For the Japanese, the Act on Prohibition of Private Monopolization and Maintenance of Fair Trade ('AMA') was the first competition law,[3] and Japan had no prior experience whatsoever with competition law.[4] But the AMA has as long a history of enforcement as the Treaty of Rome does, in its various amended forms. The AMA was adopted on 31 March 1947 and it entered into force on 20 July 1947 after vigorous negotiations

1 See, e.g., David J. Gerber, *Law and Competition in Twentieth Century Europe: Protecting Prometheus* (Oxford University Press, 1998) p. 43.

2 Important momentum to the global spread of competition law was created by the imposition of decartelisation legislation and the 'export' of modern competition legislation into Germany and Japan after World War II. See Mark Jephcott, *Law of Cartels* (Jordan Publishing, 2011) p. 7.

3 Act No. 54 of 14 April 1947.

4 See, e.g., Shuya Hayashi, 'The Goal of Japanese Competition Law', in Josef Drexl, Laurence Idot and Joël Monéger (eds), *Economic Theory and Competition Law* (Edward Elgar, 2009) p. 57.

between the US and Japan.[5] The Japanese drafters often had to appease the Allied Occupation Forces in charge of Japan's post-war democratisation.[6] The Allied Occupation Forces criticised the Japanese economic system and introduced the Economic Democratisation Policy, which called for, among other things, the dissolution of the super-conglomerate *zaibatsu* firms. The unique background to the establishment of the JFTC was that it was set up according to the requirements of the GHQ (General Headquarters/Supreme Commander for the Allied Powers). This helped to ensure, in the early period, that the JFTC would be independent, in particular since it was modelled after the US Fair Trade Commission.[7] Some have argued that the AMA and other related measures were not adopted by Japan but were imposed by the USA. However, records indicate that the Japanese government vigorously participated in the legislative process, and that the Act reflected its views and ideas.[8] During the drafting of the original AMA, the preparatory work was allocated to the Japanese government. While the Ministry of Commerce and Industry was in charge of substantive law, the Ministry of Justice took care of procedural parts.

---

[5] As regards Japanese competition policy in the twentieth century, in particular insofar as it reflected Japanese industrial ethics, Professor Souty explains that Japan developed a competition policy adapted to its own needs, which (together with other factors) brought successful economic growth in the period from 1960 to 1990. According to Souty, although the logic of the AMA of 1947 followed Western judicial systems that were far from traditional Japanese politics, the content of the Act was drafted so that it could accommodate a dynamic post-war economy. See François Souty, 'La politique de la concurrence au Japon au XXe siècle: entre éthique et marché', in Martine Raibaud and François Souty (eds), *Europe-Asie, Echanges, Ethiques et Marchés, XVIIe–XXIe siècles* (Les Indes Savantes, 2004) pp. 189–204.

[6] Mitsuo Matsushita, 'The Antimonopoly Law of Japan', in J. David Richardson and Edward M. Graham (eds), *Global Competition Policy* (Institute for International Economics, 1997), pp. 151–97 at pp. 151–6; available at http://www.piie.com/publications/chapters_preview/56/5iie1664.pdf.

[7] The main feature allowing the US FTC to define its own agenda and priorities is its structural independence from the Executive branch (although the President does have the power to nominate Commissioners, subject to bipartisan limits). However, the FTC is subject, like other agencies, to direct and indirect pressures (including budgetary pressure) from US lawmakers.

[8] See, e.g., Harry First, 'Antitrust in Japan: The Original Intent', *Pacific Rim Law & Policy Journal*, **9** (1) (February 2000) 67–70.

This probably explains why the AMA was not a mere imitation of US antitrust law.[9] Indeed, the drafters of the AMA took into consideration criticisms of US law. For instance, the original AMA contained strict preventive provisions including severe control of international agreements using prior notification systems in response to criticism against US systems. As another example, Article 8 of the original AMA provided that a large company could be ordered to divest its assets to balance the market power between it and its competitors in the market. Although this provision was never actually used, it demonstrates a strong intention of enforcement against dominant market operators. The far-reaching nature of the provision is evident in the fact that a company could be forced to divest a part of its facilities or transfer its technology even without any infringement if the authority found a wide difference in market power between the company in question and its competitors.[10] Moreover, under Article 4 of the original AMA a cartel was considered per se illegal unless its effects were *de minimis*.[11]

1950s

The establishment of the EEC initiated a profound process of integration, and competition law has played an important role in this regard. Moreover, over time (and especially since the 'modernisation' discourse began to take hold in the 1990s), the EU Member States have modelled and remodelled their substantive competition laws in a manner largely inspired by the Community/Union model. One can take the view nowadays that Europe's ample experience with this field of law has spurred the development of a European competition culture. In Europe, the

---

[9] See Eleanor Fox, 'Economic Development, Poverty and Antitrust: The Other Path', *Southwestern Journal of Law and Trade in the Americas*, **13** (2007) 224. Fox, like others, suggests that legislation should respond to contextual problems that need to be solved, assessing local problems before adopting law. As she notes, law is not ideally generated by outsiders who try to superimpose replicas of their own laws.

[10] The GHQ's approach, which was very critical of giant companies, was influenced by the American New Deal views in a period when longstanding distrust of big business came together with a huge failure of the economy. See Eleanor M. Hadley, *Antitrust in Japan* (Princeton University Press, 1970) pp. 4–5.

[11] See, e.g., The JFTC, *AMA Policy Fifty Years History*, Volume 1 (Kosei Torihiki Kyokai, 1997) p. 4 (in Japanese). The idealistic provisions described in the text reflect ideas coming from the US during antitrust law's prosperous period.

original Member States signed the Treaty of Rome in 1957 amidst great suffering and economic strife after the war. Like Japan, competition law in Europe was created in a context of economic and human crisis, and it was fundamentally conceived as a tool to fight against the oppressive economic power of dominant companies and dominant groups of companies, partly because of their perceived role as facilitators of and feeders on militarisation.[12] Before World War II, certain European countries accepted national cartels of heavy industries. After the war, the US, as leader of the Allies and hegemon of the West, imposed its model of competition law, as well as de-concentration policy and other aspects of law and politics, on both Germany and Japan. During the first 30 years of existence, EU competition policy was a tool to speed up single market integration. Thus, the Commission's attention focused primarily on vertical distribution agreements that tended to keep the common market partitioned along national boundaries by preventing so-called parallel imports.

But in Japan, an important early turning point was the Korean War, which broke out at the beginning of the 1950s. This conflict forced Japan and the US to change many Japanese policies, including competition policy. The US wanted Japan to be a safeguard against Communism and to shift policy, radically, in order to encourage prosperous heavy industry in Japan. This policy reversal was also necessary because of a new demand for war materials in the region. Internally, it was not difficult to shift policy in this way, since Japan – whose economy had been devastated by war – needed a more pro-industry competition policy to stimulate growth and restore the national economy. For these reasons, both US and Japanese interests converged on the need to relax the originally stringent AMA, which had been opposed from the outset by most Japanese. In retrospect, it appears that competition policy in Japan swung, though not all at once, from one extreme to another. In the following decades, competition policy was often eclipsed by, or even dictated by, industrial policy.[13]

In the early period, the AMA was first amended, in light of the shifting mood just described, in 1949. Further and more far-reaching revisions

---

[12] For further details, see, e.g., François Souty, 'Droit antitrust, concurrence et innovation: réflexions sur les origines et les objectifs de la politique de la concurrence', *Revue Lamy de la Concurrence*, **31** (avril–juin 2012) 209–11.

[13] See Chapter 3 (this volume) on the structure of the AMA and its enforcement.

were made in 1953, the year after Japan regained its independence.[14] These amendments introduced an exemption for resale price maintenance of books and other publications subject to copyright, and for commodities to be designated specially by the JFTC. Furthermore, the above-mentioned Article 8 providing for divestiture was abrogated, and Article 4, which established per se illegality of cartels, was replaced by Article 2(6) AMA and Article 3 AMA, which prohibits a cartel if it substantially restrains trade contrary to the public interest. Furthermore, the scope of the Article that originally applied to 'unfair methods of competition' was widened so that it prohibits 'unfair business practices'. This broader language covers certain unfair competitive practices but it also applies to other situations such as, for example, oppressive pressure imposed by a large manufacturer on relatively small subcontractors. In this sense, although the amendments in 1949 and especially 1953 are generally considered to have weakened the AMA, with regard to vertical restraints the amendments actually strengthened its enforcement.[15] This also marked the separation of the Japanese competition enforcement from the US model. Subsequently, a number of exemptions were adopted. Articles 24-3 AMA and 24-4 AMA introduced, respectively, specific exemptions for crisis cartels and 'rationalisation' cartels. Among others, there were the Export and Import Transactions Law, which allowed the establishment of commercial associations (including export cartels), the Maritime Transportation Law, which (like other countries' laws) allowed shipping 'conferences', and the Medium and Small Size Business Organisations Law, which allowed trade associations to pursue certain restrictive activities.

At the beginning of 1955, as global demand gained momentum, the Japanese started to feel that they had finally got out of the difficult post-war period. In its 'National Income Doubling Plan', which characterised Japan's strong economic growth, the Ikeda administration claimed

---

[14] See, e.g., Hideaki Miyajima, 'Reform of Antimonopoly Act of 1953', *Waseda Shogaku*, **331**, **332**, (1989) 426 (in Japenese).

[15] Professor Ishihara explains that the Amendment made in 1953 relaxed the AMA because of the grim economic conditions in Japan, and in response to the criticism that the US pro-competitive idea was a poor fit in light of the national economic and social context. See Takako Ishihara, 'Industrial Policy and Competition Policy', available at http://www.jftc.go.jp/eacpf/05/jicatext/aug27.pdf. Professor Takigawa considers that the AMA was not weakened by the amendments, because only extreme clauses were removed as a consequence of the legislative changes. See Toshiaki Takigawa, *Competition Laws and Competition Policy in Japan, the US and the EU* (4th edn, Seirin Shoin, 2010) p. 10 (in Japanese).

that price-fixing cartels and other illegal agreements should be removed in order to achieve a more efficient economy and to protect consumer interests.[16] Subsequently, in the late 1950s, a surge of inflation also encouraged the perception that effective competition law enforcement was necessary, including in particular the fight against resale price maintenance (RPM), which had been (and later remained) a significant problem for the country.

1960–1989

In the European Economic Community, despite the importance of the 1960s especially for the adoption of Regulation 17/62 and for seminal decisions and court judgments, the enforcement of competition law remained incomplete. Suffice it to recall that in the foundational period of the Community, little action was taken in areas such as the abuse of dominance, hard core cartels, state aid or other public restraints of competition (that is, those not falling within the scope of the internal market rules), not to mention merger control. These areas of law and policy had to evolve between the 1970s and the 1990s, partly through developments in jurisprudence, partly through the adoption by the European Commission of block exemptions as delegated legislation and partly, with regard to mergers, through the intervention of the Council. In short, the development of Community competition law was a protracted process, and various obstacles had to be overcome. In the 1960s, for example, the nationalisation of industries was in vogue and was used as a major industrial policy instrument. The economic shocks of the 1970s posed further challenges for Community competition law, as sector-specific industrial policy began to play a greater role inside the European Commission.

In Japan, enforcement of the AMA by the JFTC became more active for a while in the 1960s. The JFTC examined some important merger cases and launched a serious fight against cartels. Public support for this increased activity grew in response to rising consumer prices owing to price-setting cartels, RPM and other anticompetitive conduct apparently facilitated by tight oligopolistic market structures. In 1977, the first amendment to strengthen the AMA was made, and a surcharge, which functioned as a partial disgorgement mechanism, was introduced. The use of this administrative penalty (financially quite light at that time), and the broad use of instruments such as 'warnings', accentuated the increasing differences between Japanese antitrust enforcement and the US model.

---

[16] See JFTC, supra note 11 at 127.

Despite the introduction of the surcharge, some consider that the 1977 amendments weakened the enforcement of the AMA because it introduced several exemptions.

In 1970, the high growth economy came to an end, and it became apparent that domestic demand alone could not sustain economic growth. As the ministries struggled to find solutions, the status of the JFTC and of the AMA were marginalised because they did not seem to contribute to the government's efforts to promote employment and maintain economic growth. To the contrary, the JFTC's existence was considered an obstacle to progress.

1989–1991

The Japan-US efforts to decrease their trade imbalance (see below) coincided with the conclusion of the EU-US Competition Agreement of 1991, whose goal was to enhance transatlantic cooperation in antitrust enforcement. While the EU and the US were making progress towards bilateral cooperation in specific competition cases within the framework of that Agreement, Japan and the US were laying the groundwork for further bilateral cooperation to remove regulatory barriers to trade, although bilateral exchanges and dialogue between Japan and the US had already been established in 1977.[17]

In the 1980s, the US trade deficit vis-à-vis Japan increased significantly. In response to pressures from US exporters, the Bush administration (with the participation of the DOJ's Antitrust Provision but also the FTC) launched the bilateral Structural Impediments Initiative ('SII') talks in July 1989.[18,19] The joint SII Working Group studied and identified

---

[17] See, e.g., Kazuhiko Takeshima, 'Toward the New Design of Competition Policy in Japan', Speech at the American Bar Association Section of International Law and Practice and Section of Antitrust Law, 18 September 2003, available at http://www.jftc.go.jp/en/policy_enforcement/speeches/pdf/takeshimaaba.pdf. Mr Takeshima was the JFTC chairman from 2002 to 2012 and undertook important amendments to Japan's competition policy including the introduction of the leniency policy and surcharge increase from 6 per cent to 10 per cent of an undertaking's turnover in the affected markets.

[18] Tony A. Freyer, 'Antitrust and Bilateralism: The US, Japan, and EU Comparative and Historical Relationship', in Mitsuo Matsushita and Clifford Jones (eds), *Competition Policy in the Global Trading System* (Kluwer Law International, 2002) p. 21.

[19] After September 1989, the US and Japan held four meetings in the context of SII. As a result, in April 1990 an interim report explaining the measures that both took to improve the situations and the future actions was issued. Following

structural problems in both the US and Japan that impeded trade and balance of payments adjustments. The relevant structural problems, according to the Working Group, included, among other things, competition law matters such as the openness of distribution systems in Japan. Tight distribution networks based on mutual trust and typified by long-term (and vague) commercial obligations were regarded as obstructions to market access and, in effect, as barriers to inbound investment by US companies. At least part of the necessary response, so the argument went, was stricter and more effective antitrust enforcement.

The SII talks, which clearly were aimed more at regulatory change in Japan rather than in the US, appear to have had a catalytic effect. Following the talks and the adoption of a final joint report, the level of surcharge imposed by the JFTC was increased; criminal penalties were strengthened; the JFTC became more active as an enforcer; private enforcement was promoted; and the Distribution Guidelines were issued in 1991. In short, the SII was another turning point in the history of Japanese competition policy.

1992 to the Present

In December 1989, the European Economic Community adopted its first Merger Regulation, which pre-empted application of all national competition laws within the EEA once certain turnover thresholds and control criteria were satisfied. Since 21 September 1990, 'concentrations' meeting those conditions have been subject to review by the European Commission. The Merger Regulation was amended in 2004, introducing procedural and substantive changes, and the Commission implemented a number of internal improvements to its merger procedures in response to stinging annulments of its merger decisions in 2002, but despite these adjustments EU merger control since the 1990s can also be seen as displaying substantial continuity.

Other significant European developments in the last 20 years should be mentioned briefly here. For example, as a result of an Agreement establishing the European Economic Area, which entered into force on 1 January 1994, and with the accession of Austria, Sweden and Finland on 1 January 1995, Community competition law became applicable to a broader group of Western European countries. The intensity of enforcement has also been growing. In the mid-1990s, and, particularly in the

the fifth meeting of June 1990, the final report was published. In this regard, see, e.g., JFTC, *AMA Policy Fifty Years History*, Volume 1 (Kosei Torihiki Kyokai, 1997) p. 487 (in Japanese), supra note 11.

last decade or so, the Commission has started to impose very high fines (generally the highest in the world) on companies involved in cartels. The high fines work in tandem with the Commission's Leniency Programme, which has fundamentally changed the Commission's functions and role.[20] However, as is generally known, the most far-reaching change in the EU competition law regime since the 1960s was the adoption in 2004 of a reform package designed to 'modernise' the structure of enforcement in Europe. The reform bore features of both decentralisation and centralisation, and has resulted in a quasi-federal system of EU competition law enforcement.

In Japan, following a steady rise that made Japan the number two economy in the world at that time, the economic bubble burst in 1991. The Hosokawa government initiated administrative reforms in 1993, and regulatory controls and the exemptions from the AMA were gradually abolished. The EU submitted its opinion regarding the Regulatory Deregulation Promotion Plan requesting Japan to strengthen AMA enforcement and abolish the exemptions.[21] Apparently, the SII negotiations, the Japan-US Framework for a New Economic Partnership that followed the SII and the EU's opinion regarding the Regulatory Deregulation Promotion Plan have contributed to provoke change in Japan. In the field of bilateral cooperation, Japan concluded a Competition Cooperation Agreement with the US in 1999 and then did the same with the EU in 2003, completing 'a three-way network linking the competition authorities of the trilateral economic spheres'.[22] Other cooperation initiatives have been ongoing between the JFTC and various Asian countries. These arrangements have been useful tools to tackle international cartels and multijurisdictional mergers, whose numbers have been increasing.

Another significant development at the political level concerns the Koizumi government, which between 2001 and 2006 contributed to more proactive enforcement of the AMA. In 2003, the JFTC expanded its organisational structure and it was resituated as an agency under the

[20] See, e.g., François Brunet, 'La nouvelle politique de la Commission européenne à l'égard des ententes horizontales: ententes illicites et coopération licite', in François Brune and Guy Canivet (eds), *Le nouveau droit communautaire de la concurrence* (L.G.D.J., 2008) p. 6.

[21] See JFTC, *AMA Policy Fifty Years History*, Volume 1 (Kosei Torihiki Kyokai, 1997) p. 501 (in Japanese), supra note 11.

[22] See Takeshima, supra note 17.

Cabinet Office (and thus not subordinated to a ministry). The organisational changes aimed at 'enhancing competition policy which is a key to a fair and free economic society'.[23]

Over the span of ten years under the leadership of former JFTC Chairman Takeshima, the JFTC's existence became much more visible, drawing attention from within and from outside Japan. However, partly owing to Japan's debilitating economic crisis, regarding Japan's success in raising the profile of competition law enforcement there are pressures, once again, to give priority to industrial policy over competition policy.

On the other hand, the now-global dimension of competition policy discourse and dialogue has also helped to steer the JFTC towards more aggressive and proactive enforcement. In this regard, EU competition policy has provided a particularly influential model as Japan proceeded through several rounds of amendments to the AMA. For instance, in 2005, surcharges were increased and the JFTC's investigative powers were enhanced. In 2006 Japan introduced a leniency policy and in 2007 the categories of conduct subject to surcharges were broadened.[24] Further, the notification threshold under Japan's merger control regulation was substantially revised and, following the EU model, the turnover of groups of companies was taken into consideration.

CONCLUSION

Although the AMA was created following the US model (that is, largely as an attempt to devise a hybrid blend of Sherman Act and FTC Act features), antitrust enforcement in Japan today does not always follow trends in the US. More often, enforcers and analysts in Japan carefully examine the enforcement approach and institutional choices of the EU. This observation is consistent with Professor Gerber's contention that EU competition law has been largely successful in the sense that it has gained increasing recognition and status around the world.[25]

In Japan, there are fewer indigenous elements that could enhance the AMA's status and recognition. The globalisation of competition law is relevant but it is not sufficient to secure a higher profile for Japanese competition policy, in particular when the national economy is on its

---

23 See Junichiro Koizumi, General Policy Speech to the 156th Session of the Diet, 31 January 2003, available at http://www.kantei.go.jp/foreign/koizumi speech/2003/01/31sisei_e.html.

24 For further details, see Chapter 9 (this volume) on fining policy.

25 See Gerber, supra note 1, p. 434.

knees and the world economy seems unlikely to be of much help. However, if Japan maintains a policy based on flexibility in response to the continuous change of the political and economic situations, and based on careful reflection on Japanese culture, the quality and efficiency of competition law enforcement will improve steadily, even if such improvement does not look sufficiently speedy from the outside.

3. Legal structure and enforcement

BACKGROUND

The official name of the main legislation of the Japanese competition law is the 'Act on Prohibition of Private Monopolization and Maintenance of Fair Trade', and its interpretation and enforcement are supported by various rules, including Guidelines and administrative law provisions. But the Japanese competition law is commonly called the Antimonopoly Act (*dokusen kinshi ho* in Japanese, or its often used abbreviated form *dokkin ho*). By contrast, the competition laws of major foreign jurisdictions, including the EU, are referred as to *Kyoso ho*, which literally means 'competition law' – except for US antitrust law, which is referred to simply as antitrust.[1,2] Although the term 'competition law' is becoming

[1] The term 'competition law' may also cause confusion when translated into languages other than Japanese. See David J. Gerber, *Law and Competition in Twentieth Century Europe. Protecting Prometheus* (Oxford University Press, 1998) p. 4.

[2] The first to hazard a Japanese translation of the English word 'competition' was apparently Yukichi Fukuzawa, a *Rangaku* scholar (on Fukuzawa, see the introduction in Chapter 1 (this volume)). In his famous book entitled *Fukuo jiden* (1899), Fukuzawa explained that when he translated 'competition' as *Kyoso* (which means 'compete' but also 'fight' in Japanese) for the governor of the *Tokugawa Shogunate* in the Edo period, the latter told Fukuzawa that he was not pleased with his translation, because one of the characters he used – which meant 'fight' – did not sound peaceful. Fukuzawa answered that his translation did not carry a negative connotation because traders were competing with each other to attract their customers. The governor replied with surprise that Western competition was harsh. For details regarding this story, see, e.g., Masanao Nakagawa, 'Reconsidering the Notion of "Competition" – "*Kyoso*" or "*Kyowa*"', *Jurisconsultus*, Kanto Gakuin University (January 2012), 29–30 (in Japanese). Professor Nakagawa explains that, in the Japanese industrial world, the tendency to avoid competition is deeply rooted. Although the episode described above concerning Fukuzawa happened around 150 years ago, the word 'competition' may still provoke resistance owing to Japanese social patterns. On the other hand, some argue that the word 'competition' may give a more positive impression and is replacing antimonopoly because 'competition law' gives the impression of rules apt to create a competitive atmosphere. See Hiroyuki

more popular in Japan too, it seems unlikely that the familiar expression of 'Antimonopoly Act' could be replaced by 'Competition Law' any time soon.[3] In this regard, the existence of the AMA has been already widely acknowledged and rooted in Japan's public space, whereas in the EU, competition law – despite its long history – is not an area of law commonly known to the general public, at least not in all the Member States.

COMPETITION PROVISIONS

Although the AMA was adopted following the US model, the structure of the AMA provisions does not look similar to that of the relevant US legislation. The original AMA was drafted with the contribution of US specialists who incorporated Western ideas of competition into the Japanese economic system.[4] Although the AMA has been revised several times, its structure has not radically changed since its adoption in 1947. Substantively, it is composed of four pillars: merger control, private monopolisation, unreasonable restraint of trade and unfair trade practices. In general, the scope of competition laws around the world, including EU competition law, covers unilateral conduct and joint conduct (that is, cartels and restrictive agreements) as well as merger control. As is well known, in the case of the EU, the merger control system was not established by the Treaty of Rome but was adopted much later, in 1989 (and amended in 2004).

The main substantive areas covered by the AMA are private monopolisation (unilateral conduct), unreasonable restraint of trade (joint conduct) and merger control. Unfair trade practices include the abuse of a superior bargaining position and interference with business relations that are not totally unique but nevertheless increasingly idiosyncratic categories of conduct, compared to other countries' competition laws. In

---

Odagiri, 'Why Is Competition Important?: Welfare Loss Created by Monopoly and Cartels', *The Keizai Seminar*, **625** April 2007 (in Japanese).

[3] For the definition of Antimonopoly Law, see, e.g., Tadashi Shiraishi, *Competition Law of Japan* (2nd edn, Yuhikaku, 2009) pp. 1–3 (in Japanese). Professor Shiraishi does not expect that 'competition' will replace 'antimonopoly'. See also ibid. pp. 30–31. Professor Nakagawa wonders whether the development of competition law in Japan would have been different if 'competition' had been translated not as *Kyoso* but *Kyowa,* which means 'peace' or 'harmony'. See Nakagawa, supra note 2.

[4] See Chapter 2 (this volume) on the historical background.

terms of overall structure, the AMA is composed of four parts: substantive provisions, sanctions, procedural provisions and organisational provisions.

The AMA is also supplemented by other laws, which include the Subcontract Law of 1956 and the Act against Unjustifiable Premiums and Misleading Representations of 1962. Further, other sector-specific laws such as the Telecommunications Business Act promote competition in specific markets.[5] These laws are complementary to the AMA. As regards liberalisation of the gas and electricity markets, in December 1999 the JFTC and the METI (formerly the MITI) issued the Guidelines on Appropriate Electricity Transactions, which aim to provide guidance for commercial practices in the electricity market.[6]

EU competition provisions are contained in Articles 101 to 109 in Chapter 1 of Title VII of Part Three of the TFEU, which should be interpreted in conjunction with the objectives and principles laid down in the TFEU and in the Treaty on European Union.[7] The two main provisions, Articles 101 and 102 TFEU, are supplemented by various Regulations, Notices and Guidelines. As the provisions in the TFEU are relatively concise and simple, the structure of EU competition law is perhaps clearer and easier to understand, but as in most jurisdictions it is necessary to refer to other sources, including legislation and the European Courts' precedents, to interpret and apply EU competition law with more precision.

The difference between Japan and the EU stems from the traditions and current situations in the two jurisdictions. Traditionally, Japanese laws were often written in technical language that is difficult for ordinary Japanese citizens, and the whole structure of the law is complicated: recourse must be had to several rules in order to interpret the law in a coherent way. The same applies to court judgments. To improve this situation, vigorous efforts have been made in particular by the Japanese legal community, and some laws have been amended and judgments have been written in a more natural way so that the people without a legal education can better understand the content of legislation and judgments. As regards the AMA, although the language used is not in itself so difficult (partly because the AMA is relatively new compared to other Japanese laws such as the Civil Code), the expression of provisions and

---

5 See http://www.soumu.go.jp/main_sosiki/joho_tsusin/eng/Resources/laws/pdf/090204_2.pdf.

6 See http://www.meti.go.jp/policy/tsutatsutou/tuuti1/aa499.pdf (in Japanese).

7 For further details, see, e.g., Richard Whish and David Bailey, *Competition Law* (7th edn, Oxford University Press, 2012) pp. 51–2.

the structure are not always sufficiently clear. Accordingly, in order to clarify interpretation, Japanese academics have to spend more time arguing about how to interpret the wording of rules and precedents of the JFTC and the courts; and sometimes there seems to be less emphasis on actual practice compared to the work of academics in Europe. In the EU, where more and more countries are becoming Member States and where there are now more than 24 official languages, the language used in legislation and other documents necessarily has to be clear and easily understood by EU citizens.[8] The delicate task of rendering legislation coherent across languages falls to the EU institutions' translation services. Further, the EU institutions have rich experience in numerous legislative processes in various policy areas, whose outcomes must be implemented in the 28 Member States. The task of adopting relatively clear and user-friendly rules is strictly and constantly overseen by the EU institutions and by the institutions of the Member States.

THE COMPETITION AUTHORITIES OF JAPAN AND THE EU

In Japan, the JFTC is in charge of enforcement of the AMA. Although the JFTC is attached to the Prime Minister and considered an extra ministerial organ of his Cabinet, it performs its functions independently under Articles 27 and 28 AMA. The JFTC is composed of a chairman and four commissioners who are appointed with the consent of both chambers of the Diet. The JFTC has the exclusive power to adopt administrative measures including cease and desist orders, and orders imposing administrative 'surcharges' (fines). A cease and desist order is precluded if five years have elapsed from the date on which the illegal conduct ceased. Among other things, the JFTC may order a partial transfer of business assets (Article 7(1) AMA), a dissolution of an industrial association (Article 8-2(1) AMA), or a public announcement that the relevant illegal conduct has ceased (Article 7(2) AMA, Article 8-2(2) AMA, Article 20(2) AMA). The JFTC has the exclusive power to bring criminal charges, and the Prosecutor's Office is in charge of criminal prosecution on behalf of the public.

---

8 For Official EU languages, see the European Commission's website at http://ec.europa.eu/languages/languages-of-europe/eu-languages_en.htm.

In the EU, DG Competition is, of course, the main enforcer of EU competition law. Compared to the JFTC, the Commission is less 'isolated' in fulfilling its functions because it carries out its tasks in cooperation with other Directorates General (where they have sectoral interests), with other EU institutions, and with the competition authorities and the courts of the Member States. Both the JFTC and DG Competition cooperate regularly with other competition authorities worldwide, under both formal and informal frameworks.

Several years after the moment of adoption of the AMA, the JFTC's independence from the ministers was criticised because, as was argued, executive power should be vested in the executive organ, and the government and the Prime Minister should be responsible for its functioning. Partly because the effectiveness of the JFTC was limited for many years, with just a few decisions being adopted each year, the independence of the JFTC might have been preserved until the present and not been under the direct control of other governmental organs. Otherwise, actual or potential conflicts with other government organs and with business would likely have jeopardised the JFTC's independence. As the original culture and 'spirit' of the common people of Japan are not litigious, the general expectation in a 'harmonious' social order is that the authority will settle any disputes peacefully, that is, consensually; the assumption is that the authority will not intervene in the business of the operators concerned unless strictly necessary. Thus the fact that the JFTC dealt with only a few cases annually did not seem problematic.

The Japanese system of competition law enforcement is largely centralised, apart from a modest but increasing trend of private litigation under the Civil Code (where stand-alone actions are possible). In the EU, by contrast, the original system established in 1962, which led to substantially centralised enforcement of Community law (notwithstanding the direct effect of Articles 85(1), 85(2) and 86 EEC), was radically changed in 2004 to catalyse the enforcement of EU competition law by national authorities.[9] As the EU is composed (as of this writing) of 28 Member States, it is useful to consider the allocation of roles for the sake of efficient enforcement. This allocation of roles accentuates the institutional differences between the EU and Japan, particularly in relation to the effect of the decision of the authorities. For instance, in the EU, under Article 101(2) TFEU, an illegal agreement is, in principle, automatically

---

[9] See, e.g., John Temple Lang, 'Decentralised Enforcement of Community Competition Law', available at http://ec.europa.eu/competition/speeches/text/sp1999456_en.pdf.

void. This rule of nullity reflects a basic principle that in the past was expressed in Article 3(1)(g) EC, and that now appears in the Protocol on the Internal Market and Competition: there it is stated that the Member States consider that the internal market includes 'a system ensuring that competition is not distorted'.[10,11] As Articles 101 and 102 TFEU are directly applicable in their entirety, national competition authorities and national courts can order parties to bring illegal agreements or practices to an end and/or declare them to be void. According to EU law, actions for damages in case of breach of those Articles must be entertained by national courts.

In Japan, although the public enforcement power is concentrated in the hands of the JFTC, there seems no principle to justify the universal (*erga omnes*) effect of a decision finding an AMA infringement. Thus, an illegal clause does not automatically render an agreement void; the courts decide voidness on a case-by-case basis. However, if the JFTC adopts an order declaring that an agreement is illegal, the agreement is normally unenforceable because it is considered to be contrary to the public interest and therefore void under Article 90 of the Civil Code.[12]

In terms of civil damages actions, the AMA contains a special provision. Article 25 stipulates strict liability, once the JFTC has found an infringement of the AMA. In that case, if the plaintiff can establish causation and damages, the court hearing the case must grant the civil damages award, without any need to establish intentional tort or negligence.[13]

OBJECTIVES

Japan is based on a market economy in which free decisions and activities by individuals and companies are respected. The proper objective of the AMA is to promote fair and free competition, and ultimately the AMA should protect the interests of general consumers and promote

---

[10] See Van Bael and Bellis, *Competition Law of the European Community* (5th edn, Kluwer Law International, 2010) p. 69.

[11] Protocol (No. 27), OJ 2008 C115/309.

[12] For the illegality of cartel agreements, see, e.g., the Tokyo District Court judgment of 25 October 1984.

[13] Of course, the quality of the evidence is crucial; if the causation or damages element of the plaintiff's claim are in doubt, Article 25 is no guarantee of success. See Chapter 11 (this volume) on private enforcement.

the national economy in a democratic and sound manner.[14] In general, the objective of safeguarding consumer interests is not considered a separate objective of the AMA but is rather a secondary interest that is advanced as a consequence of fair and free competition.[15] Active competition will bring benefits to consumers and competition policy should not neglect the interest in protecting them.[16] However, some argue that the objective of the AMA includes ensuring that consumers have free choice and the right to be informed.[17]

In the EU, Article 3(3) TEU declares that the objectives of the Union include the establishment of an internal market based on a highly competitive social market economy. The main goal of EU competition law is to assure undistorted competition in the internal market. As a matter of policy, Commission President Barroso in 2009 charged Competition Commissioner Almunia with the following mission: 'Your role will be to implement the competition rules to ensure that the internal market operates efficiently and without distortion, thus contributing to the welfare of businesses and consumers and the competitiveness of the European economy.'[18]

From the above mandate, and from numerous soft law instruments issued by the Commission, it is clear that promoting consumer welfare is one dimension of the Commission's mission. The European Court of Justice does not emphasise consumer welfare, an economic term, but it does accept that the competition rules are partly meant to protect consumer interests.[19] A consumer interest function is thus clearly attributed to EU competition law,[20] although it remains unclear in some cases how this interest is to be best protected. Furthermore, it seems clear from the Treaty and from the case law that there is not just a single, ultimate

---

14 Oil price agreement criminal case, judgment of the Supreme Court of 24 February1984.

15 See, e.g., Yosuke Okada and Shuya Hayashi (eds), *Economic Impact of the Antimonopoly Law: Case Studies in Recent Court and Tribunal Decisions* (University of Tokyo Press, 2009) p. 9 (in Japanese).

16 See, e.g., Noriyuki Doi, 'Competition Policy and Consumer Policy', *Kose Torihiki*, **740** (June 2012), 2–8 (in Japanese).

17 Akira Negishi and Masayuki Funada, *Japanese Antitrust Law* (Yuhikaku, 2010) pp. 33–5 (in Japanese).

18 See Barroso's letter of 27 November 2009 to Almunia, available at http://ec.europa.eu/commission_2010-2014/almunia/about/mandate/mission_letter_en.pdf.

19 See Case C-209/10, *Post Danmark A/S v Konkurrencerådet*, judgment of 27 March 2012, not yet reported.

20 For further details, see Whish and Bailey, supra note 7, pp. 20–21.

goal of safeguarding consumer interests. Rather, that goal has to be accommodated within a framework of objectives, and these include, most famously, the objective of promoting an internal market. No equivalent aim is found in relation to the AMA (or in relation to the Sherman Act, etc.), and the importance of the market integration imperative in the EU is not always sufficiently understood in Japan (or elsewhere). In the 1990s some wondered whether the goal of market integration in EC competition law would recede in importance owing to the development of the Community's internal market; but this objective remains as forceful as ever, owing in part to the inherent diversity that characterises the markets of the Member States, not to mention that new Member States are periodically added to the group and pose new challenges.

RELATIONSHIP BETWEEN COMPETITION POLICY AND INDUSTRIAL POLICY

One of the reasons why the JFTC's enforcement was not very active until the 1990s, despite the fact that it had already for several decades been equipped with a law to enforce, is that in Japan regulatory control and industrial concerns often pre-empted competition rules.[21] Since the introduction of the AMA, one of the measures for Japan's economic democratisation has been a continuous battle to reach a 'settlement' on the terms of Japan's market economy. The role of the AMA during Japan's period of rapid economic development was sometimes neglected, partly because of the idea that intervening to protect competition might impede economic growth.[22] Industrial policy played a major role in the post-war era, and the then Ministry of International Trade and Industry (MITI; today, METI) took the lead in administering this policy, whose central aim was to achieve and maintain rapid growth and competitiveness. Until the recent economic crisis, it was rather difficult to make the general public aware of the fact that competition policy is as important as industrial policy for Japan, because industrial policy brought tangible results, while competition policy's achievements were less visible. Post-war poverty and misery in Japan is not completely lost to living memory, and the many workers who dedicated their lives to specific companies take great pride in Japan's economic 'miracle' after World War II.

21 The JFTC was often criticised as 'a watchdog that does not bark'.

22 See the introduction in Chapter 1 (this volume).

Thus, enforcement of the AMA has been diluted by industrial considerations, and Japanese companies are accustomed to this regulatory approach. In general, Japanese companies' trust in and expectations of the ministries that guided them (seemingly correctly) as an expression of 'benevolent government' have been quite high. Illustrative of the prominent role of industrial policy were the frequently used instrument of 'administrative guidance' and various exemption rules. To make the Japanese economy function correctly, it was generally considered necessary to give priority to industrial policy over enforcement of the AMA. Moreover, in Japanese society, not only consensus but also hierarchy and harmony are generally more respected than in Western society.[23] This tradition also contributed to impede the development of competition policy.[24] From this perspective, the ideal solution for anticompetitive conduct was not public condemnation after an adversarial investigation but rather informal approval based on compromise and a promise between the JFTC and the operator concerned. This was particularly true when the JFTC conducted merger investigations. In this way, the JFTC could earn the companies' trust and enjoy flexibility and discretion, while the companies could negotiate in confidence with the authority. This made it possible for them to keep information disclosed between them strictly confidential. We return to the subject of administrative guidance below.

Although the general perception is that AMA enforcement was heavily influenced by the government's industrial policy, whose purpose has been to create and maintain a strong Japanese economy, some argue that in reality industrial policy made only a minor contribution to growth in Japan.[25] It is difficult to know the extent to which industrial policy contributed to Japan's dramatic growth prior to the 1990s separately from competition policy, in particular on a long-term basis. There has been resistance against allowing the JFTC to intervene in industries such as the

---

[23] See the introduction in Chapter 1 (this volume).

[24] See Eleanor Fox, 'Linked-in: Antitrust and the Virtues of a Virtual Network', *International Lawyer*, **43** (2009) 151, 153, where Fox mentions that, whereas in Asia, and in particular in Japan, the development of antitrust law was slower because of their custom of transacting business by consensus, and because industrial policy and fairness were priorities and maybe inseparable from competition policy, in the EU and the US, competition authorities do not welcome intrusions by industrial policy into competition policy.

[25] See, e.g., Marcus Noland and Howard Pack, *Industrial Policy in an Era of Globalization: Lessons from Asia* (Institute for International Economics, 2003) p. 100.

steel industry, which affects almost all the other important industries in Japan, including notably the construction and automobile manufacture sectors.

As in Japan, competition policy in the EU may sometimes be regarded as inimical to the general development of industrial policy, or vice versa, in particular when European governments try to encourage domestic companies to collaborate where this would achieve economies of scale, or more effective R&D, or create national champions.[26] For instance, the intervention of the Commission in the energy market, which provoked strong political resistance that led to a dilution of initial ambitions, was a good illustration of the fact that EU competition policy is not applied in a vacuum but remains subject to a number of industrial and political realities.[27] However, in the EU, conflict between industrial policy and competition law seems less visible than in Japan. On the one hand, competition law has a firm basis in the Treaty, whereas industrial policy has a legal base for action but one that is comparatively weak (and is indeed explicitly made subordinate to competition by the relative clause). On the other hand, the industrial policies of 28 sovereign states sometimes cancel each other out and the EU is thus precluded from adopting a coherent policy that, for example, discriminates in favour of Union-based industry and that might come into conflict with competition policy. Further, various factors influence competition policy in Japan, including in particular a degree of political judgement, economics and industrial organisation theory – though more important today than in the past – are still not a core part of decision-making, either at the level of the JFTC or at the level of the Japanese courts. This distinguishes Japan from certain other competition authorities, including the EU Commission.

ADMINISTRATIVE GUIDANCE

The particularity of public administration in Japan is enforcement through administrative guidance. Administrative guidance is an instrument of guidance, warning and advice issued by an administrative organ within its scope of function for administrative purposes. It is non-binding and it is given by the JFTC (and other agencies and ministries) to the firm concerned in various fields of business. Neither the content of the

---

[26] See Whish and Bailey, supra note 7, p. 15.

[27] France, Germany and Russia resisted the Commission's proposal to order the unbundling of the production of energy from its distribution.

guidance nor the process leading up to it is transparent.[28, 29] The purposes for which administrative guidance may be given include: the stability of product prices; consumer welfare; fair and transparent transactions; environmental protection; improved health and safety conditions; the protection of small and medium sized companies; the avoidance of excessive competition; the adjustment of demand–supply relations; the restraint of price decreases; the adjustment of conflicts between companies; and maintenance of the industrial order.

When issued by administrative organs other than the JFTC, administrative guidance can sometimes be anticompetitive and can create problems of AMA infringement. In this regard, the JFTC has issued guidelines on administrative guidance and has tried to make the procedure clear.[30] The frequency of administrative guidance is diminishing but its role continues to be important, insofar as it ensures speedy and flexible administrative practices.[31] As for the JFTC itself, it may resort to administrative guidance when it suspects a possible infringement but does not possess sufficient evidence to impose legal measures such as a cease and desist order. In that case, it can warn the company to cease its conduct or bring it more clearly into line with the law.

The nature of administrative guidance is explained in a Supreme Court judgment of 1984, which states that as long as administrative guidance does not conflict with the AMA's ultimate objective, which is to protect the interests of general consumers and to promote the national economy in a democratic and sound manner, and so long as its methods are appropriate and commonly accepted in the society, the guidance will not be contrary to the AMA.[32] In this context, the recent document issued after the Great East Japan Earthquake by the JFTC to explain anti-competitive conduct in case of emergency mentions that even conduct that was encouraged by administrative guidance may breach the AMA.[33]

---

28 Article 2(6) of the Administrative Procedure Law.

29 See Negishi and Funada, supra note 17, pp. 188–9 (in Japanese).

30 See http://www.jftc.go.jp/dk/gyouseishidou.html (in Japanese).

31 Guidelines concerning Administrative Guidance under the Antimonopoly Act (2010). See http://www.jftc.go.jp/dk/gyouseishidou.html (in Japanese).

32 See supra note 14. See also Tadashi Shiraishi, 'Regulatory Control and Antitrust Law Examined in the Osaka Bus Association Case', *Public Law Research* (Koho Kenkyu, Japan Public Law Association, 5 October 1998), at 160–61 (in Japanese).

33 See 'Hypothetical Case Study in Emergencies Including Earthquakes', JFTC, March 2012. See http://www.jftc.go.jp/info/souteijirei.pdf (in Japanese).

Although the JFTC understands the importance of administrative guidance and its capacity to respond to urgent needs, enable flexible administration and facilitate administrative objectives, it underlines nonetheless that the existence of administrative guidance cannot justify an AMA infringement.

From the perspective of the conflict between competition policy and industrial policy, the administrative practice of the European Commission is not regarded as seriously problematic in the EU. There were periods in the past – the 1970s and early 1980s – in which case assessment by the European Commission incorporated elements of industrial policy or social policy. There is also a longstanding academic debate about the extent to which non-economic criteria may appropriately be taken into account in the application of Article 101(3) TFEU. Overall, however, the development of Community/EU competition policy has not been defined by high degrees of tension between competition policy and industrial policy in a way that would be comparable to the Japanese experience. And, as already noted, in the EU the Treaty leaves little doubt about the hierarchically privileged stature of the competition rules compared to industrial policy.

EXEMPTION

There are two kinds of exemption in Japan: one is provided for in the AMA and the other category is based on separate laws. For instance, Article 21 AMA allows an exemption for conduct that would otherwise constitute an AMA infringement if the conduct relates to the legitimate use of intellectual property rights. Article 22 AMA provides an exemption for cooperative association mutual aids such as in the agricultural field, and Article 23 AMA allows resale price maintenance under certain conditions.[34] The number of exemptions compared to the 1980s has decreased dramatically. However, some exemptions continue to be applied. To cite one notable example, an exemption for a collusive agreement to pass on a consumption tax was adopted and its revision is under consideration in view of an increase in Japan's consumption tax.[35]

---

[34] See, e.g., Mitsuo Matsushita, *International Trade and Competition Law in Japan* (Oxford University Press, 1993) p. 157. The numbering of Article 24.2 changed to Article 23 owing to the recent amendment. For more recent detailed explanation, see, e.g., Shiraishi, supra note 3, p. 389.

[35] See Chapter 4 (this volume) on cartels.

In the EU too, the number of exemption regulations has tended to decrease. The Commission's general policy is to phase out sector-specific EU antitrust regimes. Currently, there are nine block exemptions still in force in the EU.[36] For instance, the Commission will not renew the set of guidelines on the application of EU competition rules to maritime transport services, which is supposed to expire in September 2013.[37] Unsurprisingly, in some cases it is claimed that an exemption from the competition rules is necessary for a sector's survival. For instance, the extent to which EU competition law should be applicable to the farm production sector is under discussion, and the European Parliament is calling for a strengthening of the position of farmers. The balance between the objectives of the EU's Common Agricultural Policy and competition law has become even more complex owing to enforcement actions by the Member States' authorities.[38]

There is also occasionally some interaction between the Japanese regulatory regime and EU law-based exemptions, which may affect EU competition investigations. For instance, appeals brought by airline companies against the Commission in the air cargo cartel case include claims that Japan's regulatory regimes were assessed erroneously.[39]

STATE AID

The distinctive objective of market integration (see above) creates various important divergences between the EU and Japan. State aid control is a case in point. The EU's state aid regime is a complementary tool for the achievement and maintenance of an internal market. It is not only one of the pillars of EU competition law; it also influences various European policies and regulations, and interacts with the EU's Cohesion Policy and

---

36 For an explanation of these block exemptions, see Whish and Bailey, supra note 7, pp. 169–70.

37 The purpose of these guidelines was to facilitate the transition from a specific regime to a general EU competition regime for the maritime transport sector after the repeal of the Block Exemption regulation for liner conferences in 2006. See the Commission's press release of 25 September 2006, IP/06/1249.

38 See EU Competition Framework Policy and Agricultural Agreements: Collation and Comparative Analysis of Significant Decisions at National Level, European Parliament (2012), IP/B/AGRI/CEI/2011-097/E011/SC1, available at http://www.europarl.europa.eu/committees/en/agri/studiesdownload.html?languageDocument=EN&file=75231.

39 See, e.g., T-48/11-*British Airways v Commission*, judgment of the General Court of 12 March 2011, not yet published.

Structural Funds. State aid control also affects other areas of competition law, such as the liberalisation of regulated sectors. For instance, in the air transport sector, before 1987, aviation markets were fragmented along Member States' borders across the EU. Although, in the 1990s, the EU liberalised the air transport sector in order to create a single European market. Increasing competitive pressures prompted Member States to try to protect their own air carriers by granting them state aid, for example in the form of loan guarantees that reduce the cost of credit. In Europe, a major concern reflected in the Treaty's state aid rules is that when one Member State grants selective economic benefits to a particular undertaking or a particular industry, there is a risk that this could lead to a subsidy race and new national entry barriers, harmful to competition and trade within the EU. It is thus considered that the EU's state aid rules – which include *ex ante* control by the Commission – must be enforced in order to create a level playing field across Europe.

Both the EU and Japan are, of course, members of the WTO, and are both subject to the anti-subsidy disciplines contained in the WTO Agreements. However, the EU state aid regime, with its *ex ante* control system and its fairly strong enforcement mechanisms (whereby a Member State must claw back state aid that it has illegally granted to an undertaking), goes well beyond the WTO anti-subsidy rules.

With regard to Japan, from an internal perspective a state aid regime similar to the one applicable in the EU would seem to make little sense because the Japanese market is already integrated. Thus, the fact that state aid is currently under discussion in the Japanese Diet may come as a surprise.[40] Where a company in financial difficulty has received advantageous financial aid from the government, some legislators contend that its competitor should be able to complain that the public aid distorts what should be a level playing field, even if the aid itself was permitted by law. As of this writing, no legislative action has been taken but there is ongoing debate regarding the necessity of EU-like Guidelines on state aid. Absent more affirmative hard or soft law measures, the solution might take the form of monitoring and investigating the conduct of the favoured (or rescued) firm to ensure that its conduct conforms with the requirements of the AMA.

---

[40] See the proposal submitted by the Liberal Democratic Party on an 'Act enduring conditions of fair competition': 'Make clearer the rules for restructuring support of companies by public funding!', *Gendai Business*, available at http://gendai.ismedia.jp/articles/-/33504 (in Japanese).

CONCLUSION

A more prosperous future for Japanese industry will likely depend on a delicate balance of both industrial and competition policy.

During the last decade, the importance and visibility of the AMA in Japan have certainly increased.[41] However, in the EU, competition law's practical impact and visibility are greater, partly because the process of European integration enhances the imperative nature of competitive markets. EU competition law has been – in combination with the EU's free movement rules – a major foundation for a unified market in Europe.[42] As explained above, in Japanese competition law there is no constant endeavour to preserve the unity of a 'single' market.

Despite that distinction, EU law and practice have been influential in Japan, where successive reforms seem to be bringing JFTC enforcement tools and strategies closer to an EU-type model. It may be doubted whether the famously high fines imposed in the EU could be transposed to the Japanese context, but in Japan, too, the 'surcharge' has been increased repeatedly. With regard to other enforcement tools, the EU has often provided a basic model, such as was the case when Japan adopted its leniency programme in 2005. Indeed, most of the new tools of competition enforcement that have emerged in the EU could also be introduced in Japan with certain adjustments, as the competition culture that has grown in Japan is not so different, now, from Europe's own. As seen in the introduction to this book, Japan has a long history of incorporating European ideas into its own culture. An illustrative development, in the context of enforcement, is that the JFTC is currently incorporating the use of economic analysis into its activities. In the EU, the use of economists and the use of economics across practically all policy fields (and especially in merger control) have significantly increased since the 1990s. At present, the number of economists working in the JFTC is limited, and economic analysis based on quantitative data

---

41 However, it is still observed that while the domestic reputation is that the JFTC takes a more and more active role, the JFTC is not always considered as an active agency compared to other foreign competition authorities outside Japan. This may be because of difficulties of understanding the details of the assessment of an individual case investigated by the JFTC and the low impacts of surcharges. See the remarks of Akinori Uesugi and Toshiaki Tada, the Spring Discussion, 'Future Image of the JFTC: Concrete Suggestions to Become a Respectable Existence', *Kosei Torihiki*, **723** (January 2011) 28–9.

42 See Gerber, supra note 1, pp. 1–2.

has not often been used. The more active role of economic analysis will constitute yet another profound change of the JFTC's traditional enforcement practice.[43]

[43] See, e.g., Louis Vogel, *Droit Européen de la Concurrence* (SAS LawLex, 2010) 16–17.

4. Cartels and bid rigging

HISTORY OF CARTELS IN JAPAN AND THE EU

In Japan, it may be the case that cartels are an even more serious and complicated issue than in the EU, in particular because horizontal coordination has often been rooted in the traditional business practices of Japanese companies. Professor Hadley, an economist who was sent to Japan to join the US General MacArthur's headquarters in Tokyo after World War II, wrote that Japan did not have a long tradition of cartels based on explicit agreement before the 1920s but was rather typified by 'cordial oligopoly', which characterised the handful of combines dominating the economy.[1] In the 1930s, however, cartels were encouraged by the government, and for a time were even mandatory in a variety of sectors as industry became an instrument for increasingly militant policies. In addition, as the European economy recovered after World War I, the markets of the colonial territories to which the Japanese small and medium sized enterprises had been selling daily commodities were taken by the European companies. Accordingly, the Japanese small and medium sized companies started to sell cheap products of low quality to compete with the European competitors in these markets. As a result, the Ministry of Commerce and Industry (now METI) established the export association system to limit the sale of low quality products manufactured by threatened Japanese enterprises.[2]

As suggested above, bid rigging has been the main problematic area of cartel control in Japan, particularly in the construction sector. The legal framework for construction tenders was established at the end of the 1800s. The Accounting Act, which provided the principle of general bidding, was adopted in 1889 and the Civil Code, which governed subcontracting relations, was adopted in 1896. However, in practice this

1 See, e.g., Eleanor M. Hadley, *Antitrust in Japan* (Princeton University Press, 1970) pp. 358, 362.

2 See Takehiko Yasuda, 'Activate Economy through Competition: Maintain Strength of Small and Medium Sized Companies', *Nihon keizai shinbun* (30 January 2009) 23 (in Japanese).

legal framework was honoured more in the breach than in the observance. Above all, bid rigging was regarded as a justifiable practice to prevent bankruptcy, maintain employment and avoid 'dumping' in the form of cut-rate service and defective construction. Even after the Criminal Code criminalised bid rigging in 1940 and after the AMA, which confirmed the illegal nature of bid rigging, was enacted in 1947, the idea that collusive bidding was illegal was not absorbed as part of societal norms.[3] In Japan, during World War II, the pricing, production and sales allocations of almost all materials including machines, airplanes, steels, oil, cars, lumbers, agricultural and sea products were under the control of the government but its policies were implemented under delegation by private 'control associations'.[4] After the war, in order to demilitarise and democratise Japan, the basic laws that had created these associations were abolished and new distribution regimes were introduced.

Analogous events occurred in Europe. In Germany, cartels played a key role in the wartime regulatory scheme, and the government compelled cartel behaviour in many sectors so that it could control economic activities more directly.[5] However, in Europe, the idea that a cartel could damage consumers and the economy already existed in the 1890s. During that time, the harms caused by cartels became increasingly serious and provoked public concern, whereas in Japan, with its traditional culture of respect for harmony and cooperation, a cartel was not considered 'bad' by its nature (and was later viewed, as noted above, as a necessary evil even after cartels formally became illegal). In Europe, legal sanctions against cartels were established as early as in the nineteenth century.[6] For instance, in Germany, the Weimar government attempted to control cartels; however, the National Socialists took a radical turn in their approach to economic policy, enacting, among other measures, the Compulsory Cartels Law in 1933. This legislation authorised new cartels

---

[3] For detailed discussion on the history of bid rigging in Japan, see Toshifumi Hienuki, 'Lack of Competition Culture in the Japanese Administrative Organs: The Example of Public Bidrigging', *Hokkaido Journal of New Global Law & Policy*, **17** (2012) at 312–13 (in Japanese).

[4] See JFTC, *AMA Policy Fifty Years History*, Volume 1 (Kosei Torihiki Kyokai, 1997) pp. 21–2 (in Japanese).

[5] See David J. Gerber, *Law and Competition in Twentieth Century Europe: Protecting Prometheus* (Oxford University Press, 1998) p. 116.

[6] See, e.g., Gerber, ibid., pp. 53, 60. Professor Gerber explains that an Austrian statute of 1803 was designed to prevent merchants from capitalising on shortages caused by the Napoleonic wars, and at the end of the nineteenth century, even after interesting debates, Austria failed to adopt the cartel law.

and indeed forced companies to join cooperative agreements for the sake of the national economic interest and welfare.[7] In Japan, following the sharp decline in AMA enforcement in the 1950s, cartel investigation became more active in the 1960s, not least because of price-fixing cartels and other illegal activities that were contributing to a rise in consumer prices.[8] Through the 1970s the number of cartel cases investigated by the JFTC increased, but the main cases concerned cartels implemented through industrial associations. Further, more than 90 per cent of the cases concerned price-fixing cartels.[9]

Under the GHQ's policy, an ambitious campaign was launched to dissolve the mega-conglomerate *zaibatsu* groups. Dissolution of the *zaibatsu* was ironically one of the reasons why cartels of suppliers in Japan became active in the post-war period. Mainly aimed at cost reduction, it became more common to see makers of finished products purchasing parts from suppliers operating outside of the *zaibatsu* corporate structures. This created uncomfortable competition among parts suppliers, who then resorted to cartel conduct since they could no longer benefit from the stable demand of producers belonging to the *zaibatsu*.

A famous cartel case in Japan was triggered by the first oil crisis as a result of OPEC's role in restricting the supply of oil worldwide. The crisis prompted 12 Japanese oil companies occupying around 85 per cent of the market to act in their turn as a cartel, a move that hardly endeared them to the public. The JFTC issued a decision finding that the companies had fixed prices in violation of the AMA, and a criminal investigation was also conducted.[10] Following a long saga of litigation and appeals, the Supreme Court of Japan in its judgment of 24 February 1984 stated that 'unreasonable restraint of trade' is defined as business activities by which any companies, by contract, agreement or any other concerted practices, irrespective of the name given to it, with other companies, mutually restrict or conduct their activities in such a manner as to fix, maintain or increase prices, or to limit production, technology, products, facilities, customers or suppliers, thereby causing, contrary to

---

[7] See Tony A. Freyer, *Antitrust and Global Capitalism 1930–2004* (Cambridge University Press, 2006) pp. 63–4.

[8] See Chapter 2 (this volume) on the historical background.

[9] Supra note 4 JFTC at 234. Less than 10 per cent of the cartels between 1970 and 1976 concerned quota allocation and distribution channels and equipments.

[10] Oil cartel criminal case, judgment of the Supreme Court, 24 February 1984.

the public interest, a substantial restraint of competition in any particular field of trade.[11]

In the same case, the Supreme Court interpreted the definition of 'public interest' for purposes of applying Article 2(6) AMA and Article 3 AMA. According to the Court, in an exceptional case where, after balancing free competition, the integrity of the economic order and other interests affected by the conduct concerned, if it is found that collusive conduct can in fact be reconciled with the final objective of the AMA, that is, the 'protection of general consumers' interests and the promotion of national economy in a democratic and sound way', the conduct will be deemed not to fall within the category of 'unreasonable restraint of trade'. In this case, the Court concluded that the parties had failed to refute the JFTC's finding that their price-fixing agreement harmed consumers, even if, as the companies argued, their conduct might have prevented extremely high prices in the future. This resulted in a judgment condemning ten companies and 13 individuals.

Despite the generally positive ruling in the oil cartel case and despite the strengthening of the AMA in 1977, the perception of outside observers was that antitrust enforcement in Japan was still falling short of its potential. However, adjustments were made in the 1990s, and particularly in the last decade the JFTC's pursuit of cartels and bid rigging has become more proactive in enforcement of cases and clarification of illegal conducts. Among other initiatives, for example, on 26 June 2001, the JFTC adopted Guidelines concerning joint activities for recycling under the AMA in order to establish general principles as to how such joint activities will be treated under the AMA.[12]

As a result of several bid rigging cartels in which the construction companies exchanged sensitive information on their general strategy in relation to the bids involving Ministry of Land, Infrastructure, Transport and Tourism in 2007, 2009 and 2012, the JFTC requested the Ministry to take actions to prevent public bid rigging involving this ministry under

---

11 Ibid.

12 JFTC, the Guidelines Concerning Joint Activities for Recycling under the Antimonopoly Act, as revised, available at http://www.jftc.go.jp/dk/risaikuru.html. Similarly, the JFTC issued the Guidelines Concerning Joint Research and Development under the Antimonopoly Act in 1993 and the Guidelines on Standardization and Patent Pool Arrangements in 2005. Available at http://www.jftc.go.jp/en/legislation_gls/imonopoly_guidelines.files/jointresearch.pdf.

the Act on Prevention of Bid Rigging in Public Procurement.[13] This demonstrates that the bid rigging control in Japan is still weak and ineffective.

More and more firms appeal against the JFTC's cartel decisions before the Japanese courts. In February 2012, the Supreme Court rendered the first judgment regarding the the JFTC's bid rigging decision and upheld the analysis of the JFTC in terms of the evidence that established unreasonable restraint of trade under Article 2(6) AMA.[14]

LEGAL STRUCTURE OF CARTELS AND BID RIGGING IN JAPAN AND IN THE EU

Cartel behaviour is governed under Article 2(6) AMA and Article 3 AMA in Japan. Collusive conduct that unreasonably restrains trade is prohibited; and in order to sanction such conduct the JFTC can impose surcharges that essentially claw back at least some of the ill-gotten gains. Further, Article 8 AMA provides for a special prohibition of acts of a trade association if they substantially restrict competition. The inclusion of the latter provision is explained by the fact that, in the past, cartels in Japan were often conducted through or with the aid of trade associations. In addition, an international agreement that amounts to a cartel is prohibited under Articles 6 and 8 AMA. And, particularly given Japan's notorious history of problems with collusive tenders, it is also relevant to note the existence of a special law for public bid rigging.[15]

In contrast to the EU competition rules (but like several other jurisdictions), in Japan it is possible to impose penal sanctions on individuals and companies involved in collusive behaviour mainly under Articles 89(1) and 95 AMA; and Article 96-3 of the Criminal Code provides an additional basis for action where a company's employees obstruct a tender. In 1990, in a context in which perceptions on the part of foreign observers that antimonopoly enforcement in Japan was weak, the JFTC published Guidelines stating that it would thereafter indict

13 *Nihon Keizai Shimbun*, 17 October 2012 (in Japanese).

14 Tama Dango case, the judgment of the Supreme Court of 22 February 2012.

15 Act on Elimination and Prevention of Involvement in Bid Rigging, etc. and Punishments for Acts by Employees that Harm Fairness of Bidding, etc., Act No. 101 of 2002 ('Act on Prevention of Bid Rigging in Public Procurement'). Available at http://law.e-gov.go.jp/htmldata/H14/H14HO101.html (in Japanese).

serious cartels more proactively.[16] However, the number of cartels, and in particular bid rigging cases, is not decreasing. For 2011, in relation to bid rigging cases, the total number of companies subject to measures adopted by the JFTC was 252, and the JFTC imposed fines of 16.69 billion yen (approximately 130 million euros) on 229 companies.[17]

As is widely known, Article 101 TFEU is the main provision that governs EU cartel control, and the Commission may impose administrative fines to sanction an illegal cartel in accordance with the EU's procedural rules. At a very theoretical level, even a cartel is not automatically excluded from the possibility of qualifying for an exemption under Article 101(3) TFEU, but for practical purposes cartels (in contrast to legitimate collaborations and joint ventures between competitors) amount to illegal conduct that is beyond redemption. Therefore, it is not an exaggeration to speak of per se illegality in relation to price-fixing, output-restricting or bid rigging cartels under EU law.[18] The current Japanese rules have a somewhat different emphasis: by virtue of Article 3 AMA: a cartel is illegal if it substantially restrains competition in the relevant market and if it is contrary to the public interest. In this sense, under the Japanese rules, a cartel is not regarded as per se illegal. This ostensibly more flexible rule may partially reflect the traditional idea of Japanese business that a cartel is a necessary evil that has positive features, for example because it is perceived as yielding greater stability and enhanced certainty.

EU CARTEL INVESTIGATIONS AND JAPANESE FIRMS

The first case in which a Japanese company was involved in an EU cartel investigation was the *Quinine* cartel case of 1969.[19] In another case, in

---

[16] The JFTC's Guidelines of Filing Criminal Accusations against Violations of the Antimonopoly Act of 20 June 1990.

[17] See JFTC, Towards the Prevention of Bidrigging: AMA and Act on Elimination and Prevention of Involvement in Bid Rigging, etc. and Punishment for Acts by Employees that Harm the Fairness of Bidding, etc. (November 2012) 1, available at http://www.jftc.go.jp/kansei/honbun.pdf (in Japanese).

[18] The Commission's Fining Guidelines mention that the basic amount of the fine will be related to a proportion of the value of sales, and the proportion of the value of sales taken into account for cartels will generally be set at the higher end of the scale. See the Guidelines on the Method of Setting Fines Imposed Pursuant to Article 23(2)(a) of Regulation No 1/2003, OJ C 210, 1 September 2006, pp. 2–5, paras 19 and 23.

[19] *Quinine* Commission decision of 16 July 1969, OJ 1969 L192/5.

1974, the Commission declared that an agreement between French and Japanese companies to limit Japanese imports into Europe constituted an infringement of Article 85(1) EEC (now Article 101(1) TFEU).[20] In this case, French companies had asked the members of a Japanese export cartel to reduce their sales of ball-bearings in Europe, to increase their prices and to control the value and volume of their exports. The Japanese manufacturers accepted this request to participate in the European market in a more 'harmonious' way with their European counterparts.[21] The Commission issued its Opinion relating to imports into the European Community of Japanese products covered by the Treaty of Rome on 10 November 1972, in which the Commission clarified that Article 85 EEC Treaty was applicable as a measure intended to limit imports of Japanese products into the Community or control their prices and quality and recommended companies to notify any such agreements.[22] In this particular case, fines were not imposed because, according to the Commission, the voluntary restraint agreements concerning imports into the European market took place prior to the publication of the Commission's Opinion.[23] However, the Commission later initiated an antidumping investigation on imports of certain ball-bearings after receiving a complaint submitted by the Community roller-bearing industry and, in 1977, Council Regulation (EEC) No 1778/77 imposed a definitive antidumping duty on the Japanese bearing makers.[24]

---

20 Franco-Japanese Ball-bearings Agreement, Commission Decision of 29 November 1974 OJ 1974 L343/19. The Commission held that the agreement did not qualify for an exemption under Article 85 (3) not only because it had not been notified but also because it considered that it did not create any consumer benefits. See Jean-François Bellis, 'International Trade and the Competition Law of the European Economic Community', *Common Market Law Review*, **16** (1979) 647–83, at 659.

21 See Commission's press release of 4 December 1974, IP (74)214.

22 Opinion relating to imports of Japanese products in the Community falling under the Treaty of Rome OJ 1972 C111/13.

23 See the Commission's press release, supra note 21. It mentions that the Commission decided not to fine the companies in view of the special circumstances of the case, in particular the fact that the agreement was concluded before the Commission's Opinion was published. See also supra Bellis note 20 at 660.

24 Regulation No. 1778/77 OJ 1977 L 196/1. In Japan, export cartels were exempted from the AMA by the Export and Import Transaction Act. See, e.g., Mitsuo Matsushita (ed.), *EC Economic Law* (Yuhikaku, 1993) pp. 72–3 (in Japanese).

It was in the Seamless steel tubes cartel of 1999 that three Japanese companies were fined for the first time by the Commission for collusive conduct. As of 2012, the number of EU cartel cases in which Japanese companies were involved was 24, and around 50 Japanese companies have been fined.[25] Against this background, Japanese companies continue to make efforts to win leniency races to obtain immunity or leniency from the Commission when they discover their involvement in cartels affecting the EU market.[26] In the *Marine Hoses* cartel in January 2009, the Commission imposed fines totalling approximately 131 million euros on five companies for their role in market-sharing and price-fixing between 1986 and 2007.[27] A Japanese company that had participated in the cartel together with another Japanese and four Western firms applied successfully for immunity and thus were not fined by the Commission.

VERTICAL CARTELS AND PUBLIC BID RIGGING

The term 'vertical cartel' is sometimes used in Japan. It refers to mutually restrictive relations between undertakings operating at different levels of trade and may also refer to vertical restraints under EU competition law. This issue is related to the interpretation of the wording of Article 2(6) AMA ('mutually restrict or conduct their business activities in such a manner as to [...]') and in particular to the question of whether this definition can apply to parties only if they are horizontal competitors.[28] If that were the case, then the JFTC would have to resort to the provision prohibiting unfair trade practices, that is, Article 19 AMA – with its comparatively softer remedies and deterrent effects. Initially, in 1953, the Tokyo High Court found that, in order to be caught by Article 2(6) AMA and Article 3 AMA, the parties must indeed be

---

[25] The details and statistics were explained by Eric Van Ginderachter (Director of the Cartels Directorate at DG Competition) in his speech 'Fights against Cartels in the EU: Practice and Impact on Japanese Businesses, Cartel Enforcement in the European Union? – Why Japanese Business Should Care' at the Keidanren seminar in Tokyo on 1 November 2012.

[26] See Chapter 9 (this volume) on fining policy.

[27] *Marine Hoses* COMP/39406, Commission Decision of 28 January 2009 OJ 2009 C 168/6. See also the Commission's press release IP/09/137. On appeal, the General Court partially reduced the fines. Case T-146/09 *Parker ITR Srl & Parker-Hannifin Corporation v Commission.*

[28] For a theoretical development of this issue and possible solutions, see, e.g., Tadashi Shiraishi, *Competition Law of Japan* (2nd edn, Yuhikaku Publishing, 2009) pp. 132–6.

competitors, and furthermore restrictions in the contested agreement must be mutual. In a subsequent judgment, however, the Tokyo High Court relaxed its position and held that, to be a cartel participant, the companies need only be competitors 'in essence', and that the parties can be active at different levels of trade.[29] The JFTC's Guidelines also confirm this interpretation.[30] Although this more flexible approach may facilitate the JFTC's fight against the most frequently seen pattern of cartel conduct, called *kansei dango*, the specific practices of the Japanese Courts and the JFTC in this regard are not clear.[31] The term '*kansei dango*' denotes bid rigging that involves not only bidders themselves but also the public bureaucrat that organises the call for tender; normally, the collusion is in fact instigated by the relevant public officer. While the negotiations among bidders are horizontal, the agreement between the public officer and the bidding firms is regarded as vertical. *Dango taishitsu* (which roughly translated means 'tendency to collude') is the source of the biggest problems in Japan. It facilitated the manipulation of public tenders, and it has been difficult to terminate this kind of bid rigging notwithstanding the fact that the JFTC has intensified enforcement against such collusion since the mid-1990s. At present, the liability of the public officer does not arise under the AMA but results instead from the Act on Prevention of Bid Rigging in Public Procurement[32] and from Article 96-6 of the Criminal Code, which criminalised public bid rigging.

The increasing attention given to *dango* by the JFTC may engender friction with public purchasing authorities but the motivation behind it is clear. Bid rigging causes public money to be wasted, and it amounts to a serious infringement of the AMA. The JFTC issued its Guidelines on bid rigging in 1994 and then, in 2002, the legislature adopted the Act on Prevention of Bid Rigging in Public Procurement, which provides, inter alia, for criminal sanctions.[33] The JFTC has also issued a compliance manual to explain the rules on and penalties for bid rigging. Penalties include not only the surcharges imposed by the JFTC and criminal

29 Seal bid rigging criminal case, Tokyo High Court judgment of 14 December 1993.

30 See Distribution Guidelines, 1.2.3, Note 3.

31 See Shiraishi, supra note 28, at 133. It is submitted that since, in most of the cases, the facilitator was not an independent trader but an employee of one of the cartelists, it should be explained by analogy with accomplice liability under criminal law.

32 See supra note 15.

33 For the Guidelines, see http://www.jftc.go.jp/dk/kokyonyusatsu.html (in Japanese).

sanctions but also restrictions imposed on an infringer that preclude for a set period of time its future participation in public bids, a potentially very costly measure. Furthermore, in light of the changing environment, contracts awarded following a successful bid now commonly contain a clause providing for remedies in case the bid was made in violation of the AMA.[34]

Although the JFTC's fight against bid rigging has become more effective, and although it has drawn significant public attention, cultural factors still preclude a perfect solution to the *dango taishitsu* problem. In Japanese society, where hierarchy is generally highly respected, vertical cartels may not be sufficiently stigmatised. From a social perspective, it may still appear acceptable for a public authority, imbued with superior 'rank', to impose restrictions on lower 'ranks', that is, bidding firms. This seems to be the case even if it is fallacious to regard the collusion as being imposed, since it enhances the bidders' overall profits calculated across a large number of tenders. This respect towards hierarchy has continued even in modernised Japan also because it fits economic and social orders as well as political systems.

Public bid rigging was accepted in part because public organisations, such as regional governments, fulfilled the duty assigned to them by the central government to protect the regional economy by 'correctly' distributing the work to all the members of the regional industry. This reflected the values described above: respect for hierarchy between the central government and the regional government as well as trust of the companies towards public organisations and civil servants. Thus, the termination of bid rigging was not necessarily appreciated by the general public because it was perceived by some as a threat to social systems that functioned together with bid rigging.[35] In certain companies, there were employees with special responsibility for bid rigging, and their 'know-how' and contacts were transferred to successors when they retired or changed positions. These 'skilled' employees typically lost their jobs when it started to become clear that bid rigging would no longer be tolerated. The new policy momentum also had some unintended consequences because, in certain regional construction tenders, there was in fact no construction company that was eligible to submit a bid because all the companies in the area had been penalised for bid rigging and precluded from participating in a tender for a fixed period.

---

[34] Actual situations of Cartel and Economic Theory Analysis, JFTC Competition Policy Research Center (March 2008), available at http://www.jftc.go.jp/cprc/reports/cr-0307.pdf (in Japanese).

[35] See Hienuki, supra note 3 at 314 (in Japanese).

Further, in the Saitama Saturday Association *Dango* case, the corruption in the construction industry revealed complex relations between politicians and construction companies. In this case, the JFTC issued its decision in June 1992. Subsequently, it was discovered that a vice president of an implicated construction company had offered money to the Minister of Construction to avoid criminal indictment of the JFTC. Further investigations revealed that numerous central and regional politicians such as a mayor and a governor were involved in corruption in construction bid riggings, provoking derivative suits of construction companies.[36] Moreover, in 2011, the JFTC found bid riggings in engineering and road pavement construction works in the Ibaraki Prefecture and for the first time requested remedial measures to the governor of the Ibaraki Prefecture under the Act Concerning Elimination and Prevention of Involvement in Bid Rigging, etc.[37]

Times have changed, however. Today the controls imposed on bid rigging in Japan have become very strict. As explained above, because a vertical cartel is considered illegal just as horizontal cartels are, not only bidders who colluded but also the bid organiser who participated in a conspiracy can be sanctioned. Most bid rigging cases in Japan involve public bids but the number of private bids under investigation is increasing. These are treated in a similar manner.

The EU approach to bid rigging is somewhat different. As regards the idea of a 'vertical cartel', such an arrangement is considered by the European Commission to be a vertical infringement but not a cartel. In the *Nintendo* case, the Court of First Instance (now the General Court) distinguished between a cartel of a horizontal nature and an agreement of a vertical nature.[38] According to longstanding principles, Article 101(1) TFEU applies to each. However, in the EU, bid rigging is not a special and separate category of cases but rather is considered to be similar to other types of collusion such as market-sharing cartels and production quota cartels.[39] Bid rigging often consists of coordinated bids in procurement events by private companies in the EU and manipulating tender

---

[36] See, e.g., JFTC, Analysis of Actual Situations of Cartel and Theoretical Analysis (March 2005), p. 5. Available at http://www.jftc.go.jp/cprc/reports/cr-0307.pdf. See *Saitama Saturday Association*, JFTC decision of 4 June 1992.

[37] Ibaraki Construction bid rigging, JFTC decision of 4 August 2011.

[38] Case T-13/03, *Nintendo Co., and Nintendo of Europe GmbH v Commission* (2009) ECR II-947.

[39] Article 101(1) TFEU refers to agreements to fix prices and to limit production, as among other examples, but it does not mention bid rigging explicitly. The examples given are non-exhaustive, however, and the scope of the

procedures is often only one element of a cartel. For instance, in the *Marine Hoses* cartel, which is regarded as a textbook bid rigging case, the arrangement between the companies on the whole amounted to a classic cartel involving the fixing of prices and quotas.[40] Likewise, in the *Pre-insulated Pipes* case, the Commission uncovered a cartel that engaged in market sharing, price fixing and bid rigging in the European pre-insulated pipe market.[41] In Raw Tobacco – Italy, the coordination of bids at a public auction was cited as one of the forms of wrongdoing in addition to allocation of quantities and the fixing of trade conditions for purchase.[42,43] In European practice, bid rigging generally involves a conspiracy on the part of the bidders but without the implicit or explicit cooperation of the purchasing authority; public-private collusion (*kansei dango*) is not so common. Thus, although bid rigging is considered to be just as serious as other hard core cartel behaviour under EU competition law,[44] the main enforcer, that is, the Commission, is not obliged to devote special attention to bid rigging in general or *kansei dango*-type arrangements in particular. Also in the EU, a cartel participant who is not a competitor but is rather considered a facilitator in a cartel can be sanctioned under EU cartel control, but unlike the *kansei dango* scenario, this person is usually not a government official. For example, in the *Marine Hoses* cartel case, an ex-employee of one of the firms concerned assumed the role of a coordinator with whom cartel members exchanged

---

prohibition is quite flexible as long as an agreement or concerted practice has the object or effect of restricting competition.

[40] See, e.g., Maurits Pino, 'The Marine Hoses Cartel', *Competition Policy Newsletter*, **2** (European Commission, 2009) 53.

[41] Pre-insulated pipes, COMP/35691, Commission decision of 21 October 1998. For appeals to the then CFI, see Cases T-21/99 *Dansk Rørindustri v Commission* [2002] ECR II-1681, T-9/99 *HFB and others v Commission* [2002] ECR II-1487, T-17/99 *KE KELIT v Commission* [2002] ECR II-1647, T-23/99 *LR AF 1998 v Commission* [2002] ECR II-1705, T-15/99 *Brugg Rohrsysteme v Commission* [2002]ECR II-1613, T-16/99 *Lögstör Rör v Commission* [2002] ECR II-1633, T-31/99 *ABB Asea Brown Boveri v Commission* [2002] ECR II-1881. For appeals to the ECJ, see Cases C-189/02 P, C-202/02 P, C-205/02 P, to C-208/02 P and C-213/02 P.

[42] Raw Tobacco – Italy, OJ L353, p. 45 of 13 December 2006, Case T-11/06 *Romana, Tabacchi Srl v Commission*, Case T-19/06 *Mindo Srl v Commission* and Case T-39/06 *Transcatab SpA v Commission.*

[43] For bid rigging under EU competition law, see, e.g., Van Bael and Bellis, *Competition Law of the European Community* (5th edn, Kluwer Law International, 2010) pp. 377–8.

[44] See, e.g., Mark Jephcott, *Law of Cartels* (2nd edn, Jordan Publishing, 2011) p. 88.

sensitive information regularly.[45] However, under Article 23 of Regulation 1/2003 the Commission has no power to fine individuals separately except in the rare case where an individual acts as an undertaking.[46] As regards undertakings, consistent with the increasing vigorous enforcement of the Commission against cartels, the Commission started to impose fines on cartel facilitators.[47]

In the EU, a 'cartel' is a concerted practice between competitors that (unlike some efficient forms of collaboration) cannot be justified. A 'vertical cartel' covers the coordination of certain market functions, such as an agreement between a supplier and a distributor, and it can be assessed case by case.[48] As noted above, since Article 101 TFEU covers both horizontal and vertical agreements and concerted practices, the distinction between a horizontal cartel and a vertical cartel does not appear important under EU competition law insofar as the scope of the prohibition is concerned. However, since horizontal collusion is generally considered to be the most economically damaging form of conduct under the competition rules, horizontal conduct generally is given clear priority as a matter of policy, although maybe it depends on the kind of vertical conduct that is at stake.[49] Further, in the EU, there is a highly elaborate set of rules that apply to public procurement and date back to the 1970s, and rigging of a public bid generally is not in the EU level but of a national nature of a cartel case, which is the subject of an investigation conducted by the EU Member States' competition agency.[50] Thus bid rigging cannot become a principal pattern of cartel conduct in the EU.

---

45 *Marine Hoses*, COMP/39406.

46 Pino, supra note 40, at 54.

47 See, e.g., organic peroxides cartel case: an independent Swiss consultancy was given a nominal fine of 1000 EUR and then fined again (this time, 174 000 EUR) in relation to a heat stabilisers cartel in 2009 for its role as facilitator in each case. Case T-99/04 *AC Treuhand v Commission* [2008] ECR II-1501 and Case T-27/10 *AC Treuhand v Commission*.

48 François Souty, *Le droit et la politique de la concurrence de l'Union européenne* (4th edn, Montchrestien, 2013) pp. 48, 54–5.

49 See Souty, ibid. p. 51.

50 See, e.g., Alberto Heimler, 'Cartels in Public Procurement', *Journal of Competition Law and Economics*, 8 (4) (2012) 862. It explains why there are few leniency applications in relation to bid rigging agreements although the EU leniency programme has been highly successful.

PASSIVE MEMBERS OF A CARTEL

In Japan, a passive bid rigging participant, that is to say, a participant who did not make any effort to win a bid but cooperated by remaining passive so that the prearranged winner of the public contract would be successful, is not considered to have infringed the AMA.[51] This issue concerns the interpretation of the term 'mutually restrict' under Article 2(6) AMA. The JFTC and the majority of legal scholars consider that, in the case of a cooperative but passive member as described above, there is no mutual restriction, because only the bid rigger that won the bid enjoyed the benefit.[52] In contrast, the European Commission assesses the passivity of a cartel participant only at the stage of calculating the fines after identifying him as a cartelist. Although, in the 1998 Fining Guidelines, the Commission could grant a fine reduction for purely passive behaviour, the 2006 Fining Guidelines do not provide for this possibility.[53] Considering the increasingly severity of the Commission against cartels, lenient treatment for a passive cartelist has become less likely. The differences between the application of the EU rules and of the AMA in Japan may not be fully appreciated by Japanese firms under investigation by the European Commission.

For example, in the *Gas Insulated Switchgear* cartel case, the Commission fined 11 groups of companies a total of over 750 million euros for cartelising gas insulated switchgear products, used for the regulation of high-voltage power transformers and protection of related equipment.[54] Between 1988 and 2004, Japanese and European companies engaged in a variety of collusive activities including, among other things, the rigging of procurement bids. A European company was granted full immunity from fines under the Commission's leniency programme. The companies had agreed that the Japanese companies would not sell in Europe, while

---

[51] See, e.g., *Fukuoka Construction and Gardening Bid Rigging* case: the JFTC decision of 12 September 2001 became final owing to the withdrawal of the action for annulment of the JFTC decision on 7 May 2002. In this regard, see also the JFTC's Annual Report of 2002 (in Japanese).

[52] See Shiraishi, supra note 28, pp. 133–4.

[53] See Augustijn Van Haasteren, 'The Judgments in the Nintendo Case', *Competition Newsletter*, **2** (2009) 51.

[54] *Gas Insulated Switchgear* COMP/38.899. The decision, which was re-adopted after the appeal before the European General Court, is available at http://ec.europa.eu/competition/antitrust/cases/dec_docs/39966/39966_295_15.pdf.

the European companies would not sell in Japan. The Japanese companies were fined, to their surprise, despite their nearly total absence from the EU market for gas insulated switchgear. The Commission considered that the agreement to abstain from EU tenders contributed directly to the restriction of competition on the EU market. It was not easy for Japanese companies to understand why the Japanese companies in this cartel, despite their passive role, were sanctioned with such a high fine.[55,56]

ILLUSTRATIVE CARTEL CASES IN THE AUTOMOTIVE PARTS SECTOR

Automotive parts cartels are currently under investigation in several major jurisdictions, including in Japan and the EU. The relevant competition authorities have been coordinating their parallel investigations. A brief survey of these cases follows.

In the wire harness cartel (the relevant products being used in automotive electrical distribution systems), the JFTC in February 2010 inspected the Japanese manufacturers. The investigation started almost at the same time as did the EU investigation.[57] On 19 January 2012, the JFTC issued cease and desist orders, and surcharge payment orders against three manufacturers of automotive wire harnesses and related products, finding that they had substantially restrained competition in the field of automotive wire harnesses and related products.[58]

In March 2012, the JFTC conducted inspections of the premises of various manufacturers of another car part, headlamps, and issued cease and desist orders together with surcharges of 4.7 billion yen on 22 March 2013.[59] In July 2011 and March 2012, the JFTC also inspected the premises of the four main producers of bearings for an alleged price-fixing cartel.[60] Subsequently, in April 2012, the Tokyo District Prosecutor's Office and

---

55 The fine imposed on one of the Japanese companies was the second highest fine ever for Japanese companies in EU cartel control.

56 'Disclosed by the European *Gas Insulated Switchgear* cartel: the 'essence' of the risk to which the Japanese companies are exposed', *Weekly Diamond* (9 May 2007) 14, 15.

57 See the JFTC's decision of 19 January 2012.

58 Ibid.

59 Headlamps and rear combination lamps, the JFTC decision of 22 March 2013.

60 See *Kosei Torihiki Jyoho*, **2320** (19 March 2012). One of the companies announced to have received a questionnaire from the Commission in relation to a car parts cartel.

the JFTC conducted further inspections. In March 2013, the JFTC imposed surcharges totalling 13 billion yen on three bearing companies and one company who escaped a surcharge was an immunity applicant.[61]

For automotive starters, radiators, generators and other automotive components, a Japanese company applied for immunity in Japan and, in July 2011, the JFTC raided the premises of seven Japanese companies (cooperating in the investigation with the Antitrust Division of the US Department of Justice). As a result, in November 2012, the JFTC imposed fines on four companies of over 3.3 billion yen (around 29 million euros) for their cartel conduct.[62]

In the EU, in November 2008, the Commission issued a decision imposing fines on four companies, including Japanese firms, for their alleged cartel behaviour in the car glass sector. In this case, the fines imposed on a French company (Saint-Gobain) were at that time the highest ever imposed on a company, partly explained by an extra penalty for recidivism.[63] In February 2010, the Commission, together with the US Department of Justice and the JFTC, carried out coordinated dawn raids at the offices of manufacturers of automotive electrical and electronic components and in the EU, the Commission conducted dawn raids in several Member States as part of its investigation into the automotive parts cartels.[64] Subsequently, in August 2012, the Commission opened an investigation into the wire harness cartel case.[65] In the meantime, the Commission carried out another unannounced inspection at the premises of producers of car parts such as safety systems, bearings and thermal systems.[66]

The series of cartels described above did not concern public bid rigging but they did feature manipulation of private procurement. This type of conduct is commonly found in both the EU and Japan. As noted above, since the dissolution of the *zaibatsu*, suppliers selling parts operating outside of the *zaibatsu* corporate structures have had a tendency to collude in Japan. This series of car parts cartel cases reveals that

---

[61] Bearing cartel, the JFTC decision of 29 March 2013.

[62] See the JFTC's decision of 22 November 2012, available at http://www.jftc.go.jp/en/pressreleases/121121%20press%20release_docx.pdf. The JFTC initiated the investigation at almost the same time as the US authorities.

[63] See the Commission's cartel statistics at http://ec.europa.eu/competition/cartels/statistics/statistics.pdf.

[64] The Commission's MEMO/10/49 of 25 February 2010.

[65] See the Commission's press release of 9 August 2012, available at http://europa.eu/rapid/press-release_IP-12-894_en.htm?locale=en.

[66] For safety systems, see MEMO/11/395; for bearings, see MEMO/11/766; and for thermal systems, see MEMO/12/563.

this collusive practice among Japanese parts producers, partly based on Japanese history, appears to cover the EU market and also reveals that, in the EU, there is a similar collusive practice among European car parts manufacturers. In this case, cooperation among different competition agencies is essential to tackling such cartels, and has proven to be successful.

CARTEL EXEMPTIONS

In Japanese, the word 'cartel' is translated as *dango,* which means collusion; or as *karuteru,* which is a phonetic representation of 'cartel'.[67] Another Japanese word that means a cartel is '*yami-karuteru*'. *Yami* means secret, hidden or unauthorised. Traditionally in Japan, these different expressions implied that there are different types of cartel: one type is hidden and illegal by nature; but then there are open and public cartels that should be tolerated. What is more, as opposed to a *yami-karuteru,* a *karuteru* may mean a legally authorised cartel, in particular one that qualifies for an exemption. However, as awareness of AMA enforcement and of the illegal nature of cartels has grown with time, the distinction between *yami-karuteru* and *karuteru* is blurring. Furthermore, the number of exemptions has decreased radically over the decades. Today there are few exempted cartels, although certain exemptions are still applicable under exceptional circumstances. In the EU, there is no common distinction between a cartel and a '*yami*' cartel. In EU usage, the term 'cartel' is itself negative, and refers to horizontal collusion that is beyond redemption. Such cartels are almost always secret until they are exposed. To speak of an exempted cartel would be quite odd, although in the past liner 'conferences' in the shipping sector were block exempted. Horizontal coordination that benefits from an exemption under Article 101(3) TFEU or under a block exemption is generally referred to as a joint venture, or as a cooperation agreement, or patent pools, standard-setting organisations, and so on.

In Japan, a 'crisis cartel' exemption is stipulated in Articles 24-3 and 24-4 AMA, and the conditions that must be satisfied to benefit from such an exemption are similar to the conditions under Article 101(3) TFEU. In

[67] In relation to 'karuteru', Professor Shiraishi considers that, because the Japanese word 'karuteru' is used for various meanings, the use of this word (as opposed to the statutory language, 'unreasonable restraint of trade') is inadequate for accurate legal analysis. See Shiraishi, supra note 28, p. 123 footnote 34.

practice, an exemption is accepted only under very limited circumstance in both jurisdictions.[68]

At a very early stage of AMA enforcement (the mid-1950s), such an exemption applied to a production cartel among hemp yarn producers for about five years and six months.[69] Later exemptions were more limited in time, with duration from three months to two and a half years. The relevant industries varied from sugar to diesel engines.[70] Perhaps surprisingly, given Japan's persistent economic troubles, the last case in which the crisis cartel exemption rule was applied was terminated in 1989. The crisis cartel was abolished amid efforts of deregulation in the Japanese market, triggered by foreign pressure.[71]

Currently, the creation of a similar exemption is under discussion.[72] One is to allow small and medium sized companies to discuss among themselves how to pass on price increases owing to Japan's consumption tax to their buyers and how to indicate this increase in their prices.[73] In Japan, the consumption tax law was enacted in 1988 and the conflict between the AMA and the SMEs' 'passing on' cartel was an issue.[74] In order to introduce the consumption tax smoothly, a temporary exemption for such 'passing on' cartels (two-thirds of whose members were small and medium sized companies) between 1988 and 1991 was adopted together with accompanying Guidelines. Notification was required and the total number of notifications was 4589.[75] Today, the purpose of the exemption is to protect SMEs from powerful buyers upon the envisaged

---

[68] Details are provided in the submissions of the EU and of Japan to the OECD's recent survey on crisis cartels: OECD, 'Policy Roundtable: Crisis Cartels' (2011) available at http://www.oecd.org/daf/competition/cartelsandanti-competitiveagreements/48948847.pdf.

[69] See JFTC, supra note 4, p. 112.

[70] See JFTC, supra note 4, p. 430.

[71] Akira Negishi and Masayuki Funada, *Japanese Antitrust Law* (4th edn, Yuhikaku, 2010) p. 395.

[72] See, e.g., *Nihonkeizai Shinbun*, 31 May 2012. Another exemption rule regarding the increase of the consumption tax was adopted when the consumption tax was introduced in Japan in 1989. See also Chapter 3 (this volume) on legal structure and enforcement.

[73] See JFTC, supra note 4 at pp. 549–50.

[74] See, e.g., Shoji Takahashi, 'Summary of Passing On of Consumption Tax and Antimonopoly Act', *Jurist*, **931** (1 April 1989) 64.

[75] For a detailed explanation on this issue, see JFTC, supra note 4, pp. 389–95. The idea of 'consumption tax pass-on of cartels' is not known to Europe. In this regard, see, e.g., Tomoki Yamada, 'Nature and Scope of AMA Exemption: Focused on the Issues Regarding Consumption Tax "Pass-On" of Cartels', *Nihon University Journal of Legal Research*, **32** (2002), 136.

introduction of a consumption tax of 8 per cent in 2014 and 10 per cent in 2015.[76] Compared to the EU, the consumption tax has generally been very low in Japan, and its increase has provoked strong objections from industries. In order to realise the increased consumption tax smoothly, the government may try to alleviate the burden on companies that have to pass on the tax to consumers.

Under the EU rules, a practice that might be caught by Article 101(1) TFEU is examined (if plausibly relevant) under the Block Exemption Regulations and if it is not block exempted, it may still be possible to qualify for an individual exemption under Article 101(3) TFEU.[77] The Commission explained the limited circumstances in which an exemption is possible after the Irish beef and crisis cartels[78], which aim to reduce industry overcapacity. Exemption can be justified in situations where structural overcapacity cannot be remedied by market forces alone within a reasonable period of time and is most likely where giving up capacity is costly for the firms in stable, transparent and symmetric market structures.[79]

CONCLUSION

As seen above, in Japan, there are mainly two kinds of cartel that are problematic. The first kind is the classic textbook cartel, common worldwide, in which firms conspire to fix prices, restrict output, boycott third parties, and so on, to the detriment of consumers. The second kind, traditionally more prominent in Japan, involves the practice of *kansei dango*, where, with the explicit or implicit understanding or encouragement of purchasing authorities, companies collude on public tenders. Eradication of the latter practice seems likely to require special strategies

---

[76] See JFTC, 'Basic Guidelines on Smooth and Appropriate Passing On and Indication of Consumption Tax', 26 October 2012, available at http://www.kantei.go.jp/jp/singi/shouhizei/pdf/kettei_121026.pdf. However, a new administration assumed power in December 2012 and Taro Aso, the new Finance Minister, stated that a decision concerning the envisaged increase of consumption tax would not be made until October 2013. *Sankei News*, 27 December 2012, available at http://sankei.jp.msn.com/politics/news/121227/stt12122708420005-n1.htm.

[77] See Chapter 3 (this volume) on legal structure and enforcement.

[78] Case C-209/07, *Competition Authority v Beef Industry Development Society Ltd and Barry Brothers (Carrigmore) Meats Ltd*, (2008) ECR I-8637).

[79] See OECD, DAF/COMP/GF/WD (2011) 20 of 27 January 2011.

and instruments, whereas more pedestrian cartels can be tackled in the same way as in the EU and elsewhere.

With regard to *kansei dango*, the JFTC is making continuous efforts both to detect and punish bid rigging and to promote compliance through dissemination of information and by encouraging specific compliance training programmes addressed to specific groups of people and companies. By contrast, international cooperation among competition agencies, including, for example, simultaneous or quasi-simultaneous dawn raids, is essential for the worldwide fight against cartels. Needless to say, another crucial factor in cartel enforcement is the leniency programme, which in Japan has enhanced the JFTC's ability to uncover and punish collusive conduct.

Although the field of cartels is one of the areas in which global convergence has advanced significantly in the last two decades, there are still some differences between Japan and the EU. This may require greater attention since, for both authorities and firms involved in international cartel investigations, harmonisation of the law and procedure of cartel control will be quite beneficial. As seen above in connection with the automotive parts cartels, numerous cartels are now being investigated simultaneously in different jurisdictions and companies may have to prepare multiple leniency applications and provide waivers of confidentiality to allow agencies to disclose information submitted to them to another agency. Moreover, since the European Commission is not obliged to take into account fines imposed on companies in jurisdictions outside the EU when it sanctions them, even though the same worldwide cartel may be at stake,[80] the firms in question may be exposed to disproportionate fines at the end of the day if cartel analysis is not harmonised.[81]

---

80 See the graphite electrodes cartel, Case C-308/04, *Commission v SGL Carbon*, judgment of the Court of Justice [2006] ECR I-5977. The ECJ confirmed that, in setting the fine, the Commission was not obliged to take account of penalties paid by SGL Carbon in other jurisdictions such as the US and Canada in the graphite electrodes cartel. See also the Commission's MEMO/06/258 of 29 June 2006.

81 For instance, discussion with the Commission regarding direct and indirect sales into the EU to define the product concerned is sometimes done bearing in mind the possibility of a similar investigation in the country of origin.

5. Vertical restraints

HISTORY OF VERTICAL RESTRAINTS IN JAPAN AND THE EU

The AMA was adopted under the strong influence of the US, when Japan was occupied by the Allied Occupation Forces.[1] However, the Japanese market featured particular distribution systems uncommon to the US market. Further, the peculiarities of distribution systems in Japan, such as the high density of small retail stores, the relatively limited number of large stores and complex wholesale channels was a longstanding tradition that could not easily be changed. *Keiretsu* is one of the examples of traditional vertical arrangements in Japan[2] and has long been considered by critics to be problematic (or by supporters to be efficient). The term refers to a business network of companies whose members own stakes in each other as a means of achieving mutual security and the integration of large industrial and banking operations. In some respects, *keiretsu* are similar to *zaibatsu*, which were (originally) family-owned corporate groups typical of the pre-World War II economy. Under *keiretsu*, relations between the companies are rigidly fixed and their commercial transactions are often based on vague conditions without any formal contracts. They sometimes impose unfair conditions on a smaller party. 'Production *keiretsu*' take the form of arrangements at a production level between a manufacturer and a supplier of raw materials and components, while 'distribution *keiretsu*' is formed, for instance, between a supplier and a distributor. In addition to vague conditions and occasionally unfair practices and trading conditions, *keiretsu* often employ RPM, exclusive conditions, territorial restrictions, tying and rebates. *Keiretsu* may generate economic efficiency, for example by reducing transaction costs or the costs of production or distribution. Like other forms of vertical relations, however, *keiretsu* have at least the potential to foreclose markets to a

[1] See the introduction in Chapter 1 (this volume).

[2] *Keiretsu* can refer to both vertical and horizontal commercial relations. The focus in this chapter is on vertical distribution channels.

significant degree, and they are therefore often considered to be in tension with Japan's competition rules.

The 1953 amendment of the AMA is generally considered to have weakened the AMA, but in one specific context it reinforced control of vertical relations by prohibiting the abuse of a superior bargaining position in commercial transactions. The first important difference in the regulation of vertical restraints between the EU and Japan concerns their historical backgrounds. Japan's policy on vertical restraints and its enforcement activities have been strongly influenced by its traditional business practices, and by pressure from the US. The main provision of the AMA that deals with vertical restraints is Article 19, the unfair trade practices provision. Originally this provision was based on Section 5 of the US Federal Trade Commission Act of 1914 (unfair methods of competition). A principal purpose behind Section 5 FTC was to provide the US Fair Trade Commission with civil enforcement powers equivalent to those of the US Department of Justice.[3] In light of the distinctive historical background to Section 5, which was specific to the US, it has been argued that in Japan it was unnecessary to incorporate Article 19 into the AMA. Furthermore, it has been claimed that, because of this provision, the AMA became complex and very different from the structures of other jurisdictions' vertical rules. This may create problems to the extent that Japan seeks to harmonise its rules on vertical restraints with those of other jurisdictions.[4]

The JFTC's Distribution Guidelines were first adopted in 1991. Originally the Guidelines were adopted as one of the JFTC's responses to the Structural Impediments Initiative ('SII') talks between Japan and the US. The complaint on the US side was that enforcement was too lax with regard to illegal conduct that excluded foreign companies from the Japanese market. During the SII talks in July 1989, the SII Working Group identified structural problems in both countries that impeded trade and prevented an adjustment of the balance of payments between the two countries. The structural problems that were identified included antitrust law matters such as distribution systems in Japan in certain sectors. The Guidelines were quite different compared to other then existing Guidelines in terms of clarity and practical usefulness in explaining the rules of distribution, and they took into account issues relevant to specific sectors.

---

3 There are also long-running debates about whether and how far the scope of Section 5 of the FTC Act extends beyond that of Sections 1 and 2 of the Sherman Act.

4 See, e.g., Masahiro Murakami, *Hanrei Times*, **1331** (15 November 2010) 29.

Consequently they became a useful tool, and they remain a pertinent instrument for both the JFTC and business.[5]

In the EU, beginning in the mid-1990s the control of vertical restraints has changed substantially compared to prior practice. Since then, the experience with the Commission's Vertical Agreement Block Exemption Regulation (VABER) and Guidelines on Vertical Restraints has been positive, as these instruments have generally helped firms to comply with the EU's rules on vertical restraints while reducing the need for the Commission to use resources pursuing infringers.[6]

The 'modernised' approach to vertical restraints was formally introduced by Regulation 2790/1999, which entered into force on 1 June 2000.[7] This replaced the old block exemptions for exclusive distribution, exclusive purchasing and franchising, and it signalled an 'effects-based' analysis, in contrast to the more formulaic approach taken by the older block exemptions. On 1 June 2010 Regulation 2790/1999 was superseded by Regulation 330/2010, of the current version of the VABER, and the Guidelines on Vertical Restraints were updated. These latest reforms maintained substantial continuity with the modernised regime and only made relatively minor changes, for example by providing additional clarifications with regard to hard core restrictions.[8] The VABER and the Guidelines are based on the idea that for a proper assessment of a vertical agreement it is necessary to analyse its actual or likely effects on the market, both negative and positive. The same approach has been introduced in other block exemption regulations and guidelines regarding the

---

[5] Tadashi Shiraishi, *Competition Law of Japan* (2nd edn, Yuhikaku, 2009) p. 432. The Guidelines influence the practice of the JFTC and the Courts render their judgments based on the Guidelines although it is not legally binding.

[6] Mr Peeperkorn has explained that the framework of 1999, which introduced an effects-based approach, was strongly supported by respondents to the public consultation, and the principle of a market share threshold was also well accepted. Although, since 2004, most enforcement has been conducted by national authorities and courts, the Commission continues to ensure a consistent application of the EU vertical rules across the EU. See Presentation of Luc Peeperkorn, 'New EU Competition Rules for Purchase and Distribution Agreements', Belgium, Japan Association Chamber of Commerce, Seminar on Vertical Agreements (Brussels, May 2011).

[7] Commission Regulation 2790/1999 of 22 December 1999, OJ 1999 L336/21 of 29 December 1999.

[8] Regulation 330/2010 OJ L102 of 23 April 2010; Guidelines, OJ C130 of 19 May 2010.

application of Article 101 TFEU, such as those concerning technology transfer agreements and horizontal cooperation agreements.[9]

A side effect of the more restrictive interpretation of the prohibition in Article 101(1) TFEU as it applies to vertical agreements, together with the legislative change in 2004 whereby Article 101(3) TFEU became directly applicable (Regulation 1/2003), is that the enforcement of competition law in the field of vertical restraints has become predominantly a matter for national competition authorities. Since the entry into force of Regulation 2790/1999, the Commission has issued only a few decisions specifically relating to vertical restraint issues while the number of cases dealt with by national agencies and courts has increased significantly. The attendant risk is of diverging analytical approaches, although this may be mitigated to some degree by the instruments described above.

LEGAL FRAMEWORK OF VERTICAL RESTRAINTS

In Japan, vertical restraints within the meaning of Article 19 AMA encompass various forms of conducts as in the EU. In this regard, the JFTC issued a Notice designating 15 categories of conduct as unfair trade practices under the AMA (General Designations).[10] In addition to these General Designations, which are shown in Table 5.1, there are a few sector-specific Special Designations covering the newspaper industry and other industries.

However, in enforcing the rules on unfair trade practices in order to defend small and medium sized companies, the JFTC has drawn criticism, particularly when the targets of enforcement have been foreign undertakings.

As we saw, the AMA provides for prohibitions of private monopolisation, unreasonable restraints of trade, unfair trade practices and merger control. The provisions on unfair trade practices have historically been

---

[9] Commission Regulation No. 722/2004 on the application of Article 81(3) of the Treaty to categories of Technology Transfer Agreements, L123/11 of 27 April 2004. Guidelines on the applicability of Article 101 of the Treaty on the Functioning of the European Union to Horizontal Cooperation Agreements OJ C11, 14 January 2011, p. 1.

[10] The JFTC's Notice on Designation of Unfair Trade Practices, No. 15 (1982, revised in 2009). An English translation is available at http://www.jftc.go.jp/en/legislation_guidelines/ama/unfairtradepractices/index.html.

Table 5.1 JFTC Designations of Unfair Trade Practices

Article 2(9) AMA	(These conducts are subject to surcharges)	(1)	Refusal to supply		
		(2)	Discriminatory pricing for supply		
		(3)	Unjust law price		
		(4)	Resale price maintenance		
		(5)	Abuse of superior position		
	(These conducts are not subject to surcharges)	(6)	General Designations	1	Refusal to purchase
				2	Refusal to deal
				3	Unjust low price for purchase
				4	Discriminatory treatment in terms of commercial conditions
				5	Discriminatory treatment within a trade association
				6	Unjust low price sales
				7	Purchase at an excessive price
				8	Deceptive customer inducement
				9	Deceptive customer inducement by unjust benefits
				10	Tying
				11	Dealing under exclusive conditions
				12	Dealing under restrictive conditions
				13	Unfair interference with the appointment of an officer of its trading partner
				14	Interference with a competitor's transactions and business
				15	Interference with internal operation of a competitor

viewed as preventive measures against monopolisation[11] because they are not very clear and can be flexibly interpreted.[12] But beyond this concept of 'preventive measures', the unfair trade practice provisions are more actively used than the prohibition on unreasonable restraints of trade in

[11] See Mitsuo Matsushita and John D. Davis, *Introduction to Japanese Antimonopoly Law* (Yuhikaku, 1990) pp. 8–9.

[12] See Hiroshi Iyori and Akinori Uesugi, *The Antimonopoly Laws and Policies of Japan* (Federal Legal Publications, 1994) pp. 107–8.

cases of apparent overlap, where a practice could arguably be qualified either as an unfair trade practice or as an unreasonable restraint of trade.

Under the Japanese rules, the provisions on vertical restraints are essentially separated from those on horizontal restraints.[13] The distinction stems from a judgment of 1953, in which the Court established that Article 3 AMA (unreasonable restraints of trade) covered only horizontal agreements.[14] Consequently, it was Article 19 (unfair trade practices) that became the primary means to regulate vertical restraints. In contrast, under EU competition law, Article 101 TFEU applies to all agreements irrespective of whether they are horizontal or vertical. Under EU law, vertical restraints are defined as restraints in agreements between operators at different levels of trade.

While Article 101(1) TFEU can only apply to agreements, concerted practices or decisions by associations of undertakings, and thus contemplates only bilateral or multilateral conduct, in Japan the situation is rather different. Under Article 19 AMA it is not necessary to have an agreement or concerted practice, as long as an obligation imposed on a distributor can be established. According to the Powdered milk (*Wakodo*) judgment, the obligation is not necessarily contractual, if it is secured by any economic sanctions.[15] The point was also made apparent by the JFTC's Distribution Guidelines, which stated that a restraint 'includes' an agreement.

SUBSTANTIVE TEST

In the EU, there is a relatively liberal economics-based approach to restrictions imposed in vertical agreements. In many cases, anticompetitive effects are only likely to be found where the suppliers imposing restrictions have individual or collective market power. Negative effects of vertical restraints include anticompetitive foreclosure of other suppliers or other buyers, damage to active competition in the market, facilitation of collusion between a supplier (or a distributor) and its competitors and, in Europe, the creation of obstacles to market integration. Article 101(1) TFEU prohibits agreements, decisions and

---

13 See Chapter 4 (this volume) on cartels and bid rigging.

14 The judgment of the Tokyo High Court of 9 March of 1953. See also, e.g., Akira Negishi and Masayuki Funada, *Japanese Antitrust Law* (4th edn, Yuhikaku, 2010) pp. 145, 146.

15 *Wakodo*, judgment of Tokyo High Court of 17 July 1971 and judgment of Supreme Court of 10 July 1975.

concerted practices that have the object or effect of preventing, restricting or distorting the competition in the EU market.[16] Thus, no actual effect on the market is necessary for the rule to apply, which corresponds to the preventive nature of the provision.[17]

In Japan, the fundamental policy goal for vertical restraints is to remove obstacles to fair and free competition in the market. With emphasis on fair and free competition, unfair trade practices are not examined under the test of 'creation, maintenance and strength of market dominance', which is used as a test for substantial restraint of competition (Article 3 AMA).

Potentially anticompetitive vertical restraints include RPM, territorial restrictions, customer restrictions and restrictions on sales methods. In Japan, the analysis of anticompetitive effects is conducted using a form-based approach varying from conduct to conduct, as shown in Table 5.2. For instance, to examine non-compete obligations, the test is whether a restriction may make it difficult for new entrants to easily secure alternative distribution channels. As for territorial and customer restrictions, the test may be whether the price level of the products covered by the restriction is likely to be maintained. RPM is in practice considered per se illegal, while non-price restrictions are treated under a different mode of analysis.

MARKET SHARE

In the EU there is no presumption of illegality linked to market share in the field of vertical restraints. Instead, where the VABER does not apply owing to market shares that exceed the thresholds for the supplier or buyer (each fixed at 30 per cent), an individual assessment under Articles 101(1) and 101(3) TFEU will be required. In simple terms, this involves a trade-off between any appreciable adverse effects on competition in the market and countervailing pro-competitive benefits.

In Japan, market share thresholds are relevant, for instance, when the test as to whether a supplier is an influential company in the relevant market is used. The term 'influential supplier' refers to a manufacturer whose market share exceeds 10 per cent, or who is one of the three largest competitors in the relevant market. However, this 'influential

---

[16] See, e.g., Case C-56/55 *La Technique Minière Maschinenbau v Ulm GmbH* [1996] ECR 235.

[17] See, e.g., Doris Hildebrand, *Economic Analyses of Vertical Agreements: A Self-Assessment* (Kluwer Law International, 2005) p. 32.

Table 5.2 Tests for analysing anticompetitive effects of non-price restriction categories

Categories of non-price restriction	Main concerns	Possible tests used for analysis of anticompetitive effects
Non-compete obligation	Restriction of inter-brand competition	Influential supplier test Market foreclosure test
Territorial restriction	Restriction of intra-brand competition	Influential supplier test Price level test
Customer restriction (excluding restrictions on parallel trade)	Restriction of intra-brand competition	Price level test
Sales methods restriction (excluding online sales restrictions)	Restriction of inter-brand competition + intra-brand competition	Reasonable justification test

supplier' test is not applicable to all types of vertical restraint; it applies only in cases of certain restraints such as non-compete obligations and territorial restrictions.

Moreover, under EU law, where an agreement is made between companies that are not actual or potential competitors, if the market share held by each of the parties to the agreement does not exceed 15 per cent on any of the relevant markets affected by the agreement, the agreement is generally considered not to have appreciable anticompetitive effects, provided that it contains no hard core restriction.[18]

Where an agreement is made between companies that are actual or potential competitors, the agreement will only be considered not to have appreciable anticompetitive effects if the combined market share of the parties to the agreement does not exceed 10 per cent on any of the relevant markets affected by the agreement and where the agreement does not contain any hard core restrictions. Where competition in the market is restricted by 'cumulative effects' arising from networks of similar agreements concluded

[18] Commission Notice on agreements of minor importance that do not appreciably restrict competition under Article 81(1) of the Treaty establishing the European Community, OJ C368, 22 December 2001, pp. 13–15.

by different suppliers and distributors, a reduced market share threshold of 5 per cent applies for both agreements between competitors and agreements between non-competitors. For instance, intervention by the Commission is most likely where 50 per cent or more of the market is covered by selective distribution and the largest five suppliers have a combined market share equal to or greater than 50 per cent.

Compared to the 30 per cent thresholds in the VABER, the Japanese market share test is lower. As a result, in Japan it is often more important to conduct a more qualitative analysis; and the JFTC has broader discretion to determine whether a specific activity is anticompetitive. For instance, for non-compete obligations to be anticompetitive, the 'influential supplier' test (test 1) and a 'market foreclosure' test (test 2) must both be met. Accordingly, although the EU and Japan each use companies' market shares as a criterion, it seems that the Japanese rule is stricter than the EU rule. Furthermore, in Japan it may not be market shares as such but rather the relative positions of the parties that matter, in particular in cases of alleged abuse of a superior bargaining position. This approach is not generally followed in other countries, even in Asia. The reason why the market share threshold is low (10 per cent) in Japan is partly because the conduct that requires an 'influential supplier' test (non-compete obligations) often causes problems on the market where parallel networks of similar agreements are entered into by suppliers and buyers. On these markets, the share of each supplier may be relatively small but the agreements may nonetheless cause anticompetitive foreclosure.[19] In this scenario, in the EU, a reduced market share threshold of 5 per cent applies for both agreements between competitors and agreements between non-competitors; that is to say, below the 5 per cent market share it will be assumed that the agreement does not contribute significantly to the cumulative foreclosure effect.[20]

---

[19] In terms of the interpretation of the anticompetitive effects of parallel networks, there have been some developments in Japan. In *Oriental Rice Mill Factory (Toyo Seimai)*, a Tokyo High Court judgment of 17 February 1984, the Court stated that if every distributor belongs to a *keiretsu* and does not deal with outside suppliers, it is unlikely that these exclusive arrangements will distort competition. The judgment was criticised, because it implies that parallel networks of *keiretsu* do not create distortions of competition. Later, the JFTC's Distribution Guidelines of 1991 confirmed that parallel networks of *keiretsu* increase the likelihood and intensity of foreclosure effects.

[20] See De Minimis Notice Note 14, Point 8.

RPM

RPM in Japan includes longstanding traditional forms of vertical restraint. It may take the form of wholesale price fixing called *tatene*.[21] In contrast, vertical restraints by the headquarters of a company imposed on its member shops under franchise systems have been a relatively recent issue in Japan. Although the possibility of proposing specific legislation to regulate RPM was discussed long ago, the JFTC abandoned the idea of proposing such legislation in February 1968 and instead it decided to reinforce the enforcement of existing provisions to tackle RPM issues.[22]

In Japan, Article 19 AMA and Article 12 of the General Designation are the principal provisions regulating RPM. Although Article 19 AMA provides that RPM is illegal if there is no justifiable reason for it, in practice RPM is considered to be per se illegal. Since, among the various forms of vertical restraint, RPM is at least potentially the most restrictive form of competition, no arguments to justify RPM based on economic analysis have thus far been accepted. RPM is considered to limit the freedom of a buyer in determining their own sales price and restrict competition in the market. Unlike the EU, this applies irrespective of whether maximum or minimum resale prices are involved and the Distribution Guidelines do not distinguish between maximum RPM and minimum RPM. This shows Japan's rather stricter attitude against RPM, which has traditionally been seen as an obstacle to free competition in the domestic market. Even if RPM may create pro-competitive effects, it is considered that a company's freedom to decide its own sales price is essential to its business activities. On this view, the prohibition of RPM can ensure competition among players in the market and free choice of consumers;[23] pro-competitive effects of RPM will not be accepted as offsetting anticompetitive effects. Chapter 1, Section 2(1) of the Distribution Guidelines confirms that RPM by manufacturers is an unfair trade practice, and illegal. This means that RPM is illegal irrespective of the parties' market shares.

---

21 '*Tatene*' is a price fixed by a manufacturer taking into account margins (commissions) for wholesalers and retailers before putting a product in the market. It has been commonly used in various industries such as the pharmaceutical industry, and is considered a basic price for transactions in Japan.

22 JFTC, *AMA Policy Fifty Years History*, Volume 1 (Kosei Torihiki Kyokai, 1997) pp. 160–63 (in Japanese).

23 Distribution Guidelines, 1.1.1.

In the EU, the traditional hostility to minimum RPM remains essentially unchanged. RPM remains a hard core restriction despite criticism in light of the *Leegin* judgment of the US Supreme Court, according to which, as a matter of federal law, RPM is to be assessed according to the rule of reason.[24] However, in revising its Guidelines on Vertical Restraints in 2010 the Commission cautiously softened its analytical approach to a modest degree. The revised Guidelines accept that, under certain circumstances, minimum RPM, though presumed to be restrictive of competition by object, could potentially qualify for exemption on an individual assessment. Thus, RPM could possibly be exempt under 101(3) TFEU if imposed by the seller and necessary to introduce a new product, or where a company organises a short-term (two to six weeks) low price campaign in a franchise or similar uniform distribution system, or, more generally, where it is genuinely necessary to adopt such minimum prices in order to incentivise dealers to provide appropriate pre-sales services. However, the sceptical tone running through the relevant passage (particularly as regards generic free riding arguments) suggests that in many cases it will be quite difficult in practice for contracting parties, who bear the burden of proof, to show that the conditions of Article 101(3) TFEU are satisfied.

In the Powdered milk judgment of the Supreme Court of Japan in 1975, there were four companies in the market. One of them (*Wakodo*), with 30 per cent of the market, fixed both the wholesale price and the retail price of its products. *Wakodo* sold only to wholesalers and retailers who accepted the fixed prices and reduced rebates if they failed to comply. The Court refused the argument that the price fixing should be justified because the purpose was to prevent the product from being used just as a tool to encourage customers to come to the shops and eventually let them buy other products.[25]

In contrast to minimum RPM, maximum and recommended resale prices are exempted in the EU under the VABER provided that they do not amount in practice to minimum or fixed sale prices as a result of pressure from, or incentives offered by, any of the parties.[26] Unlike the EU (and the US), Japanese antimonopoly policy regards all vertical price restraints as contrary to the essential freedom of a reseller to decide their own sales price. Thus, both maximum and minimum resale price

---

24 *Leegin Creative Leather Products, Inc. v PSKS, Inc.*, 551 U.S. 877 (2007).

25 Powdered milk judgment of the Supreme Court of 11 July 1975.

26 Vertical Guidelines point 48.

maintenance is basically considered to be illegal.[27] The JFTC's Guidelines confirm this view and do not distinguish between maximum and minimum price fixing.[28]

However, despite that general rule, under a specific exemption regulation, RPM of publications such as books, magazines, newspapers, analogue records, music tapes and music CDs is exempted from the prohibition of RPM to the extent that it is considered as justifiable fair conduct – unless it harms consumers' interests.[29] No notification under the exemption regulation is necessary. RPM in the publication sector has been a focus of political discussion for a long time, but attempts to abolish special treatment for publications have met strong resistance from the industry. In the EU, there is an ECJ judgment of July 1985 stating that periodicals can be exempted[30] and in practice, in several EU Member States RPM on sales of periodicals continues to be exempted.[31] RPM can be investigated by the Commission as well as by the competition authorities of the EU Member States, which may create more complicated competition issues. For example in 2012, five companies under the Commission's investigation in relation to the sale of e-books offered commitments under Article 9 of Regulation No. 1/2003 in order to respond to the Commission's competition concerns, which related to, among other things, a suspected concerted practice with the object of raising the retail prices of e-books in the EEA. These commitments are without prejudice to national laws that allow publishers to set the retail

---

[27] See supra note 14, Negishi and Funada, p. 278.

[28] Guidelines Distribution 2.1.2.

[29] Article 23 AMA.

[30] Case C-243/83 *AMP v Binon* [1985] ECR 2015.

[31] An Austrian law allowing trade associations to fix the prices of publications was held in principle to be illegal under EU law by the European Court of Justice because it constituted a restriction on the free movement of goods and as such could only be maintained if justified by and proportionate to legitimate public interest imperatives. See *Fachverband der Buch- und Medienwirtschaft v LIBRO Handelsgesellschaft mbH*, Case C-531/07 [2009] ECR I-3717. In this case the ECJ stated that the national provisions that prohibit importers of German-language books from fixing a price lower than the retail price fixed or recommended by the publisher in the state of publication cannot be justified under Article 30 EC and 151 EC or by overriding requirements in the public interest.

price for e-books at their own discretion.[32] Thus, even if the Commission's investigation is closed, the situations including the national authorities can be still unclear.

RPM is sometimes unaccompanied by other restraints but is also often combined with non-price restrictions.[33] A rare example of a stand-alone RPM obligation in Japan was examined in the JFTC's *Shiseido* decision, where a distributor of Shiseido's cosmetic products asked Shiseido if it could fix the price cheaper than Shiseido's recommended price. Shiseido refused but instead provided sample products, which the distributor accepted.[34]

In sum, under both the EU and Japanese rules (and leaving aside the relaxed EU approach to maximum RPM), restrictions placed on the buyer's ability to determine its sale price are generally prohibited. The difference is that, while in Japan RPM is in practice per se illegal (what the AMA says about RPM being illegal absent a justification), the modifications of the Commission's Guidelines on Vertical Restraints may lead to a more flexible approach towards RPM in practice. However, since hard core restrictions have traditionally been considered as subject to an absolute prohibition, it remains to be seen how pro-competitive arguments in favour of RPM will be treated in the EU in the future.

TERRITORIAL RESTRICTIONS

Territorial restrictions can take a variety of forms. Although, in the EU, the VABER can exempt most types of distribution and supply agreement, such as exclusive and selective distribution systems, from the prohibition of restrictive agreements set out in Article 101(1) TFEU, territorial and customer resale restrictions are generally treated as hard core restrictions.

---

32 Communication of the Commission published pursuant to Article 27(4) of Council Regulation (EC) No. 1/2003 in *E-BOOKS* COMP/39.847.

33 For instance, in the *Yamaha* case (*Yamaha* COMP/37.975), where on 16 July 2003 the Commission fined the Yamaha group for imposing vertical restrictions in Europe. Yamaha Corporation Japan and its European subsidiaries distributed a wide range of musical instruments in Europe and had implemented various agreements and/or concerted practices whose object was the restriction of competition in eight EU Member States (and in the EEA). The restrictions contained in Yamaha's distribution contracts in three Member States included, among other things, obligations on official dealers to sell only to final customers, restrictions on exports via the Internet, territorial protection concerning manufacturer guarantees and RPM.

34 *Shiseido*, JFTC decision of 30 November 1995.

In particular, restrictions of parallel trade are generally regarded as serious infringements and contrary to the very idea of European cross-border integration. The possible consequences of including some forms of territorial or customer restriction in an agreement are the invalidity and unenforceability of the entire agreement and the imposition of potentially severe fines by the European Commission.

Under the VABER, exclusively allocated territories or customer groups can still be protected from active sales, while any restriction on passive sales remains in principle a hard core restriction. Thus, under the VABER, in exclusive customer allocation arrangements, in which a supplier grants a distributor the exclusive right to sell to a limited group of customers, the obligation on a distributor not to make active sales to a limited group of customers allocated to another distributor is allowed.

In Japan, the Distribution Guidelines take a more lenient attitude towards vertical restraints other than RPM. Territorial restrictions may be considered under the category of 'dealing under restrictive conditions' and are examined under the 'influential supplier' test and the 'price level' test to determine whether the price of the product covered by the restriction is likely to be maintained. The 'price level' test depends on the impact of the restriction on inter-brand competition, intra-brand competition, the number of competitors and their positions in the market. As in the EU, when Japanese firms adopt a selective distribution system, cross-supplies between members of the network must be allowed.[35] However, some traditional forms of selective distribution system do not permit such sales.

In addition to the Distribution Guidelines, in 2004 the Tokyo District Court rendered a judgment indicating more detailed criteria for territorial restrictions.[36] Where a manufacturer allocates a region to a distributor prohibiting sales outside the allocated region, the following tests must be met to show the arrangement is illegal: (1) the supplier must be an 'influential supplier' in the relevant market; (2) the restriction must unfairly restrict business activities; and (3) the restriction must have the effect of maintaining the price level. Thus, compared to the approach taken in the Distribution Guidelines, the District Court's judgment narrowed the scope of the prohibition as it pertains to territorial restrictions.

---

[35] For the treatment of restrictions on cross-supplies among distributors in the EU, see, e.g., Louis Vogel, *Droit Européen de le Concurrence* (SAS Lawlex, 2010) p. 174.

[36] *Sankogan* Tokyo District Court judgment of 15 April 2004. This case was settled during the appeal before the Tokyo High Court.

Thus, in Japan, where 'an influential supplier in the relevant market' allocates an exclusive territory to a distributor and if the price level of the contract product is likely to be maintained, the restriction is illegal as unfair trade practices.[37] However, it is not illegal for a manufacturer to adopt location clauses or to allocate areas of responsibility to its distributors for their active sales activities in order to develop effective sales networks or to establish better systems for after-sales services.

CUSTOMER RESTRICTIONS

As seen above, customer restrictions are treated in a similar way to territorial restrictions in the EU, and the VABER identifies restrictions on customers to whom the buyer can resell as hard core restrictions.[38] However, a buyer may be legitimately prevented from actively selling to a group of customers exclusively allocated to another buyer or exclusively reserved to the supplier.[39]

As in the EU, a supplier in Japan sometimes imposes on a distributor the obligation not to sell the products to other distributors and discount retailers. The supplier may also sometimes impose on a wholesaler the obligation to deal only with designated retailers. This may reinforce the *keiretsu* commercial structure. An example of a traditional pattern of distribution is *nakama torihiki no kinshi* (ban on transactions among friends), where a manufacturer prohibits a distributor from selling to the manufacturer's other distributors.[40]

In the JFTC's *Nippon Kogaku* decision of 1972, a Japanese company, *Nippon Kogaku*, which imposed resale prices on its wholesalers, also prevented them from freely choosing their own retailers by allocating retailers to them.[41] This system is called *itten choaisei* and has been another typical pattern of traditional customer restrictions in Japan that

---

[37] In this case, the influential supplier test was not examined as provided for in the Distribution Guidelines. According to the Guidelines, an influential supplier has a market share exceeding 10 per cent or is one of the three largest companies in the market. The Court used wider discretion to examine whether the company was regarded as an influential company. See Toshiaki Takigawa, *Competition Law and Competition Policy in Japan, the US and the EU* (4th edn, Seirin Shoin, 2010) p. 334 (in Japanese).

[38] VABER, Article (b) 4.

[39] Ibid.

[40] Distribution Guidelines, 2.1.4(3).

[41] *Nippon Kogaku*, JFTC Decision of 30 June 1972.

the JFTC now essentially considers anticompetitive and is not often seen in Europe.[42]

As explained above, under the Japanese rule a supplier is not allowed to impose customer restrictions on a distributor outside its territory if the price level of the relevant product is likely to be maintained ('price level' test). The same applies to customer restrictions imposed on wholesalers as well.

A selective distribution system typically involves, among other things, customer restrictions and restrictions on sales methods. A company whose market share is small, for instance less than 10 per cent, may adopt a selective distribution network in Japan without infringing the AMA. As occasionally seen in other jurisdictions including the EU, in some Japanese industries, including the cosmetics industry, if one supplier adopts selective distribution, other suppliers tend to follow suit. As a result, such industries are typified by a degree of market rigidity and it may be difficult for outsider retailers to gain a foothold or survive.

PARALLEL IMPORT RESTRICTIONS

The EU approach to territorial restraints is linked to protection of parallel trade outside a supplier's authorised distribution network. As already explained, the imperative of protecting parallel trade (and, relatedly, the protection of intra-brand competition) is crucially related to Europe's market integration objective.[43] Thus, impediments to parallel trade can attract high fines even though parallel traders often 'free ride' on the investments of the supplier and its (possibly quite costly) authorised distribution network.[44]

Two exemplary cases can be cited here. First, on 16 July 2003, the European Commission fined the Yamaha group for RPM and for restrictions of trade between EEA Member States.[45] The Commission found that Yamaha Corporation Japan and its European subsidiaries, which distributed a whole range of musical instruments in the EU, implemented various agreements and/or concerted practices that had as their object the restriction of competition in eight Member States. A second example is

---

42 See Yasumi Ochi, *Japan, the US and European Competition Law* (Shojihomu, 2005), p. 412.

43 Van Bael and Bellis, *Competition Law of the European Community* (5th edn, Kluwer International, 2010) p. 212.

44 Ibid., p. 213.

45 *Yamaha* COMP/37.975.

the *Pokemon* case of 2004, where the Commission adopted a decision imposing a fine on Topps, a producer of collectible products such as stickers and trading cards featuring soccer players or cartoon characters. The Commission found evidence that Topps had developed a strategy to prevent imports from low price countries into high price countries.[46]

In Japan, restrictions on parallel imports of products with valid trademarks may be viewed as harmful because they reduce price competition in the market, at least as between sellers of products of the same brand. As in the EU, the protection of trademarks can justify restrictions on parallel imports.[47] A problem of restrictions on parallel imports often happens where a company appoints an exclusive distributor covering the entire Japanese market. Exclusive distribution is considered to reduce the cost and risk of market entry, and it is often used when a foreign company enters into the Japanese market. According to the Distribution Guidelines, although exclusive distribution is generally considered to be pro-competitive, it may distort competition in the relevant market under certain circumstances. With regard to parallel imports, the Japanese view is that they encourage competition in the market and restrictions on such trade should therefore be illegal if it aims at maintaining prices. However, under the AMA, parallel imports of trademarked goods may be restricted to protect the trademark.

Under the Distribution Guidelines, a restriction whereby an exclusive importer prohibits a domestic distributor from dealing with a foreign manufacturer may be considered dealing under restrictive conditions. By contrast, it is likely that where an exclusive importer imposes on a foreign supplier an obligation not to allow its foreign distributor to deal with a domestic parallel importer, this is viewed as unlawful interference with a competitor's business. Furthermore, in the *Parker* judgment of the Osaka District Court (1970), the Court stated that parallel imports of products legally put on the market are not illegal.[48] In the *Herend* decision of the JFTC (1996), Hoshi Shoji K.K. was Herend Porcelain's exclusive importer in Japan.[49] In 1992, Hoshi Shoji discovered an advertisement of a parallel importer that sold the products at a 30 per cent discount off Hoshi Shoji's own price. After checking the serial numbers and consulting the manufacturers, Hoshi found that there was an exclusive importer in Hong Kong. Parallel imports from Australian and

---

46 *Souris-Topps* COMP/C-3/37.980.

47 See the Distribution Guidelines, 3.3.1(2).

48 *Parker* judgment of Osaka District Court of 27 February 1970. It was confirmed in *Fred Perry* judgment of the Supreme Court of 27 February 2003.

49 *Herend*, JFTC decision of 22 March 1996.

Italian agents were also discovered. Hoshi asked Herend to take any measures to stop the parallel imports from reaching Japan (and driving prices down). When Herend obliged, the JFTC found that its conduct violated Article 19 AMA (interference with competitors' transactions: General Designation 15). In the JFTC's *Trading Card Game* decision (1997), Hobby Japan was the exclusive importer of Wizards of the Coast, a US-based producer of the popular card game called 'Magic: The Gathering'. Hobby Japan, which marketed the original English version of this game as well as the Japanese version, sought to block parallel imports and to maintain product prices in Japan. In 1995, Hobby Japan suspended its deliveries of the English version of the game to any dealers knowingly selling to parallel importers. Later, it started to refuse to supply the Japanese version of the game to retailers who dealt with parallel importers. The JFTC then intervened and found that Hobby Japan had breached Article 19 AMA.[50]

In relation to patent, the question as to whether the parallel import of a patented product sold in a foreign country is allowed is examined case by case in Japan and a licensor deems to allow parallel imports except for the case in which a licensor expressly prohibits imports to Japan. The JFTC has not issued any further Guidelines on this issue. As regards copyright, the Japanese Copyright Act provides exhaustive doctrine. Further, as for music records and CDs, specific law prohibits parallel imports.

ONLINE SALES

Restrictions on Internet sales create certain concerns in some cases in the EU. For instance, in 2002 the European Commission approved B&W Loudspeakers' notified selective distribution network on condition that the company remove several hard core restrictions including a clause prohibiting authorised distributors from selling over the Internet.[51]

In its 2010 review of the VABER Guidelines on Vertical Restraints, the Commission expressed concern over the use of selective distribution in concentrated markets by leading suppliers where they exclude pure retailers or other price discounters. The most contentious issue seems to be the extent to which suppliers can restrict Internet sales.

The Commission's Guidelines provide examples of restrictions of online sales that amount to hard core restrictions of competition, whose

---

50 *Trading Card Game*, JFTC decision of 28 November 1997.

51 See the Commission's press release IP/02/916 of 26 June 2002.

object is to segment markets to the detriment of consumers and the internal market. For example, any obligations on distributors to automatically reroute customers located outside their territory, or to terminate consumers' transactions over the Internet if their credit card data reveal an address that is not within the distributor's territory, are viewed as hard core restrictions.

Although suppliers may only want to sell to distributors that have one or more physical points of presence, once a supplier has allowed a distributor into its distribution system, in principle it cannot prevent that distributor from having a website and selling products online. Similarly, any obligation that dissuades distributors from using the Internet as a sales medium, such as a limit on the proportion of overall sales that a distributor can make over the Internet, or a requirement that the distributor pay a higher purchase price for units sold online ('dual pricing'), is considered to be a hard core restriction. In an exclusive distribution system a distributor must also remain free to sell to customers who contact it on their own initiative (passive sales). Since Internet sales are an important means of entering other national markets, the Commission's policy concerning restrictions of online sales is clearly driven by the EU's internal market objective.

Certain vertical restraints on online sales can in some cases be justified on the ground that they benefit consumers. For instance, in a selective distribution system a supplier may prohibit its distributor from selling online through a website that does not meet agreed quality standards, or from selling to unauthorised distributors. However, the European Court of Justice has held in its preliminary ruling of 13 October 2011 that where a contractual clause in a selective distribution system amounts to an absolute ban on Internet selling, the clause is considered a restriction by object within the meaning of Article 101(1) TFEU unless it is objectively justified and consequently falls outside the scope of the prohibition.[52] Only in exceptional circumstance, by reason of the nature of the goods or the customers to whom they are sold, can agreements prohibiting online sales be allowed, but in practice it is very unlikely that restriction by object can be exempted under 101(3) TFEU.

---

[52] C-439/09, *Pierre Fabre Dermo-Cosmétique SAS v Président de l'Autorité de la concurrence and Ministre de l'Économie, de l'Industrie et de l'Emploi*, judgment of 13 October 2011, not yet reported. In *Pierre Fabre*, the ECJ considered the restrictions in question in light of the 1999 version of the VABER, but the principles articulated in the judgment apply equally to the amended block exemption, Regulation 330/2010.

Nevertheless, in a selective distribution system a supplier can impose quality and service standards on Internet sales by its distributors equivalent to the standards it applies to sales made by them through brick-and-mortar outlets. In selective distribution a supplier can also require a distributor to have one or more physical shops.

In Japan, in terms of restrictions on a distributor's resale methods in general, the rule is that where there is a reasonable justification, the restriction is allowed. The *Shiseido/Kao* case reflects a relatively relaxed approach to restrictions on a distributor's resale methods (the imposition of face-to-face sales and counselling sales were in issue).[53] Thus, for instance, dual pricing, which is a restriction of a resale method, may not be illegal unless its purpose is to exclude online discount retailers.

Online sales restrictions may be categorised as restrictions on sales methods and prohibited under the concepts of 'dealing under restrictive conditions' or 'dealing under exclusive conditions'. In the JFTC's *Johnson & Johnson* decision (2002) case, the JFTC issued a warning to Johnson & Johnson, indicating that its conduct was considered dealing on restrictive terms. Johnson & Johnson produced disposable contact lenses on the basis of a medical doctor's prescription.[54] The company prevented online retailers, whose prices were generally lower than those of offline shops, from selling disposable contact lenses. Today, Johnson & Johnson is itself selling disposable contact lenses on the Internet in Japan and this has resulted in quite active price competition in this market.

The relevant precedents in Japan have taken a relatively relaxed approach to restrictions of a distributor's resale methods. Where there is a reasonable justification, the restriction may be allowed. For instance, in the *Shiseido/Kao* case, Shiseido and Kao – which are cosmetics manufacturers using selective distribution – imposed on their retailers an obligation to provide face-to-face consultations with their customers in the retailers' premises. The retailers had to explain how to use the products, to indicate which products were suitable and to answer customers' questions.

One retailer started to sell Shiseido's products via telephone or fax order after sending catalogues to customers, and continued to do so after being admonished by Shiseido. Shiseido then terminated the retailer's contract. In the parallel case, Kao included in its distribution agreements

[53] *Shiseido*, judgments of Tokyo District Court of 27 September 1993, Tokyo High Court of 14 September 1994 and Supreme Court of 18 December 1998. *Kao*, judgments of Tokyo District Court of 18 July 1994, Tokyo High Court of 31 July 1997 and *Shiseido/Kao* Supreme Court of 18 December 1998.

[54] *Johnson and Johnson*, JFTC decision of 1 December 2010.

a prohibition on sales to Kao's other appointed distributors. Ignoring this restriction, one retailer started to sell Kao's products to another Kao distributor. This retailer's contract was also terminated.

NON-COMPETE OBLIGATIONS

Although non-compete obligations are not restrictive by object within the meaning of Article 101(1) TFEU, they may constitute restrictions of competition by effect if they foreclose a market by restricting to an appreciable extent the ability of suppliers to find buyers for their products. According to the European Commission's Guidelines on Vertical Restraints, non-compete obligations may also have positive effects and may be justified under Article 101(3) TFEU.[55] As regards efficiencies, free riding between suppliers, hold-up problems and capital market imperfections may be particularly relevant.

The VABER sets specific conditions under which non-compete obligations can benefit from an exemption. When the conditions are not fulfilled, these non-compete obligations are excluded from the VABER but the VABER will continue to apply to the rest of the vertical agreement, if that part of the agreement is severable and assuming that the other conditions of the VABER are met.

In general, any foreclosure effects resulting from non-compete obligations will increase in proportion to their duration. A non-compete obligation will be exempted under the VABER provided its duration is not indefinite and does not exceed five years. Non-compete obligations that are tacitly renewable beyond a period of five years are deemed to be of indefinite duration.

Moreover, the VABER exempts post-term non-compete obligations provided four conditions are met cumulatively: (1) the obligation is related to goods or services that compete with the contract goods or services; (2) the obligation is limited to the premises and land from which the buyer has operated during the contact period; (3) the obligation is indispensable to protect know-how transferred by the supplier to the buyer; and (4) the duration of the obligation is limited to a period of one year after termination of the agreement. There is no specific number of years indicated under the AMA and the Distribution Guidelines.

If a non-compete obligation falls outside the 'safe harbour' of the VABER, it will be necessary to make an individual assessment of its

[55] Vertical Guidelines, Point 107.

compatibility with Article 101(1) TFEU and whether it qualifies for an individual exemption under Article 101(3) TFEU.

In Japan, non-compete obligations are regulated as a refusal to deal, or dealing under restrictive conditions (General Designation 12), or dealing under exclusive conditions (General Designation 11). They are examined under the 'influential supplier' test and the 'market foreclosure' test (which does not differ substantially from the price level test). A non-compete obligation may cause anticompetitive foreclosure of other suppliers or other buyers by raising barriers to entry and preventing them from easily finding alternative distribution channels. It can be justified, however, where supported by a legitimate reason, such as where it is necessary for the protection of know-how.

Under Japanese rules, restrictions that preclude a buyer from purchasing competing goods are illegal where a manufacturer has a market share above 10 per cent or where it is one of the three largest companies in the relevant market and where there is a risk that it will be too difficult for a new player or an existing competitor will not be able to find an alternative channel of distribution. Furthermore, in principle, after the expiration of an agreement, a supplier cannot impose non-compete obligations on its former distributor because it prevents a distributor from entering into the relevant market. However, if the obligation is limited to the extent necessary for any reasonable purpose such as the prevention of disclosure of business secrets including know-how, it is allowed. Again, there is no specific number of years indicated under the AMA and the Distribution Guidelines.

In *Nikomart*, a supermarket franchisee of *Nikomart* was bound by a non-compete obligation in its franchise agreement. The Courts decided that, where there are any justifiable reasons such as the protection of business secrets, a non-compete obligation is not anticompetitive, provided that the scope of restrictions is reasonable.[56]

TYING

In the EU, tying may constitute a vertical restraint where it results in a single branding type of obligation for the tied product. In Japan, tying is viewed as distorting fair competition in the market and reducing consumer choice. However, in Japan, no clear distinction is drawn between

---

[56] The judgments of the Tokyo District Court of 12 January 1994 and of the Tokyo High Court of 28 March 1996. See also supra note 14, Negishi and Funada, p. 267.

'tying', which is a category of conduct covered by unfair trade practices, and the 'abuse of a superior bargaining position'.[57] Most of the tying cases are categorised as unfair trade practices, possibly because it is unnecessary in a tying case to examine the details of the difference in the parties' positions in individual commercial relation. Technically, assessing a restraint as an unfair trade practice seems easier because analysis of market shares is not essential.

According to an early decision of the JFTC called *Taisho* (28 March 1955), concerning the pharmaceutical sector, the relationship between unfair trade practices and private monopolisation is that in an unfair trade practice scenario, a restriction of competition is not enough to substantially restrict competition in the market but it may be enough to distort fair competition to some extent.[58] This is because the prohibition of unfair trade practices may in some sense be seen as a preventive measure against private monopolisation.

In the *Toshiba Elevator Technics* case (1993), decided by the Osaka High Court, Toshiba Elevator Technics, whose business was the maintenance of Toshiba elevators, sold elevator parts.[59] An owner of a building who installed Toshiba elevators tried to purchase elevator parts from them, but Toshiba Elevator Technics refused because the owner did not ask for maintenance at the same time.

ENFORCEMENT

Although the Commission's main vertical restraints cases since 2000 involve Japanese companies such as Nintendo, Yamaha and Pokemon, and although companies from Japan seem to figure more prominently than firms from other countries, this does not mean that the Japanese rules for vertical restraints substantially diverge from the European rules and that it is therefore difficult for Japanese companies to comply with the EU rules. It may be that, because more Japanese companies are actively engaged in business in the EU than certain other foreign firms, for example from Russia or China, the number of Japanese companies involved in EU investigations seems significant. However, to the extent that Japanese companies take steps to divide up the EU's internal market

---

57 For details regarding the abuse of a superior bargaining position, see Chapter 6 (this volume) on abuse of dominance.

58 *No 1 Taisho Seiyaku*, JFTC decision of 28 March 1953.

59 *Toshiba Elevator Technics* case, judgment of the Osaka High Court, 30 July 1993.

and to prevent arbitrage between Member States (as in the *Nintendo* case), they may well attract more intense antitrust scrutiny from the European Commission than they might in Japan or in other jurisdictions.

Whereas an agreement that breaches Article 101 TFEU may be subject to fines in the EU (especially where restrictions of competition by object are concerned), in Japan, not all vertical restraints that qualify as unfair trade practices are subject to surcharges. Indeed, absent dominance the only vertical restraint considered serious enough to warrant surcharges is RPM. Despite this difference, in the EU vertical restraint cases now tend to be handled by national competition authorities, and not by the European Commission. The block exemptions and guidelines (and the abolition of notification in 2004) that have been adopted have borne fruit, in the sense that the Commission is now able to focus its resources on the most economically detrimental form of private conduct – cartels.

As regards the EU Member States, Council Regulation 1/2003 regulates the conditions in which the national competition authorities must apply Articles 101 and 102 TFEU. Like the Commission, the national authorities have the power to impose substantial fines in the event of a competition law infringement. Coherent enforcement of the competition rules in the field of vertical agreements is ensured by the VABER and the Guidelines on Vertical Restraints, and by the Commission's continuous monitoring through the European Competition Network.

Where the requirements of the VABER are not met, and where appreciable anticompetitive effects occur, the presumption of legality conferred by the VABER may be withdrawn where a vertical agreement, considered either in isolation or in conjunction with similar agreements enforced by competing suppliers or buyers, falls within the scope of Article 101(1) TFEU and does not meet all the conditions of Article 101(3) TFEU. While the Commission has the exclusive power to withdraw the benefit of VABER in respect of vertical agreements restricting competition on a market that is wider than the territory of a single Member State, national authorities may withdraw the benefits of the VABER in respect of vertical agreements whose anticompetitive effects are felt in the territory of the Member State concerned or a part of thereof, if the relevant national or local territory has all the characteristics of a distinct geographic market.

Whereas the European Commission has become increasingly less active in relation to vertical restraint cases, in Japan the JFTC continues to adopt decisions in this field.[60] As a recent example, on 12 April 2011, Adidas AG's Japanese unit was raided by the JFTC for allegedly pressuring retailers not to discount its popular EasyTone muscle-toning shoes.[61] Adidas Japan was suspected of pressuring retailers to sell the product for 10 000 to 15 000 yen (87 to 130 euros), and of suspending shipments to stores that did not comply.

Moreover, in 2009, as a result of the reform of law, more types of anticompetitive conduct became subject to fines. RPM is one of the new illegal types of conduct that are subject to surcharges. However, for reasons of legal certainty and modesty principle, it is considered that first-time RPM offences should not attract fines; rather, the JFTC should first establish a pattern of such behaviour and a genuine threat of harm to competition in a relevant market. Thus, under current policy, RPM must be repeated before it can be subject to fines. Criminal sanctions are not imposed on companies for employing vertical restraints considered a violation of unfair trade practices.

CONCLUSIONS

Overall, the Japanese approach to vertical restraints appears, at least to some modest degree, to be more lenient than the European approach. This can be attributed to the fact that the AMA is concerned mainly with the traditional varieties of competition concerns, and has never been linked to an additional requirement, such as that inherent in the TFEU, to ensure an integrated single market.

Although most of the individual categories of illegal vertical restraint under the AMA look the same as those caught by Article 101 TFEU, the structure and analysis of rules are sometimes different. In fact, the EU and Japan take an almost identical analytical approach to RPM. However, a clearer categorisation of illegal conduct is provided in the EU (where, for example, the difference between vertical restraints and the abuse of dominance is clearer).

In the EU, in general, there is a relatively liberal economics-based approach (something akin to a post-Chicago orientation) to restrictions imposed in vertical agreements. In practice, anticompetitive effects are only likely to be found where the suppliers imposing restrictions have individual or collective market power. However, the protection of parallel

---

60 See, e.g., the JFTC's Annual Report of 2011, available at http://www.jftc.go.jp/info/nenpou/h23/index.html.

61 JFTC Decision of 2 March 2012.

trade and the market integration concept, as well as hostility to RPM, remain fundamental policy goals. Even if the legal analysis seems different, the practical results of illegal vertical arrangements appear almost the same. In both jurisdictions, owing to potential efficiency gains from vertical restraints, such restraints are less likely to be problematic than horizontal restraints. However, the EU and Japan still share the common problem of large retailers, such as department stores, which often impose one-sided conditions in their transactions with much smaller suppliers.

Finally, in the EU the problem of the interpretation of the EU rules on vertical restraints by national courts has been highlighted in particular since the revision of the VABER of 1999 and the modernisation of competition policy in 2003, because, first, firms have to 'self-assess' their agreements based on the VABER, the Guidelines and the Commission's De Minimis Notice; and, second, because national judges now routinely examine agreements in proceedings before them on the basis of EU law.[62] Although the capacity of judges examining antitrust cases is sometimes discussed in Japan, the issue is not as complicated as in the EU because in Japan there is only a single legal order; judges are not faced with complexities such as, for example, the legal effects of a supranational competition agency.

The EU and US antitrust regimes are famously different in the field of vertical restraints, particularly as regards territorial restrictions and minimum RPM. Since the Japanese distribution system is still largely closed to new entry, and since the underlying business culture reflected in Japanese firms' distribution systems is more analogous to traditions in the EU than to those in the US, an approach more closely aligned to that of the EU seems more appropriate.[63]

---

[62] For further analysis, see, e.g., Jean-François Bellis, 'L'usage des règlements d'exemption et des lignes directrices par les juges. L'exemple des restrictions verticales', in Anne Spiritus-Dassesse, Cyril Nourissat and Robert Wtterwulghe (eds), *Le juge de commerce face au droit communautaire de la concurrence* (Faculté Universitaire Saint-Louis, 2007) pp. 169–70.

[63] See Takigawa, supra note 36, p. 347.

6. Abuse of dominance

THE LEGAL STRUCTURE IN JAPAN AND THE EU

Abuse of dominance is the area where any harmonisation of the approaches taken by the EU and Japan would be rather difficult. The Japanese rules are generally more complicated than the EU rules, as in Japan there are two categories of regulated unilateral conduct, namely, private monopolisation and abuse of a superior bargaining position. Since the latter category may trigger the antimonopoly rules even in the absence of dominance,[1] an important difference between the Japanese and EU regimes becomes immediately apparent. Furthermore, the concept of 'private monopolisation' is somewhat narrower than the abuse of dominance under Article 102 TFEU, which applies to both private and public undertakings, so long as the defendant is engaged in an economic activity. Furthermore, in Japan private monopolisation and abuse of a superior bargaining position are treated separately in terms of enforcement.

1 Private Monopolisation

The prohibition of private monopolisation is set forth in Articles 2 and 3 AMA, and was not frequently enforced until recent times. But the number of cases in relation to exclusionary monopolisation in utility sectors is gradually increasing, together with the liberalisation of the public sectors. Article 2(5) AMA defines 'private monopolisation' as the situation where an undertaking, singly or in conspiracy with other undertakings, excludes or controls other companies' business activities and thereby substantially restricts competition in a manner contrary to the

[1] In a manner analogous to the laws of certain EU Member States, the rules on abuse of a superior bargaining position in Japan are not aimed purely at competitive impact; they are more concerned with the regulation of commercial relations. See Joji Atsuya, *The Introduction to Antimonopoly Law* (7th edn, Nihonkeizai Shinbunsya, 2012) p. 169.

public interest. Private monopolisation refers to unauthorised monopolisation as opposed to traditionally authorised monopolisation in public sectors, such as electricity, postal services and so on. As the definition above implies, monopolisation of a market can be achieved by a collectively dominant group of undertakings. The definition also refers to two categories of conduct: exclusionary private monopolisation and private monopolisation by 'control'. Monopolisation by control means suppression of free decision making in a company's business activities.[2] Recently, enforcement of this area of law, and in particular the investigation of exclusionary private monopolisation, has become more vigorous in Japan. In some cases, the JFTC has found that undertakings have engaged in both exclusionary private monopolisation and private monopolisation by control.[3] The substantive test for private monopolisation under the AMA is whether competition in the relevant market is harmed.

In the EU, Article 102 TFEU establishes that undertakings holding a dominant position within the internal market or a substantial part of it must not abuse their dominant position where conduct may affect trade between EU Member States. In the EU, it is common to equate the legal concept of dominance with the economic concept of substantial market power.[4] Since Article 102 TFEU prohibits one or more undertakings from abusing a dominant position, the provision applies not only to a situation of single firm dominance but also to a situation where two or more undertakings jointly or collectively hold a dominant position on the relevant market. In order for two or more companies to be considered dominant in the context of an Article 102 TFEU case, it is generally necessary to show that they present themselves or act together on a particular market as a collective entity from an economic point of view. On 3 December 2008, the Commission issued its Guidance on enforcement priorities in applying Article 82 EC (now Article 102 TFEU) to

---

2 Ibid. Atsuya, p. 193.

3 *Toyo Seikan*, JFTC decision of 18 September 1972.

4 The legal definition of dominance, which emphasises the economic strength and capacity for independent behaviour of the undertaking concerned, is laid down in *United Brands*, judgment of 14 February 1978, *United Brands v Commission of the European Communities Court of Justice of the European Communities*, Case 27/76 [1978] ECR 207, paragraph 65. See also, e.g., Richard Whish and David Bailey, *Competition Law* (7th edn, Oxford University Press, 2012) p. 180.

abusive exclusionary conduct by dominant undertakings.[5] The Commission generally uses an effects-based approach both to set its enforcement priorities and to assess whether an infringement has occurred.

As regards single-firm dominance, on the basis of ECJ case law, an undertaking that holds a market share of 50 per cent or more on a relevant market is generally presumed to have a dominant market position.[6] However, a company may be found to be dominant even with a market share of less than 40 per cent, since market shares are not always an accurate reflection of market power.

In Japan, the JFTC issued Guidelines for Exclusionary Private Monopolisation under the AMA on 28 October 2009. In the Guidelines, the JFTC referred for the first time to a market share test, explaining that if, as a result of the conduct, the share of the product supplied by a company exceeds roughly 50 per cent of the market share in the relevant product market, and if the conduct is considered to largely affect the lives of citizens, the JFTC will investigate such conduct as a matter of priority. This statement does not refer to a substantive test but rather indicates that the conduct should be serious to trigger an investigation.[7] In practice, most JFTC investigations of private monopolisation concern firms with market shares of 80 to 100 per cent. However, Japanese markets have traditionally been characterised by numerous small to medium sized companies, and the number of large firms in most industries is relatively low.

Under the Japanese rules on exclusionary private monopolisation, the question of whether conduct is considered exclusionary is examined first. The next question is whether the conduct substantially restricts competition. The methodology thus differs from the approach under Article 102 TFEU, where the existence of a dominant position is traditionally ascertained before the issue of abuse is resolved.[8] Under the Japanese rules, it is emphasised that exclusionary conduct does not imply market power.[9, 10]

---

5 Commission Communication C(2009) 864 final.

6 For the Commission's guidance on defining relevant markets, see OJ C372 of 12 September 1997, pp. 5–13, available at http://eur-lex.europa.eu/LexUriServ/LexUriServ.do?uri=OJ:C:1997:372:0005:0013:EN:PDF.

7 Guidelines on exclusionary private monopolisation under the Antimonopoly Act, available at http://www.jftc.go.jp/dk/haijyogata.pdf (in Japanese), p. 3. See also, e.g., Akinori Uesugi, *Handbook on International Competition Practices* (Shojihomu, 2012) p. 291 (in Japanese).

8 In a concrete investigation, the sequential separation between a finding of dominance and a finding of abuse may not be clear-cut. For example, the fact

In Japan, following the 2005 and the 2009 amendments to the AMA, the JFTC may impose surcharges on a dominant company for either exclusionary private monopolisation or private monopolisation by control. Thus, both exclusionary private monopolisation and private monopolisation by control are subject to surcharges. In the EU, the Commission is entitled to impose fines in order to sanction infringements of Article 102 TFEU and has done so in a number of high-profile cases.

2 Abuse of a Superior Bargaining Position

As noted above, the AMA also prohibits the abuse of a superior bargaining position. This type of conduct is governed by Article 2(9)5 AMA, Article 19 AMA and the General Designations. The General Designations are the Notice issued by the JFTC that describes the kinds of conduct that are considered unfair trade practice.[11] In addition, three Special Designations deal with sector-specific varieties of abuse of a superior bargaining position.[12] Under these provisions, it is prohibited for a firm to unfairly exploit its superior position relative to another party. For instance, if pricing conduct constitutes predatory pricing under General Designation Section 6, which is adopted under Article 2(9) AMA, this conduct is prohibited under Article 19 AMA. However, if it substantially restricts competition in the relevant market, it will be subject to the prohibition of private monopolisation under Article 2(5) AMA and Article 3 AMA. Article 19 AMA is being applied more frequently now since the abuse of a superior bargaining position became subject to fines in 2010.[13]

---

that abusive conduct is observed may provide a significant context for the analysis of dominance. Abusive conduct may, for example, result in significant entry barriers that contribute to the incontestability of the undertaking's position on the market.

[9] Uesugi, supra note 7, pp. 290–91.

[10] See, e.g., Louis Vogel, *Droit Européen de la Concurrence* (SAS LawLex, 2010) p. 215.

[11] JFTC Notice on Unfair Trade Practices of 18 June 1982.

[12] Special Designation for Large Retailers (JFTC Notice No. 11 of 13 May 2005); Special Designation for the Newspaper Industry (JFTC Notice No. 9 of 21 September 1999); Special Designation for Logistic Distribution (JFTC Notice No. 1 of 8 May 2004).

[13] For the background to the reform of Japan's rules on predatory pricing and abuse of a superior bargaining position, see Mitsuo Matsushita, 'The Control of Below-Cost Selling in the United States, Europe and Japan', *Journal of the Japanese Institute of International Business Law*, **33** (2) (2005) 145–6 (in

In 2010, the JFTC issued the Guidelines Concerning Abuse of Superior Bargaining. The definition of a 'superior bargaining position' is not clear, but the term is generally thought to refer to the situation where two companies need to have commercial relations and one of them is more powerful than the other.[14] Clearly, the objectives behind the prohibition of this special form of abuse include the protection of traders that are relatively weak compared to the party with whom they do business.[15,16] In this sense, antimonopoly law crosses over into social policy and becomes an instrument by which to protect smaller businesses. Accordingly, the existence of a 'superior position' is examined based on the difference in the degree of power of the parties, the dependence of the weaker one upon the stronger, and the trust and confidence between the parties in the light of Japanese-style business relations. Market shares are thus only one of the elements that may be taken into consideration in the assessment.[17] In the case of a supplier and a retailer, for instance, even a retailer with a relatively small proportion of the market may be regarded as being in a superior bargaining position vis-à-vis its supplier.[18]

Thus, the use of market shares as a measurement in assessing market power and barriers to entry in Japan differs from their use in the EU. In the EU, the central initial indicator of market power is a firm's market share in the relevant market. The definition of the relevant market –

Japanese). It was industry itself that claimed more serious sanctions for the abuse of a superior bargaining position, in particular in the form of 'predatory' pricing. This demand for vigorous enforcement is explained by the fact that small and medium sized companies represent 97 per cent of all Japanese companies. Many of these companies who are competitors of the big companies were suffering, or claimed to be suffering, from the abuse by large companies of a superior bargaining position and trying to create a level playing field.

14 See JFTC, Guidelines Concerning Abuse of Superior Bargaining Position in Service Transactions under the Antimonopoly Act, available at http://www.jftc.go.jp/dk/itakutorihiki.html (in Japanese). See also, e.g., Tadashi Shiraishi, *Antimonopoly Act* (2nd edn, Yuhikaku, 2009) pp. 265–9 (in Japanese).

15 Available at http://www.jftc.go.jp/dk/yuuetsutekichii.pdf (in Japanese), pp. 2–3.

16 The basic objective of Articles 101 and 102 TFEU is to support the establishment and maintenance of the internal market that includes a system ensuring undistorted competition in the EU. Cf., e.g., *Hoffman-La Roche v Commission* [1979] ECR 461, paragraph 38.

17 Market shares would not reflect, for example, whether a company is part of a *keiretsu*; such firms typically enjoy strong support from banks and from *sogo sosha*, i.e., general trading companies of a unique nature that conduct a broad range of business all over the world.

18 See, e.g., Jiro Tamura, 'Recent Trends Regarding Abuse of Superior Bargaining Position', *Japan Fair Trade Commission Watch*, **January 2011**.

despite the pitfalls of market definition in some circumstances, such as where there is significant product differentiation – remains very important in practice. By contrast, market share does not necessarily carry great weight in Japan. In the past, the abuse of a superior bargaining position was an important field of AMA enforcement in particular because Japanese distribution often involved vertical relations between a powerful supplier (or buyer) and its trading partner; this caused problems constantly in the Japanese market.[19] Market share was de-emphasised because it did not accurately reflect the power of the supplier (buyer) in its individual relations with its distributor (supplier). In the EU there is an argument that supports a stronger emphasis on market shares: since the EU is composed of 27 Member States with different cultures and traditions and since enforcement is to a significant degree decentralised, the need for a clear, universal and relatively objective test may contribute to the uniform or quasi-uniform application of EU competition law.[20]

After establishing an Abuse of Superior Bargaining Position Taskforce, the JFTC's enforcement in this area became increasingly active.[21] In 2011, the JFTC imposed fines on powerful retailers in the *Sanyo Marunaka* case of 2011 and the *Toys 'R' Us Japan* case of 2011.[22] In the former case, the JFTC alleged that the defendant had forced its suppliers to provide undue payments and services. In 2012, the JFTC issued a cease and desist order and fined Edion approximately 43 million euros after finding that Edion, an electronics retailer, had abused its superior position by ordering its (dependent) suppliers to send technical staff or service helpers to Edion free of charge.[23] Apart from the *Edion* case, the market power of larger retailers has been an issue for a long time in

---

[19] See, e.g., Masahiro Murakami, *Antimonopoly Act* (Iwanami Shoten Publishers, 2005) p. 137 (in Japanese).

[20] In relation to unilateral conduct, Regulation 1/2003 permits Member States to enforce national regulations stricter than Article 102 TFEU, and several of them do.

[21] See JFTC, Actual Situations of the JFTC Cases regarding Abuse of Superior Position in 2011, available at http://www.jftc.go.jp/pressrelease/12.june/120606betten.pdf (in Japanese).

[22] For the *Sanyo Marunaka* and *Toys 'R' Us Japan* cases, see respectively http://www.jftc.go.jp/en/pressreleases/archives/individual-000307.html and http://www.jftc.go.jp/en/pressreleases/uploads/2011-Dec-13.pdf. *Sanyo Marunaka*, JFTC decision of 22 June 2011 and *Toys 'R' Us Japan*, JFTC decision of 13 December 2011.

[23] See http://www.jftc.go.jp/en/pressreleases/uploads/2012_Feb_16.pdf. For more details, see *Kosei Torihiki Jyoho* (*Fair Trade Information*), **2316** (20 February 2012) 1–5 (in Japanese).

Japan. Since, in this kind of case, *competition* on the relevant market may not be substantially damaged, a private monopolisation theory of harm is unavailable. Types of illegal condition imposed on suppliers include compulsory fee payments, onerous participation in retailer events and the compulsory purchase of stock.[24] In the EU, problems caused by large retailers do arise, but Article 102 TFEU is not specifically designed to tackle this issue.[25]

A notable recent case involving an abuse of a bargaining superior position arose in Japan's energy sector in 2012. TEPCO, the incumbent electric company, was cautioned about its decision to increase electricity prices in a manner not stipulated in its agreement with a buyer.[26] The JFTC published the detailed contents of its warning to the company (these are not normally disclosed) because electricity prices concern the general public.[27] This shows that the abuse of a superior bargaining position in a sector that concerns the general public is treated with more care by the authority, even if, as in this case, an increased tariff is fixed on the basis of suggestions made by METI.[28]

Article 2(9)5 AMA regulates the abuse of a superior position towards 'the other party'. It is not clear who is covered as 'the other party' under this provision. The JFTC's interpretation seems to be that abuse of a superior position only covers conduct between businesses and does not cover exploitation of an individual consumer. However, it has been

---

[24] Sectors in which abuse of superior position is often problematic include those with large retailers, financial institutions, franchise businesses, manufacturing, hotels, etc. For more details regarding abusive conduct in these sectors, see, e.g., Yasuo Daito, 'Practical Analysis – In Which Sectors Should You Be Particularly Careful about Abuse of a Superior Position?', *Business Homu* (Chuo Keizai Sha), August 2012, pp. 112–16 (in Japanese).

[25] In the EU, cases in which buyer power raised concerns include *Kesko/Tuko*, *Rewe Meinl* and *Carrefour Promodès* (*Tesko/Tuko* COMP/M.784, *Rewe Meinl* COMP/M.1221 and *Carrefour/Promodès* M.1684). In other cases, buyer power can serve as a factor (among others) facilitating the approval of reviewed transactions. See *Enso/Stora COMP/M* 1225, Commission decision of 25 November 1998 OJ 1999 L254/9 and *Procter & Gamble/Gillette* COMP/3732, Commission decision of 15 July 2005 OJ 2005 C 239/12. See Takahiko Suzuki and Toshihiko Maki, '28th Competition Policy Research Centre Seminar: Effects of Buyer Power in Distribution Markets' (seminar summary), *Fair Trade*, **740** (June 2012), 38–41.

[26] See the JFTC's press release of 22 June 2012.

[27] *Fair Trade Information*, **2333** (25 June 2012) 1.

[28] See Masaru Endo, Tsuyoshi Yamashita and Yoichi Yako, 'Treatment of Alleged AMA Infringement Case against TEPCO', *Kosei Torihiki*, **743** (September 2012), 82 (in Japanese).

argued that it is inappropriate to limit the application of the concept strictly to business relations.[29] This issue regards the interaction between consumer protection law and competition law. Consumer welfare is one of the objectives of the AMA, but this may not be decisive since, for example, many forms of regulation may also undermine consumer welfare, yet that does not automatically mean that the JFTC is competent to act. On the other hand, exploited individual consumers, who may be disadvantaged owing, for example, to asymmetry of information, should not be left unprotected.[30] In contrast to the uncertainty regarding Article 2(9)5 AMA, in EU law, particularly in the context of Article 102 TFEU, it does not matter who 'the other party' is, because abuse of a dominant position concerns the behaviour of a dominant undertaking that affects a market. Even in the case of an exploitative abuse such as excessive pricing, the general test is whether the price of the dominant firm bears no reasonable relation to the economic value of the product concerned, such that the price can be said to be 'unfair'. This can be a price applied to other businesses purchasing an input, but it can equally be a price charged to final consumers.

In this regard, as in the EU, in Japan patterns of abuse include various types of conduct including obligations imposed by the superior party in longstanding commercial relations. In Japan, the most important categories of abuse include excessive pricing and discriminatory pricing. In these categories, a lot of cases involve various sectors such as gasoline, alcoholic beverages and medicines. Further, it is common to see cases where a firm is forced to sell certain products, to send assistant staff to shops and/or to pay a financial subsidy called *kyosankin.* This area of law has sometimes been interpreted and enforced to protect weaker companies, for instance subcontractors against bigger manufacturers. A typical abuse of dominance case in the EU may be different. Furthermore, whereas in the EU exclusionary and exploitative conduct share the same economic logic and are examined under Article 102 TFEU, exclusionary conduct does not fall within the scope of an abuse of

---

[29] See, e.g., Tadashi Shiraishi, *Competition Law of Japan* (2nd edn, Yuhikaku Publishing, 2009) p. 264 (in Japanese).

[30] For discussion, see, e.g., Shuya Hayashi, 'Consumer Transactions and Control of Abuse of Superior Position: Behavioral Economics and Competition Law', *NBL*, **981** (15 July 2012) 107 (in Japanese). Professor Hayashi explains that the wording of Article 2, Section 9(5) AMA does not limit its application to business transactions but could also cover consumer transactions.

superior bargaining position as understood in Japan.[31] In the EU, the typical anticompetitive scenario is one in which a firm reduces competition through anticompetitive means (exclusion) in order to reap the benefits of higher market power (exploitation), although not all exploitation is rooted in exclusionary conduct.[32]

REBATES

In the *Intel* case, the JFTC investigated rebate and advertising payments, referred to as a 'market development fund', for purchases of Intel's microprocessors.[33] Intel, which was a major CPU manufacturer together with two other competitors in the Japanese market, discouraged the five major Japanese OEMs (Original Equipment Manufacturer) from buying competitors' CPUs for all or most of their requirements, using the rebate and the market development fund. Intel's market share was approximately 89 per cent while competitors' shares were about 10 per cent and 1 per cent respectively. On 13 April 2005, the JFTC adopted a decision on the ground that the behaviour violated the prohibition of private monopolisation under the AMA.[34] The authority also ordered Intel to conduct an effective competition compliance auditing.[35]

Some argued that Intel's rivals were actively competing with Intel in the market, and it could not be shown that Intel's conduct substantially restricted competition. It is argued that having a large share of the market is not in and of itself a violation of the AMA, and that the relevant conduct and its effects are what matter. For instance, if a company introduces a machine efficient enough to turn out products at a much lower cost, the company should not be penalised for having made this innovation. Furthermore, it is argued that the JFTC should adopt measures that can be

---

[31] See, e.g., Akira Negishi, 'Important Point of Abuse of Superior Position', *Franchise Ages*, **1** (Japan Franchise Association) (2012), 27.

[32] Professor Röller explains that both are consistent with the same economic logic. See Lars-Hendrik Röller, 'Exploitative Abuses', in Claus-Dieter Ehlermann and Mel Marquis (eds), *European Competition Law Annual 2007: A Reformed Approach to Article 82 EC* (Hart Publishing, 2008) p. 525.

[33] JFTC decision of 13 April 2005; Tsuyoshi Okumura, 'AMA infringement case by Intel', *Kosei Torihiki*, 660 (October 2005) (in Japanese), 56–61. For the press release in English, see http://www.jftc.go.jp/e-page/pressreleases/2005/March/050308intel.pdf.

[34] The JFTC press release is available at http://www.jftc.go.jp/eacpf/cases/intel.pdf.

[35] Ibid.

enforced without hampering competition. Measures that restrict vigorous competition may be more harmful to the market than no measures at all.

Similar analysis and criticism had been claimed against the case law of the European Court regarding rebates.[36] In the European *Intel* case, where an appeal is currently pending before the EU General Court, the Commission issued its decision in line with established case law of the European Courts concerning the grant of rebates under Article 102 TFEU.[37] According to judgments such as those in *Michelin II* and *British Airways*, a rebate provided by a dominant company in exchange for exclusivity is in principle abusive, unless it can be objectively justified. To respond to the criticisms, however, in *Intel* the Commission also carried out an economic analysis to demonstrate that Intel's rebates scheme was successful in excluding a firm that was as efficient as Intel itself (anticompetitive foreclosure).

BLANKET LICENSING AGREEMENTS

In some cases, the JFTC relies on the prohibition of private monopolisation to solve competition problems that in the EU would normally be governed by Article 101 TFEU, the provision regulating restrictive agreements or concerted practices.

On 16 July 2008, the European Commission issued a decision prohibiting the practices of 24 collecting societies in the field of licensing. The collecting societies had entered into agreements specifying the conditions of management and licensing of public performance rights for musical works relating to the use, in reciprocal representation agreements, of the membership restrictions contained in the model contract of the International Confederation of Societies of Authors and Composers (the 'CISAC model contract'), or the de facto application of those membership restrictions.[38] All the European collecting societies belonged to CISAC (the Confederation of Societies of Authors and Composers), which is the world organisation of authors' societies. The Commission considered that a series of measures, including membership restrictions and territorial restrictions, incorporated in the reciprocal representation

---

[36] Ekaterina Rousseva, *Rethinking Exclusionary Abuses in EU Competition Law* (Hart Publishing, 2010) p. 200.

[37] Intel COMP/C-3/37.990, Commission Decision of 13 May 2009.

[38] CISAC COMP/C2/38.698, Commission decision of 16 July 2008 relating to a proceeding under Article 81 of the EC Treaty and Article 53 of the EEA Agreement.

agreements concluded between the collecting societies constituted infringements of Article 101 TFEU. However, in a judgment of 12 April 2013, the General Court annulled the principal part of the Commission decision, which is an allegation that CISAC's European members had engaged in an illegal concerted practice to restrict the territorial scope of their reciprocal representation agreements, owing to insufficient evidence.[39]

In Japan, meanwhile, a similar case in 2009 was examined under Article 2(5) AMA – the rule on private monopolisation.[40] In this case, the Japanese Society for Rights of Authors, Composers and Publishers ('JASRAC'), which manages the copyright portfolios of music authors, which in fact was dominant in the music licensing market before the market was liberalised in 2001, had concluded Blanket Licensing Agreements with all the broadcasters. The Blanket Licensing Agreement allowed a licensee to use JASRAC's wide variety of repertoires of music, and licensing fees were fixed at 1.5 per cent of the licensee's turnover from its broadcasting business of the previous year. Then, in 2006, E-license entered the market. Further, if a broadcaster wished to use music managed by another collecting society, it had to pay additional fees to that society, separately from the fees paid to JASRAC. In its cease and desist order, the JFTC took the view that the conditions imposed by JASRAC effectively prevented broadcasters from using music managed by other societies; this amounted to private monopolisation. However, the JFTC's cease and desist order was not supported by the JFTC's hearing officer, who was unconvinced by the evidence. In a final decision (*Shinketsu*), the JFTC annulled its own order in 2012.

Although JASRAC has numerous regional licensing offices in Japan, they all belong to JASRAC and form part of the organisation. In the EU, by opening up the European market to more competition, without finding each national collecting society to be dominant in its respective domestic market, the Commission sought to improve their services and functions to the benefit of both music authors and commercial users.[41,42] Since Japan has neither a market integration objective nor constituent Member

---

[39] Case T-442/08 *CISAC v Commission*, judgment of the General Court of 12 April 2013, not yet published.

[40] JFTC decision of 27 February 2009. For further details regarding the procedure and content of the JFTC's order, see, e.g., Tadashi Shiraishi, 'Analysis of Shinketsu of JFTC regarding JASRAC', *Law and Technology*, **57** (October 2012). See also Chapter 3 (this volume) on procedure.

[41] See, e.g., Alain Andries and Bruno Julien-Malvy, 'The CISAC decision – creating competition between collecting societies for music rights', *Competition*

States, the JFTC's aim was rather to protect commercial users simply by applying the AMA provisions on private monopolisation.

CONCLUSION

Whereas in the US the enforcement of antitrust rules against dominant companies has been comparatively lenient, in particular owing to key judgments of the US Supreme Court, the EU and Japan generally assume a more vigilant posture with regard to dominant firms.[43,44] In that regard, the balance between abuse of dominance and legitimate competition in both of these jurisdictions is often influenced to a large degree by the structure of the market of reference.

In the EU and Japan, the structure of the relevant provisions is different owing to varying objectives. In addition to the EU-type abuse of dominance, Japan puts emphasis on the protection of weaker businesses in asymmetric business relationships. The protection of small and medium sized companies is clearly one of Japan's policy objectives, and this extends to the application of competition policy. The Small and Medium Enterprise Agency, which is a governmental organ established to promote small and medium sized companies and their businesses, actually conducts visits to large companies to monitor whether they are abusing a superior bargaining position in transactions with small and medium sized companies. The role of such smaller companies in the Japanese economy is seen as crucial, since they often create business

---

Policy Newsletter, **3** (2008) 55, available at http://ec.europa.eu/competition/publications/cpn/2008_3_53.pdf.

[42] See, e.g., Fumio Sensui, 'Decision in a Case Regarding the Japanese Society for Rights of Authors and Future Issues', *Kosei Torihiki*, **743** (September 2012) 68 (in Japanese).

[43] On a policy and enforcement level, with the re-election of President Obama in the United States, strong pursuit of antitrust cases is predicted. However, given the constraints imposed by the case law of the Supreme Court, the activities of the DOJ's Antitrust Division can be expected to focus above all on cartel enforcement and close scrutiny of horizontal mergers. Monopolisation claims may arise occasionally, but the unanimous decision of the FTC (with a Democrat chairman) to settle the *Google* dispute may possibly reflect an environment in which it is difficult for the US federal antitrust enforcers to maintain such cases and litigate them successfully in court.

[44] See, e.g., Yosuke Okada and Shuya Hayashi (eds), *Economic Impact of the Antimonopoly Law: Case Studies in Recent Court and Tribunal Decisions* (University of Tokyo Press, 2009) p. 7.

opportunities and reflect entrepreneurialism while contributing to technical innovation and promoting economic activity.

Confucian ethics is just an enlargement of the family ethic, and society and the State are merely a notional enlargement of the family; the State is composed of a sovereign 'father' and his subject 'son'.[45] 'Benevolence', which is the idea that Confucius emphasised as the supreme virtue, is roughly equivalent to humanitarianism, that is, the compassion of man towards his fellow man.[46] Metaphorically, a case involving abuse of a superior bargaining position is about the father protecting a small son from a bigger brother in order to re-establish harmony within the family order.

On the other hand, small and medium sized companies in Japan, while enjoying the fatherly protection of the State, are also subject to behavioural constraints. In particular, and in contrast to EU law (but not altogether unlike certain national laws), small and medium sized companies in Japan must generally refrain from selling goods or services at a loss.[47]

45 He Zhaowu and Peng Gang, *A Critical History of Classical Chinese Philosophy* (New World Press, 2009) p. 63.

46 Ibid. p. 57.

47 Masayuki Funada. 'How Do the Japanese Commercial Practices Change?', *Shoseki no Mado* (April 2010), 17.

7. Merger control

HISTORY OF JAPANESE MERGER CONTROL

In the field of merger control, the Antimonopoly Act in Japan was in some ways the forerunner of the approach that is now typical in competition regimes around the world. The original AMA already provided for merger control in its Chapter 4, under which the JFTC approved a merger only under strict conditions, although in most other jurisdictions, provisions concerning mergers had not yet been adopted.[1] In 1949, Japan introduced a prior notification system of merger clearance,[2] many years ahead of Germany (1973), the US (1976) and the European Community (1989). When the Japanese Antimonopoly Act was reformed in 1953, it was clarified that the substantive criterion was a 'substantial restraint of competition' test, which has become a worldwide standard. One of the particularities of the history of Japanese merger control is that, although the framework was established at an early stage, its enforcement was sometimes criticised for being heavily affected by the Japanese industrial policy. The balance between competition policy and industrial policy, in particular during the period of rapid economic growth, was a serious issue, although some argue that industrial policy made only a minor contribution to growth in Japan.[3]

In the EU, after much discussion in the 1970s and 1980s, the Merger Regulation was finally adopted in 1989 and all kinds of concentrations including full mergers, acquisitions and certain types of joint ventures fell under the Commission's control, provided that they had a 'Community dimension'. Adoption of the Merger Regulation proved difficult partly because of the concerns of certain Member States, whose power to investigate a merger would be limited by an exclusive competence at the

---

[1] See JFTC, *AMA Policy Fifty Years History*, Volume 1 (Kosei Torihiki Kyokai, 1997) p. 52 (in Japanese).

[2] The acquisition of shares was not subject to prior notification until the reform of 2009.

[3] See, e.g., Marcus Noland and Howard Pack, *Industrial Policy in an Era of Globalization: Lessons from Asia* (Institute for International Economics, 2003) p. 100.

level of the Community. Since Japan was an integrated market, such concerns were not an issue. However, another organ of the government, in particular, MITI (now METI) limited AMA enforcement, insofar as it could do so, in order to defend Japan's industrial policy. From the perspective of Japanese companies, the strict scrutiny of the JFTC, which had the exclusive power to clear mergers, did not seem to promote industrial policy but rather tended to discourage companies from growing. With a longstanding hostility between the JFTC and MITI, the JFTC had to make efforts and use its energy to protect its competition policy against ministries such as MITI (METI) rather than to develop and advance it. However, the tension between the JFTC and MITI was not so visible at the moment the AMA was adopted. Japan's original merger control provisions aimed at the dissolution of the *zaibatsu* and the prevention of a general concentration in the Japanese market after the dissolution. Thus, Article 1 AMA provides that excessive concentration is to be prevented and Chapter 4 of AMA provides measures to realise this principle.[4]

Another characteristic of Japanese merger control is that the fear of a 'reincarnation' of *zaibatsu* was an important factor driving enforcement of the AMA by the JFTC. This concern explains why Japan introduced a prior notification system for mergers at an early stage.[5] As seen in the introduction to this book, the animosity between the JFTC and MITI was not yet prominent when the AMA was reformed in 1953. In the 1960s, the JFTC examined some important merger cases including *Yawata Steel/Fuji Steel* (1969).[6] In the *Yawata/Fuji* merger case, despite the concerns of academics, in particular economists warning that approval of the merger would lead to a giant monopolist, the JFTC cleared the transaction even though there was no competitor strong enough to restrain the merged company in the market.[7] The underlying message was that AMA enforcement should not be interpreted in a rigid way that

---

4 See, e.g., Akira Negishi and Masayuki Funada, *Japanese Antitrust Law* (4th edn, Yuhikaku, 2010) pp. 74–5.

5 Share transactions were subject to an *ex post* notification obligation until the reform of 2009 because it was considered that such transactions could be rectified later.

6 *Yawata Steel/Fuji Steel* JFTC decision of 30 October1969.

7 Yawata and Fuji were originally one company but they were split into Yawata and Fuji after World War II owing to GHQ's decentralisation policy. Thus, the merger of the two companies was considered a symbol of the decline of AMA policy between the 1950s and 1960s. See, e.g., Yasumi Ochi, *Japan, U.S. and European Competition Law* (Shojihomu, 2005) pp. 816–19.

could hamper Japan's economic growth. After World War II, MITI's efforts were focused on fostering and developing key industries such as steel and petrochemicals. By the end of 1976, however, owing to external pressure, industrial protectionism was gradually attenuated and the measures taken for the protection of difficult industries were limited to temporary ones.

A theoretical change came in the 1980s. In Japan, merger control had been merely complementary to the control of private monopolisation. From 1992, the cases started to be published. More and more merger cases were notified to multiple authorities and this trend has motivated Japan to develop a system roughly equivalent to other jurisdictions such as the EU. At the end of the 1990s, with increasing pressure from global competition, a surge in M&A activity was observed. It started in the traditional industries such as paper, oil and steel and then spread towards other industries including the financial sector. Responding to these developments, Japanese merger enforcement has grown more serious since 2002. As we will see later, the JFTC has issued various guidelines to clarify its procedures and substantive issues.

Starting in 2011, there was another increase in M&A activity, motivated partly by a temporarily strong yen but also by the survival strategy of Japanese companies in an adverse global business environment. The concern that prolonged economic stagnation and a decreasing population would lead to a shrinking Japanese market triggered acquisitions of foreign companies, in particular after the Great East Japan Earthquake of 2011. Against this background, the latest merger reform was carried out in 2011.[8]

In the EU, the introduction of the Merger Regulation (Regulation 4046/89) in 1989 was the most important addition to EU competition law since its inception. It altered the role of the Commission within the competition system and transformed the landscape of competition policy.[9, 10] The Merger Regulation was revised in 2004 with the aim of adapting it to more economically sound decisions, and to overcome a perceived rigidity that, according to some observers, made the substantive

---

[8] For details of the 2011 merger control reform, see Etsuko Kameoka and Mel Marquis, 'Recent Developments in Japanese Merger Control', in Philip Lowe and Mel Marquis (eds), *European Competition Law Annual 2010: Merger Control in European and Global Perspective* (Hart Publishing, 2013) p. 287.

[9] Regulation No. 4064/89 of 21 December 1989.

[10] See David J. Gerber, *Law and Competition in Twentieth Century Europe: Protecting Prometheus* (Oxford University Press, 1998) p. 380.

test for prohibition underinclusive.[11,12] Subsequently, implementing Regulation 802/2004, various Notices and Guidelines and Best Practice Guidelines have been published.[13] Furthermore, in 2013, the Commission made a proposal to amend the EU Merger Regulation to simplify procedure and to introduce merger review for non-controlling minority shareholdings.[14]

LEGAL STRUCTURE OF MERGER CONTROL IN JAPAN AND THE EU

As we have seen, Article 1 AMA is geared towards preventing excessive concentration while Chapter 4 of the Act stipulates particular measures to that end. Whereas the EU Merger Regulation establishes substantive provisions, and various procedural regulations and best practices deal with procedural issues, in Japan, Articles 9 to 16 AMA provide for different patterns of transaction. Under the AMA, a merger that substantially affects competition in the market is prohibited. As the conditions of this prohibition are relatively abstract, in 2004 the JFTC issued Guidelines to specify the substantive standard and the elements taken into account when the JFTC reviews a proposed transaction.

The JFTC's Merger Guidelines are generally consistent with the approach adopted in other jurisdictions, including in particular the EU. These Guidelines have been revised more often than guidelines that concern other areas of the AMA, perhaps because merger control principles could be more easily aligned with global standards (see Table 7.1). The reform of 2004 adopted almost the same substantive standards familiar in the EU and the US, and it can generally be said that merger control in Japan is harmonised with the regimes of the EU and the US.[15]

---

11 See Council Regulation (EC) No. 139/2004 of 20 January 2004 on the control of concentrations between undertakings (the EC Merger Regulation) OJ L24, 29 January 2004, pp. 1–22.

12 François Brunet and Guy Canivet, *Le Nouveau Droit Communautaire de la Concurrence* (L.G.D.J., 2008) pp. 519–20.

13 Commission Regulation (EC) No. 802/2004 implementing Council Regulation (EC) No. 139/2004 OJ L133, 30 April 2004, pp. 1–39. Amended by Commission Regulation (EC) No. 1033/2008, OJ L279, 22 October 2008, pp. 3–12.

14 The Commission's press release of 27 March 2013. IP/13/288.

15 Between the EU and the US, there is a framework of more close cooperation. See, e.g., Best Practices on Cooperation in Merger Investigation, 14 October 2011.

Nevertheless, there is still some divergence on basic issues, including the interpretation of market power. Whereas in the US market power is defined as the ability profitably to maintain prices above competitive levels for a significant period of time, in the EU the Commission's Guidelines on non-horizontal mergers indicate that an increase in market power refers more broadly to the ability of one or more firms to profitably increase prices, reduce output, offer choice of quality of goods and services, diminish innovation, or otherwise negatively influence parameters of competition, and is likely to deprive customers of the benefits of effective competition.[16] In Japan, a merger is prohibited if competition is substantially restricted in certain fields of trade and if the merger is likely to create, maintain and strengthen market power. There is an ongoing debate as to whether market power covers only the power to control price, or whether it also includes the power to exclude competitors. Supporters of the latter position emphasise the need to maintain open markets, even where price conditions are unlikely to change.[17]

PROCEDURE AND ENFORCEMENT OF MERGER CONTROL

The basic procedural arrangements in Japanese merger control have become increasingly similar to those in the EU. The notification requirements are examined based on total domestic turnover of the parties including its group companies. Under the current provisions of the AMA, 30 days after a notification of a transaction, the first stage investigation is terminated and if there is any remaining problem, a second stage investigation is initiated. During this period, a transaction cannot be executed, although this period can be shortened. Compared to EU merger investigations, the Japanese investigation generally does not require the submission of a voluminous notification. However, the parties may be requested to voluntarily submit various data to the JFTC piece by piece.

---

[16] See, DOJ/FTC Horizontal Merger Guidelines of 19 August 2010. Available at http://www.justice.gov/atr/public/guidelines/hmg-2010.html; Commission Notice, Guidelines on the assessment of non-horizontal mergers under the Council Regulation on the control of concentrations between undertakings, 18 October 2008, OJ C-265/6 25.

[17] See, e.g., Chizuru Ikeda, 'Purpose and Grounds of Merger Control in Competition Law: Focused on Developments of Conglomerate Merger in EC Competition Law', *Yearbook of Japanese Economic Law Association*, (2008) 123 (in Japanese).

Table 7.1 Main recent developments of the Guidelines in relation to merger control in Japan

Year of adoption	Guidelines
2002	Guidelines Concerning Companies which Constitute an Excessive Concentration of Economic Power
2002	Guidelines Concerning Authorization of Acquisition and Holding of Voting Rights by Banking and Insurance Companies under the Provisions of Section 11 of the Antimonopoly Act
2002	Policies dealing with Prior Consultation regarding Business Combination Plans (revised in 2007)
2004	Guidelines to Application of the Antimonopoly Act Concerning Review of Business Combination (revised in 2011)
2011	Policies Concerning Procedures of Review of Business Combination

Although the parties respond to the JFTC, they often cannot obtain feedback from it, and are sometimes therefore left in the dark. Like the European Commission, the JFTC sends questionnaires to interested parties such as customers. However, even if third parties claim that an envisaged merger could cause competition concerns, there is no guaranteed opportunity for the parties to respond to each submission of an interested party. However, the Japanese procedure may be more flexible than the one in the EU, and it takes into consideration various aspects. For instance, in a Japanese merger investigation, a JFTC official may come to visit the relevant premises to examine the situation on the ground.

The reforms of 2011 were designed to achieve more transparent procedures, as transparency has seemingly been a perpetual issue in Japan.[18] Under the new framework, when the JFTC requests a report

[18] These took the form of an amendment to the JFTC's notification rules and a revised set of guidelines. For translations of the Rules on Applications for Approval, Reporting and Notification ('Notification Rules'), the Guidelines on the Application of the Policies Concerning Procedures of Review of Business Combination ('Procedural Guidelines'), and the revised Guidelines on the Application of Antimonopoly Act Concerning Review of Business Combination ('Revised Guidelines'), see http://www.jftc.go.jp/en/policy_enforcement/mergers/

from the parties it should indicate the purpose of its request, thus giving the parties a better understanding of what precisely is needed.[19] At the parties' request, the JFTC should also explain its concerns.[20] This was already a matter of informal practice but it is now made explicit. Also under the new system, when the JFTC decides to initiate a second stage investigation, it will publish the announcement and ask concerned parties for their views.[21]

With regard to substantive analysis, the revised Guidelines also provide more detailed explanations of the elements that determine whether a merger will substantially restrain competition. These include, among other things, the supply posture of other producers, competitive pressure from neighbouring markets, and any competitive pressure exerted by customers.[22]

In Japan, economic analysis is gradually becoming more common in merger cases. Although blunt concentration measures have been giving way to more refined tools in the most sophisticated jurisdictions, in Japan the Herfindahl-Hirschman Index (HHI) is used regularly as an indicator. The HHI after a merger, rather than the 'delta' (increase in the HHI), is regarded as important because the JFTC pays close attention to market structure. On the other hand, the SSNIP test (let alone the UPP test) has not so far been very actively used, although the Guidelines mention the SSNIP test, and in some cases such as the *Nippon Steel Corporation/ Sumitomo Metal* merger case it was used.[23,24] In general, the majority of professional people such as officers and scholars involved in AMA policy are legally educated but there are not many economists working on cases. This may sometimes amount to not only inefficient merger control but may also reflect a lack of basic understanding of the merits of competition policy.[25]

---

pdf/110713.2.pdf; http://www.jftc.go.jp/en/policy_enforcement/mergers/pdf/rules_on_applications.pdf; and http://www.jftc.go.jp/en/pressreleases/uploads/110620attach2.pdf.

19 Notification Rules, Article 8; Procedural Guidelines, Section 6(1).

20 Procedural Guidelines, Section 4.

21 Ibid., Section 6.

22 Ibid., Section 4.

23 See, e.g.,Yosuke Okada and Shuya Hayashi, *Economic Impact of Antimonopoly Law* (University of Tokyo Press, 2009) p. 21 (in Japanese).

24 See the Guidelines point 1.2. See also JFTC's press release of 14 December 2011, available at http://www.jftc.go.jp/pressrelease/11.december/11121403.pdf.

25 Fumio Otake, 'The Merits of Market Competition', *Sanseiken Forum*, **80** (2008) 34 (in Japanese).

In the past, the JFTC tended to look only at the shares of the parties in the domestic market, and prohibited mergers because of high shares in the narrowly defined geographic market. However, the JFTC's attitude seems to have changed, at least in cases involving companies active in innovative fields such as IT. In the *Google/Yahoo* case, for example, the JFTC approved the transaction, even though Google's post-merger share of the search engine market would exceed 90 per cent.[26]

EFFICIENCY GAINS IN MERGER CONTROL

The question as to how to interpret productive efficiencies created by a merger has been discussed for a long time in Japan, although this has not been clearly indicated in the JFTC's decisions. In Japan, efficiency gains in horizontal mergers can be considered as an analysis of competitive effects when the improvement in efficiency is expected to bring, among other things, lower prices, better quality or innovations that can be shared with consumers.[27] Generally, it is considered that a true trade-off between efficiency gains and anticompetitive effects is not acceptable.[28] In contrast, the EU accepts the possibility of a trade-off whereby efficiency gains can be weighed against anticompetitive effects created by a merger, although in practice it is difficult for the notifying parties, who carry the burden of proof, to put forward decisive efficiency claims.[29,30] However,

---

26 In the *Google/Yahoo* case, the JFTC issued the result of its investigation on 2 December 2010 after deciding that the alliance would not cause problems. See the JFTC's press release, available at http://www.jftc.go.jp/houdou/pressrelease/h22/dec/10120202.files/10120202.pdf#search=グーグル (in Japanese).

27 Professor Nihoul notes that the word 'efficiency' would not have the same connotation in each region or community, because connotations are attached to words with varying cultural and social features. Paul Nihoul, 'Do Words Matter? A Discussion on Words Used to Designate Values Associated with Competition Law', in Daniel Zimmer (ed.), *The Goals of Competition Law* (Edward Elgar, 2012) p. 221. The connotation of '*koritsusei*', the Japanese translation of the word 'efficiency', may not be identical to the English word 'efficiency'.

28 See supra note 23, Okada and Hayashi, p. 77. For more recent arguments in favour of such a trade-off, see, e.g., Shingo Seryo, 'New Developments of Establishing Market Dominance in Merger Control: Focused on Horizontal Merger Control' *Yearbook of Japanese Economic Law Association*, (2012) 35.

29 Council Regulation No. 139/2004 on the control of concentrations between undertakings (2004) OJ L24/1, recital 29 and Guidelines on the assessment of horizontal mergers under the Council Regulation on the control of concentraions between undertakings, OJ C31, 5 February 2004, paras 76–88. See also, e.g., Lars-Hendrik Röller, Johan Stennek and Frank Verboven, 'Efficiency

the method of analysing efficiency gains was not clear, and this was criticised as an example of the lack of transparency in Japanese merger enforcement.[31] In response to this, in 2004, the JFTC's Merger Guidelines referred to efficiency gains, but stated that where market power is created, maintained or reinforced and where it is likely that consumer interests are damaged a merger will not be approved unless the parties propose adequate commitments.[32]

COMMITMENTS AND REMEDIES

In the EU, approximately 3 per cent of all cases that are transferred go beyond Phase I and make it to Phase II, an in-depth investigation. In around 42 per cent of the cases that go to Phase II, the parties submit commitments in order to secure clearance of their transaction. In Japan, although merging parties have often tried to resolve competition problems early, in a 'prior consultation' stage, commitments have been often required. It has been noted that, under the Japanese system, the parties have had the possibility to engage in consultations on possible commitments with the JFTC well before the formal notification is due, whereas under the EU rules formal remedy discussions are not initiated until competition concerns have been identified.

Since Japan's prior consultation system was formally abolished as a result of the 2011 merger control reforms, the traditional practice is expected to change, although even now if the parties so request they can still consult the JFTC before the official notification. In the EU, since pre-notification consultations are considered important, the Commission

---

Gains for Mergers', available at http://ec.europa.eu/dgs/competition/economist/efficiency_gains.pdf.

30 It has been asserted that some undertakings have not made vigorous arguments on the basis of efficiencies for fear that the European Commission might take this as a defensive or desperate signal. See Lars-Hendrik Röller, 'Efficiencies in EU Merger Control: Do They Matter?', in Philip Lowe and Mel Marquis (eds), *European Competition Law Annual 2010: Merger Control in European and Global Perspective* (Hart Publishing, 2013) p. 61.

31 See Kuninobu Takeda, *Merger Control and Efficiency Defense* (Taga Shuppan, 2001) p. 241.

32 See Okada and Hayashi, supra note 23, p. 13. For comparative discussion of the efficiency defence in merger cases in the EU and Japan, see also Etsuko Kameoka, 'Efficiency Claims in Japanese Merger Control: A Comparative Overview', in Gustavo Ghidini, Berardino Libonati and Piergaetano Marchetti (eds), *Concorrenza e Mercato*, 13-14/2005-2006 (Giuffré, 2007) p. 255.

actively encourages use of this system.[33] However, the outcome of the Japanese reform does not seem to make a substantial difference between the abolished prior consultation systems and still existing consultation system, because of the remaining possibility of voluntary prior consultations. But the amendment will contribute to procedural convergence between the EU and Japan, because the system promotes a more efficient and transparent procedure, a goal pursued equally in the EU. The advantages of harmonising merger control procedures may also affect the treatment of commitments. For instance, in the acquisition by Toshiba of Westinghouse, the JFTC defined the relevant geographic market as the Japanese territory and unconditionally approved the transaction, while in the EU the Commission approved it only subject to commitments.[34]

Under the JFTC's Merger Guidelines of 2007, both structural and behavioural remedies can be ordered. Although the Japanese procedure has moved closer to the Commission's system, commitments submitted to the Commission are mainly structural and quite detailed, and the Commission sets a strict deadline for execution compared to the JFTC. Moreover, commitments submitted to the JFTC do not seem to legally bind the parties. According to the JFTC, if the parties do not comply with their commitments, it can restart an investigation and take legal action. Where divestitures are concerned, the parties are expected to report compliance to the JFTC.[35] In the EU, where approval of a merger is made subject to commitments, the parties will be fined if they breach their obligations. In contrast, in Japan, the content of the commitments is not always publicly known. When the JFTC decides not to issue a cease and desist order against the transaction, the notification is considered not to raise competition concerns.[36] Although under the Japanese system competitors may not know about the content of the commitments, the JFTC's view is that it is unnecessary to resolve this problem by issuing a

---

33 See Commission Regulation (EC) No. 802/2004 implementing Council Regulation 139/2004, recital (11) and Best Practices on the conduct of EC merger control proceedings, p. 2. See also Peter Roth and Vivien Rose (eds), *Bellamy & Child's European Community Law of Competition* (6th edn, Oxford University Press, 2008) p. 693.

34 *Toshiba/Westinghouse* COMP/M 4153. For the JFTC, available at http://www.jftc.go.jp/en/pressreleases/yearly-2009/jun/individual-000054.files/2009-June-9.pdf#search=westinghouse.

35 See *Kosei Torihiki Jyoho*, **2334** (2 July 2012), 9 (in Japanese).

36 See, e.g., Noboru Kawahama, 'The Result of the Merger Project between NSC/Sumitomo Metal', *NBL*, **980** (July 2012) 76.

cease and desist order together with an order to comply with commitments. If necessary to ensure the effectiveness of a commitment, such as where the obligation is to promote market entry, the JFTC will publish the commitments on its website.[37] Here again there is a hesitant attitude towards transparency and openness, since, in other cases, the JFTC does not publish the commitments.[38]

Although in the *Panasonic/Sanyo* merger case the parties initially proposed a carve-out remedy to the JFTC and the European Commission to remedy the competition concerns in a merger related to cylindrical lithium batteries (CLBs) and rechargeable coin-shape batteries, after discussion with the parties the Commission concluded that, according to the Notice on Remedies, there was a clear preference for the divestiture of an existing operation over a carve-out solution.[39] As a result, the parties committed to divest a factory to eliminate the entire overlap in CLBs and in rechargeable coin-shape batteries. Subsequently, the JFTC approved the same commitment in response to the competition concern identified in the Japanese CLBs market.

LAW ON SPECIAL MEASURES FOR INDUSTRIAL REVITALISATION

The *NSC/Sumitomo Metal* investigation was notable not only because it was the first case in which another revised piece of legislation was applied, but also because it was the first case in which the revised law addressing the perpetual problem of balance between competition policy and industrial policy was applied.[40,41]

---

37 Supra note 35 *Kosei Torihiki Jyoho*, p. 9 (in Japanese).

38 In relation to the Sumitomo Bank and Sakura Bank Merger case, the concerns raised by the JFTC and the commitments submitted by the banks are listed on the JFTC's website as one of the public cases (2000, Case 11). Available at http://www.jftc.go.jp/ma/jirei2/H12jirei11-02.html (in Japanese). For further details on this case, see, e.g., Masako Wakui, *Antimonopoly Law: Competition Law and Policy in Japan* (Arima Publishing, 2008) pp. 4, 205.

39 See Rita Devai, Tobias P. Maass, Dimitrios Magos and Robert Thomas, 'Merger Case M.5421 Panasonic/Sanyo – Batteries included or "lost in translation"?', *Competition Newsletter*, **1** (2010) 62–3. Available at http://ec. europa.eu/competition/publications/cpn/2010_1_23.pdf. *Panasonic/Sanyo* COMP/M.5421, JFTC public case (2009, Case 7).

40 See http://www.jftc.go.jp/pressrelease/11.december/11121403.pdf (in Japanese). For an English-language summary, see http://www.jftc.go.jp/en/pressreleases/archives/individual-000457.html.

In May 2011, Japan also modified its Law on Special Measures for Industrial Revitalization, and in particular introduced Article 13, which allows close contact between the JFTC and the minister in charge to expedite procedures, considering the growing need to reinforce Japan's global competitiveness. The revised law entered into force in July 2011.[42] Under this law, the minister in charge of the industrial area concerned is entitled to consult and provide comments to the JFTC regarding a pending investigation. Where this is done, the JFTC can ask for additional information, if necessary. The Japanese business community expects that, with this possibility of consultation, the arguments in favour of a merger that is likely to strengthen the position of a Japanese company in the global market will be more easily accepted.[43] Under this procedure, for example, the ministry concerned can explain the need for the creation of a larger company to face up to global competition, especially if it is expected that the JFTC will otherwise hesitate to approve the deal on account of competition problems. In the *NSC/Sumitomo Metal* case, the relevant ministry was METI. In the *Tokyo/Osaka Stock Exchange* merger case, the parties requested the intervention of Japan's Financial Services Agency and the Agency intervened.[44] In the EU, it is not unusual for a Directorate General of the Commission other than DG Competition to become involved in the investigation, sometimes as a result of the parties' lobbying activities. And, of course, the Commission's merger decision is adopted not by DG Competition but by the College of the Commissioners after receiving the non-binding opinion of the Advisory Committee (including representatives of national regulators). In this respect, although the institutional frameworks differ in the

---

41 For details see, e.g., Noboru Kawahama, 'The Result of the Merger Project between NSC/Sumitomo Metal', *NBL*, **980** (July 2012) (in Japanese).

42 Article 13 of Law on Special Measures for Industrial Revitalization. See http://www.meti.go.jp/sankatsuhou/outline/data/etc-2/sankatsuhou.pdf (in Japanese).

43 See, e.g., Information on Minutes of Meeting of House of Representatives, No. 177 Parliament, Committee on Economy and Industry, No. 7. See http://kokkai.ndl.go.jp/SENTAKU/syugiin/177/0098/17704270098007c.html (in Japanese). However, a consultation does not necessarily mean that the JFTC and the ministry in charge will discuss the existence of illegal conduct during the investigation of a pending case. According to the Secretary General of the JFTC, the JFTC's views on the breach of the AMA and its reasoning are submitted to the ministry in charge only after completing the investigation. See http://www.jftc.go.jp/teirei/h23/kaikenkiroku110518.html (in Japanese).

44 See, e.g., *The Asahi Shinbun* (4 January 2012). http://www.asahi.com/business/ jiji/JJT201201040060.html (in Japanese).

EU and in Japan, a parallel seems to emerge here, with 'triangular' dialogues in each jurisdiction among the competition authority, the parties to a merger and relevant organs of the executive.

PRIORITY AMONG NOTIFICATIONS

Two transactions in the hard disc drive ('HDD') market shed some light on the priority of merger investigations among notifications.[45] In these cases, the largest company in the 3.5 inch HDD market planned to acquire the number three company in the market, while the number two company envisaged acquiring the number four company in the same market.

In Japan, Western Digital Ireland ('WDI') notified its acquisition of the shares of Hitachi Global Technology (later renamed Viviti Technologies) on 10 June 2011. The second stage investigation was initiated on 4 July 2011, and the authority received all necessary information from the parties on 26 August 2011. Then WDI offered remedies to address the JFTC's possible competition concerns, and the JFTC conditionally approved the transaction under Article 10 AMA (share acquisitions) on 24 November 2011.

On 19 May 2011, Seagate Technology International also notified the JFTC of its intended acquisition of the HDD business of Samsung Electronics. The JFTC initiated its second stage investigation on 17 June 2011 and received all the required documents from the parties on 27 October 2011. It considered that, with the remedies proposed by the WDI in the above case, this transaction would not substantially restrict the competition in the HDD market. As a result it approved the transaction without remedies under Article 16 AMA (business transfers) on 15 December 2011.

These cases were also investigated in the EU in 2011, and the European Commission approved both transactions. When the Commission opened an in-depth investigation on 30 May 2011, it invited interested third parties to submit their observations.[46] With regard to market definition, it concluded, as the JFTC did, that separate worldwide

---

[45] Seagate Technology International/Samsung JFTC decision of 28 December 2011 and Western Digital/Vivid Technologies (/Hitachi Global Technology) JFTC decision of 28 December 2011.

[46] OJ C165/3. See http://eur-lex.europa.eu/LexUriServ/LexUriServ.do?uri=OJ:C:2011:165: 0003: 0003:EN:PDF.

markets for HDDs existed based on their form (3.5 inch or 2.5 inch) and their end use (desktop computers, mobile computers, consumer electronic devices, and enterprise business critical and mission critical applications).[47]

However, the issue of 'priority among notifications', which became an important issue in the EU, was not discussed in Japan. In the EU, the fact that notifications filed only one day apart from each other may cause unfair outcomes was criticised. While the Seagate/Samsung merger was notified to the Commission on 19 April 2011, the WDI deal was notified on 20 April 2011. After both notifications were assessed separately based on the priority rule, the former was approved without commitments, but the latter was cleared subject to commitments more than a month later.

In Japan, the parties to the WDI merger, who submitted a notification to the JFTC almost three weeks later than the notification of Seagate Technology International/Samsung, completed all the required information two months earlier than Seagate Technology International/Samsung did, and then the parties to the WDI merger offered remedies that the JFTC accepted. Accordingly, the WDI transaction was conditionally cleared on 24 November 2011. As for the Seagate Technology International/Samsung deal, the JFTC cleared it unconditionally on 15 December 2011. According to the JFTC, in light of the remedies promised by the parties in the *Western Digital/Vivid Technologies* case, the *Seagate Technology International/Samsung* transaction would not substantially restrict competition on the market.

Unlike the EU, the JFTC's rule is that the authority examines notified transactions on the assumption that both transactions are going forward.[48] The problem arises where the JFTC concludes that a substantial restriction of competition is likely. In that case, the authority will have to decide which transaction will be subject to a remedy. In the past, the JFTC has not encountered such situations, because it has not had cases in which it found that the transactions would substantially restrict competition.[49] In the above-mentioned case, although the JFTC found that the

---

[47] Western Digital Ireland/Viviti Technologies COMP/M.6203 and Seagate Technology/The HDD business of Samsung Electronics COMP/M. 6214. For the Commission's press release, see http://europa.eu/rapid/pressReleasesAction.do?reference=IP/11/1395.

[48] Tadashi Shiraishi, 'Analysis of Merger Cases and Others in 2011', *Kosei Torihiki*, **745** (November 2011) 30–31 (in Japanese).

[49] For instance, the transactions involving Sumitomo Electric/Hitachi Cable, and Furukawa Electric/Fujikura regarding the high power electric wire sector were examined as a parallel notification. JFTC press release of 23 July 2004,

mergers would substantially restrict competition, Western Digital proposed commitments of its own accord and the JFTC did not have to face the question of which set of parties should be required to come forward with a package of remedies.[50]

THIRD PARTY OBSERVATIONS AND COMPLAINTS

In *BHP Billiton/Rio Tinto*, the parties were two of the three largest producers of iron ore in the world. The parties notified BHPB's intended acquisition of Rio Tinto to the Commission on 30 May 2008.[51] The US approved the transaction but in the procedure before the European Commission, Japanese steel companies opposed the transaction, hoping that the Commission would block it to protect the steel mills from post-merger price increases in a tight oligopolistic market.[52] The Commission initiated an investigation, which went to Phase II in July 2008. However, the Commission closed its investigation under the Merger Regulation when BHP Billiton informed it that the parties were abandoning the transaction.[53] It appears that the complaint and subsequent responses to the Commission's questionnaires were useful, at least from the Commission's point of view, as they helped to establish that the concentration would be harmful.[54]

In this case, although the JFTC expected an impact on the domestic steel industry and sought to request BHP Billiton to notify the JFTC, and even used an exceptional service method through the Australian consulate to do so, BHPB refused to receive the request.[55] In Japan, this was the first foreign-to-foreign merger case that had arisen since the 1999 merger control reform. The JFTC proceeded to investigate the *BHPB/Rio Tinto* case, asking interested parties such as competitors and steel companies for cooperation and information. It was a case that was challenging for

---

available at http://warp.ndl.go.jp/info:ndljp/pid/286894/www.jftc.go.jp/pressrelease/04.july/04072304.html.

50 See Shiraishi, supra note 48, at 31.

51 BHP Billion/Rio Tinto COMP/M.4985, Commission Decision of 5 June 2008.

52 See also Porter Elliott, Kris Van Hove and Etsuko Kameoka, 'EC Merger Control in the Global Economy: *BHP Billiton/Rio Tinto* Case', *NBL*, **905** (May 2009) 40–46, at 41 (in Japanese).

53 Commission press release of 26 November 2008, IP/08/1798.

54 See Elliott, Van Hove and Kameoka, supra note 52, at 45–46.

55 See 'Legal Inside: The JFTC Seriously Conducts International Investigation', *Nihon Keizai Shibun*, (18 September 2008).

the JFTC in the sense that it raised the possibility of a JFTC decision that differed from that of other jurisdictions if the authority considered that the merger would restrict competition in the Japanese market contrary to the AMA.[56]

Subsequently, Rio Tinto and BHP Billion planned to establish a joint venture to combine the parties' iron ore assets in Western Australia. In response, the Japanese steel mills submitted a complaint to the Commission, as did the European steel industry.[57] In January 2010, the Commission opened a formal antitrust investigation into the joint venture project, in particular to examine the effects of the proposed joint venture on the worldwide market for iron ore transported by sea.[58] This time, the investigation of the parties' production joint venture was based on Article 101 TFEU, as opposed to the previous investigation of the full acquisition of Rio Tinto by BHP Billiton, because the Commission considered that the transaction was not a full function joint venture. However, the Commission closed its investigation into the proposed acquisition of Rio Tinto without adopting a final decision because the parties abandoned this transaction as well. For its part, the JFTC also conducted an investigation, including a second stage investigation with the cooperation of other jurisdictions including the EU. Although the JFTC adopted no decision on this case, this case made the JFTC consider how to enforce the AMA in a more efficient way, in particular in a case involving a transaction between foreign parties.

JUDICIAL REVIEW OF MERGER CONTROL DECISIONS

In the EU, numerous merger decisions have been challenged before the European Courts, and this litigation has contributed to improvements in EU merger procedures. For instance, on 6 June 2002, in *Airtours v Commission*, the European Court of First Instance (now the 'General Court') annulled, for the first time, a Commission decision in which the Commission had blocked a proposed transaction. The decision, adopted in September 1999, stated that the merger would have created a collective

56 Ibid.

57 See, e.g., Porter Elliott, Johan Van Acker and Etsuko Kameoka, 'EC Competition Strategy in the Global Economy: The Example of the Proposed Joint Venture between BHP/Rio Tinto', *Journal of the Japanese Institute of International Business Law*, **39** (3) (March 2011) 321–6 at 322 (in Japanese).

58 Commission press release of 25 January 2010, IP/10/45.

dominant position for the three remaining large operators.[59] The CFI held that the Commission had failed to establish that Airtours' proposed acquisition of First Choice would have amounted to the creation or strengthening of a collective dominant position in the UK market for short-haul package holidays. According to the CFI, the Commission had failed to show that the merger would have resulted in a tacitly coordinated restriction of capacity and that such coordination would be resistant to any attempts to deviate from it by the remaining major operators on the post-merger market. The Commission faced unprecedented criticism that it could not reach a high standard of proof in issuing its decisions, particularly in the wake of two more judgments of the CFI that likewise annulled prohibition decisions that had been adopted by the Commission. This forced the Commission to propose a reform package whereby, among other things, a new post of Chief Economist was created.[60] PhD-level economists now provide highly sophisticated analysis, for instance in relation to market definition.[61] The types of evidence that the Commission generally relies on to meet the high standard of proof that the ECJ has placed upon it include not only information submitted by the parties but also witness statements, industry reports prepared by independent professionals, competitor testimony and quantitative evidence. National authorities, such as the Italian Antitrust Authority, generally follow this trend.[62]

---

[59] *Airtours v Commission*, Case T-342/99, ECR [2002] II-2585. See also Etsuko Kameoka, 'Recent Developments of EU Merger Control', *Journal of the Japanese Institute of International Business Law*, **4** (April 2003) 461–6; **6** (June 2003) 795–8; and **7** (July 2003) 948–52 (all in Japanese).

[60] *Schneider/Legrand* Cases T-310/01 and T-77/02. *Tetra Laval/Side* Cases T-5/02 [2002] ECR II-4381and T-80/02 [2002] ECR II-4519. See also then Commissioner Mario Monti, 'Merger Control in the European Union: A Radical Reform European Commission', IBA Conference on EU Merger Control, Brussels, 7 November 2002, Speech/02/545; Etsuko Kameoka, 'Reform of the EU Merger Regulation', *Journal of the Japanese Institute of International Business Law*, **30** (3) (March 2002) 302–6 (in Japanese).

[61] For determination of the relevant market, see OJ C372, 9 December 1997, pp. 5–13. Available at http://eur-lex.europa.eu/LexUriServ/LexUriServ.do?uri=OJ:C:1997:372:0005:0013:EN:PDF. See also, e.g., Doris Hildebrand, *Economic Analysis of Vertical Agreements: A Self-Assessment* (Kluwer Law International, 2005) pp. 50–54. For economic analysis in *Ryanair/Aer Lingus*, see, e.g., Etsuko Kameoka, 'Recent Developments of EU Competition Law and Practical Issues', *Kosei Torihiki*, **727** (May 2011) 22–3.

[62] See Mario Siragusa, 'Antitrust and Merger Cases in Italy: Standard of Proof, Burden of Proof and Evaluation of Evidence', in Claus-Dieter Ehlermann

By contrast, in Japan, in most merger cases the JFTC did not issue a cease and desist order but terminated investigations following prior consultations. If the response to the prior consultations was negative, the parties had the opportunity to propose commitments. Where the JFTC and the parties cannot reach agreement on commitments, the JFTC can issue a cease and desist order, and the parties can seek to have it annulled by the Tokyo High Court. If the parties fail to notify a transaction that meets the notification requirements, and that is likely to restrain competition on the market, the Tokyo High Court examines the suspended execution of the deal.[63] Accordingly, in Japan the opportunity to examine merger cases before the courts and to use litigation as a tool to improve merger control is unlikely as the case law based on appeal before the court is not accumulated.

SCRUTINY OF ACQUISITIONS OF NON-CONTROLLING MINORITY INTERESTS

In relation to notifiability of acquisition of minority shareholdings, unlike the US where the test concerns the influence caused by acquisition of a minority shareholding in the market, in Japan and the EU the issue is whether an acquisition may allow the possibility of exercising important or decisive influence on the decision making of the target firm. In the EU, decisive influence may be found when minority shareholders have additional rights that allow them to veto decisions that are essential for the strategic commercial behaviour of a joint venture.[64] In Japan, the test is generally whether the acquisition of a share leads to the holding exceeding 20 per cent of the total voting rights of the company and to the creation of the largest shareholder. However, according to the Japanese Merger Guidelines, if the acquisition amounting to the holding exceeds 10 per cent of the total voting rights of the company it may be subject to Merger Control in exceptional circumstances. Currently, the European Commission is examining the issue and Commissioner Almunia is proposing two options: (1) a selective system in which the Commission identifies cases that may raise specific problems; and (2) a mandatory

---

and Mel Marquis (eds), *European Competition Law Annual 2009: Evaluation of Evidence and its Judicial Review* (Hart Publishing, 2011) 596–7.

[63] Article 70-13(1) AMA. See supra note 7, Ochi, pp. 813–14.

[64] Commission, Consolidated jurisdictional notice under Council Regulation (EC) No. 139/2004 on the control of concentrations between undertakings, OJ C95/10 of 16 April 2008.

notification system for certain types of acquisition. The latter might create a system under which significant minority shareholdings would have to be notified to the Commission.[65]

CONCLUSION

Speedy and transparent merger proceedings may be an important key to the recovery of the Japanese economy, as the promotion of a merger will lead to a restructuring of the Japanese industry facing global competition in a crisis period. The continuous development and refinement of the merger control regime in Japan will allow for an evolving environment and changing needs. In particular, the reform of 2011 may be a new turn away from Koizumi-era enforcement with greater independence and may reflect efforts to balance powerful competition policy enforcement – a global trend encouraged by the EU, among others – against other interests including, in particular, modern variants of industrial policy.

Further, the 2011 reform may relate to the protection of the Japanese economy not by the strong bureaucratic approach adopted in the past, but rather by a legalistic approach that fits global standards. As seen in this chapter, developments under the new system are moving towards international standards, and in particular towards the EU's merger procedure. Overall, the new reform brings the JFTC's merger investigations in line with the EU's procedures, a tendency begun with the reform of 2004.

---

[65] See, e.g., Joaquín Almunia, 'The Role of Competition Policy in Times of Crisis', Speech/12/917, 6 December 2012.

8. Procedure

HISTORICAL BACKGROUND TO PROCEDURAL RIGHTS IN JAPAN AND THE EU

Shintoism, the indigenous Japanese spiritual belief since approximately 500 BC, involves practices associated with often abstract natural forces. In this system of beliefs, emphasis is placed on a positive view of essential human nature; human beings are considered to be fundamentally good, and wrongdoing is thought to be caused by evil spirits. Most Shinto rituals are conducted to keep away evil spirits through purification and through offerings to the *kami*, which are the gods. In this spiritual practice, nothing prevents basic human rights from being admitted to everyone equally.

The traditional Japanese legal system, based on old Chinese legal systems that were influenced by Confucian philosophy, was modernised mainly by reference to the French and German legal systems.[1] According to Confucian teaching, a ruler should be guided in his acts by justice and virtue. Moreover, a governor should control society not by law but by the moral example set by the governor himself. Thus law is considered to be merely a tool to maintain order and enlighten the people; it does not limit the power of the governor or guarantee 'rights' for the people. Ideally, an individual conflict should be settled between the parties informally in the community rather than before the courts. Law and litigation were not welcomed as order imposed by the governor. This culture was imported into Japan from China and it continued to influence the legal system in the *Edo* period.[2] After World War II, the Japanese Constitution and judicial system were restructured under direct US control, and the novel features introduced at that time were based largely on the common law system. Against this background, the Japanese legal system is generally regarded as being based on Continental law systems, and the appearance looks similar to those typical in European countries; but in fact the legal

---

1 See Chapter 2 (this volume) on the historical background.

2 Shigeaki Tanaka, *Introduction to Law* (Yuhikaku, 2005) pp. 51–3.

culture and many public functions are quite different from European norms. Such differences have been at the root of certain trade frictions.[3]

In Europe, the common law system that emerged in England in the Middle Ages coexists with the civil law system, which developed in Western Europe. The latter system was built on an infrastructure of Roman law, and the pre-eminent method of producing law is codification, which provides people with written sets of laws to which they are subject. By contrast, in the common law tradition, judges generally follow precedential authority established by the judges that came before. In addition, legal culture in Europe is rooted in Christianity. Greek philosophy, too, has been influential, and should not be neglected even if it is not prominent.[4] In Europe's relatively recent history, Robert Schuman, one of the 'founding fathers' of the EEC/EC/EU, signed the European Convention on Human Rights (ECHR) as the French Foreign Minister in 1950, although it took almost 15 years for France to ratify the Convention.[5] Today, by virtue of Article 6(2) of the Treaty on European Union, the EU's accession to the ECHR is obligatory. It is expected that this will lead to a reinforcement of the protection of human rights through the independent external control of the EU legal system. Of course, fundamental rights protection is not new to the EU; indeed, the 2012 Nobel Peace Prize awarded to the EU acknowledges its contribution for over six decades to the advancement of human rights in Europe.[6]

In EU competition law procedures, important fundamental rights guarantees and procedural transparency requirements apply despite continuing arguments over issues such as whether 'human' rights should be fully applicable to legal persons.[7] Historically, these relatively high standards were imposed not by the European Courts but by the Commission on its own initiative, which tended to be more liberal than the

---

3 Ibid. p. 48.

4 See Frédéric Lenoir, *Petit traité d'histoire des religions* (Plon, 2008) pp. 221–2.

5 For details see René Lejeune, *Robert Schuman, Père de l'Europe*, 1886–1963 (Fayard, 2000) pp. 152–3.

6 See the official site of the Nobel Prize at http://www.nobelprize.org/nobel_prizes/peace/laureates/2012/press.html.

7 See, e.g., Mel Marquis, 'Rules that Govern Rules: Evidence, Proof and Judicial Control in Competition Cases', in Claus-Dieter Ehlermann and Mel Marquis (eds), *European Competition Law Annual 2009: Evaluation of Evidence and Its Judicial Review in Competition Cases* (Hart Publishing, 2009) pp. xlviii–xlix.

European Courts in relation to the rights of defence,[8] although the Courts today are arguably quite rigorous in ensuring respect for procedural requirements. This tendency is gradually also being followed in Japan by the JFTC, which is currently considering improvements to its procedures.

PROCEDURAL PROVISIONS GOVERNING COMPETITION CASES IN JAPAN AND THE EU

Under the EU competition rules, substantive and procedural provisions are clearly separated and the procedural provisions are provided for in separate legislation such as a Regulation or a Notice. Article 87 of the Treaty of Rome empowered the Council of Ministers to adopt a Regulation implementing Article 85 EEC and Article 86 EEC, and in 1962 the Council used this authority to adopt Regulation 17/62.[9] Currently, the EU's enforcement framework and procedural rules are found in Council Regulation 1/2003, Commission Regulation 773/2004, Commission Regulation 1033/2008, the Commission's Leniency Notice, the Fining Guidelines, a Notice on Access to File, a Notice on Co-operation between the Commission and the National Competition Authorities, and a Notice on Cartel Settlements. Procedural issues are also covered in various 'best practice' documents. The various bits of legislation and soft law regarding procedure, albeit copious, enhance procedural transparency and predictability, even if no *ex ante* guidance can achieve these objectives perfectly.

The enforcement of EU competition law is rather complicated, in particular because the Commission, European Competition Network, national authorities and courts are all involved in enforcement of EU competition law. For instance, in the EU, the initiation of an antitrust investigation may be *ex officio* or it may be triggered by immunity applications, complaints or market monitoring, but also by referrals made to the Commission by national competition authorities.[10] These multiple

---

[8] See, e.g., Ivo Van Bael and Jean-François Bellis, *Droit de la Concurrence de la Communauté Economique Européenne* (Bruylant, 1991) p. 33.

[9] Regulation 17/62 OJ 1962 204/62, OJ Sp Ed (1962) p. 87.

[10] For the issues and the approaches in relation to the practices among the Commission and ECN, see, e.g., Damien M.B. Gerard, 'Regulation 1/2003 (and Beyond): Balancing Effective Enforcement and Due Process in Cross-border Antitrust Investigations', in Jürgen Basedow, Stéphanie Francq and Laurence Idot (eds), *International Antitrust Litigation: Conflict of Laws and Coordination* (Hart Publishing, 2012) pp. 365–92.

possibilities do not have an equivalent in Japan, where, apart from private enforcement actions, enforcement remains centralised. Likewise, the complex issues that arise between the Commission and national authorities regarding the impact of the disclosure of information received under the leniency programme is unfamiliar to Japan.[11] With the various steps of the Commission's investigation – the request for information, the Statement of Objections (SO), access to file, responses by parties to the SO, the oral hearing, and so on – the Commission follows an elaborate set of procedural rules and endeavours to fully respect the rights of defence of the undertakings concerned. To the extent that the Commission's decisions are subject to independent judicial control, its power to require a company to bring infringing conduct to an end and its power to impose sanctions, including corporate fines, must be compatible with the case law of the European Courts and of the European Court of Human Rights.[12] On appeal, complainants often assert the failure by the Commission to respect the due process protections guaranteed by the general principles of EU law, by the European Court of Human Rights, and now by the European Charter of Fundamental Rights.[13]

Unlike the TFEU, the AMA contains not only substantive provisions but also prescribes the corresponding procedures. But this does not mean that procedural provisions in Japan are more robust than in the EU. Many observers have criticised the lack of sufficient procedural guarantees in the JFTC's investigations.

Under the AMA, the JFTC can issue a cease and desist order to stop illegal conduct (Article 7 AMA). For certain categories of conduct, the JFTC can also issue a separate order imposing surcharges (Article 7-2 AMA). Further, the AMA provides for criminal sanctions (Articles 89-100 AMA) and strict liability for private damages based on the

---

11 In the *Pfleiderer* case, a German court held that a claimant is allowed to have access to documents submitted to the German competition authority under the German leniency programme. The ECJ ruled in its preliminary judgment that under EU law as it stands there can be no absolute ban on the disclosure of leniency documents, and that national courts should balance, on a case-by-case basis, the importance of the EU leniency programme and the requirements for effective private damages actions. Case C-360/09 2011, *Pfleiderer AG v Commission* not yet published.

12 See Philip Lowe, 'Taking Sound Decisions on the Basis of Available Evidence', in Claus-Dieter Ehlermann and Mel Marquis (eds), *European Competition Law Annual 2009: Evaluation of Evidence and Its Judicial Review in Competition Cases* (Hart Publishing, 2009) p. 157.

13 See Wouter P.J. Wils, *Principles of European Antitrust Enforcement* (Hart Publishing, 2005) p. 157.

JFTC's decision (Article 25 AMA). The consequences of infringements include, among other things, termination of illegal conduct, surcharges and legal invalidity of illegal agreements. If the JFTC finds an infringement, it issues a cease and desist order. And even if the authority does not possess sufficient evidence to establish an infringement, the JFTC can, if it suspects an infringement, issue a warning to the undertakings concerned.[14] Moreover, if the JFTC's evidence is insufficient to justify a warning, it can issue a 'caution'.[15] Furthermore, Article 72 AMA provides that the JFTC is entitled to issue a cease and desist order that extends for five years, if necessary, after the illegal conduct ceases.[16]

HEARINGS

The hearing procedure in Japan, called *shinpan,* is based on the law of civil procedure. In the EU, the hearing proceeds according to a framework described in the terms of reference of the Hearing Officer.[17,18] The functions of the EU Hearing Officer and a hearing officer in Japan are similar but there are important differences.

The Japanese hearing officer is appointed by the JFTC, presides over the hearing and prepares a draft of the final decision, which is called *shinketsu. Shinketsu* is adopted by the JFTC. The measures to guarantee the hearing officer's neutrality are stipulated in the AMA.[19] The EU Hearing Officer works directly under the Commissioner. He is appointed

---

14 Articles 31 and 32 of the JFTC Investigation Rules.

15 See, e.g., Kosaku Uchida, 'Informal Enforcement of Antimonopoly Law', *Hikone ronso*, **393** (Autumn, 2012) 5. The number of notices is increasing, with 95 being issued in 2010 and 138 issued in 2011, while the number of warnings is just a few every year, and decreasing. See JFTC Annual Report of 2011, available at http://www.jftc.go.jp/pressrelease/12.june/120606.pdf.

16 These provisions were amended in 2009. Previously the relevant period was three years.

17 Decision 2011/695 EU of the President of the European Commission of 13 October 2011 on the function and terms of reference of the hearing officer in certain competition proceedings, OJ L275, 20 October 2011, p. 29.

18 The reason for the naming of a 'hearing officer' was the notion that no one should decide his own case, *nemo iudex in causa sua*, implying that the prosecuting service was in charge of concluding the case and organising the hearing of the company's defence. In this regard, see Ian S. Forrester, 'Due Process in EC Competition Cases: A Distinguished Institution with Flawed Procedures', *Economic Law Review*, **34** (December 2009) 835.

19 For instance, Article 56(1) prohibits appointing a person who was involved in the investigation of the case as a hearing officer. For further details regarding

by the Commission, presides over the hearing (but does not examine witnesses) and prepares a report at the end of the procedure that focuses on procedural matters including respect for the rights of the defence.[20] In Japan, the *shinpan* procedure is essentially based on written evidence but the parties can also use witness testimony as evidence. When the parties do not accept the JFTC cease and desist order, they can request a hearing. If the parties accept the cease and desist order, it will become final without a hearing. In the EU, the oral hearing is prior to the decision and provides the parties the opportunity to supplement their defence conducted in writing. More specifically, before issuing the cease and desist order and the surcharge payment order, the JFTC provides companies with advance written notice and an opportunity to present their views and submit evidence.[21] If the addressee does not agree with the order, it may request the JFTC to initiate a hearing regarding the order within 60 days after the transcript of the order was served.

Unlike an EU hearing, *shinpan* is not a closed-door meeting but rather is open to the public. The lack of guarantee of protection of parties' confidential and/or sensitive information sometimes discourages the parties from reacting openly during the procedure; as a consequence JFTC decisions sometimes appear to suffer from vagueness.

It cannot be said that a *shinpan* hearing is used systematically: the procedure is used in only around 100 cases annually. In practice, it is extremely rare for the JFTC to 'reverse' its own cease and desist order. In the JASRAC music rights society case, the JFTC's cease and desist decision was annulled in its entirety for the first time after 18 years.[22] It has been criticised because a hearing officer is appointed by the JFTC

---

the functions of a hearing officer and its neutrality, see, e.g., Tadashi Shiraishi, *Competition Law in Japan* (2nd edn, Yuhikaku, 2009) pp. 588–9 (in Japanese).

[20] For the practice concerning hearings and the functions of a hearing officer, see, e.g., Valentine Korah, *An Introductory Guide to EC Competition Law and Practice* (9th edn, Hart Publishing, 2007) pp. 3271–2.

[21] The JFTC sent its written advance notice and surcharge payment order of approximately 13 billion yen to three Japanese companies (excluding a leniency applicant) in March 2013, alleging that they were involved in the bearing cartel. See, e.g., *Nihonkeizai Shinbun*, 9 March 2013. Subsequently the authority issued its cease and desist decision on 29 March 2013. *Bearing*, JFTC decision of 29 March 2013.

[22] One example is the JASRAC case (JFTC decision of 27 February 2009), where the JFTC's order was not upheld by the hearing officer and then the JFTC had to issue an almost identical reasoning and conclusion as the draft *Shinketsu* prepared by the hearing officer. See also Chapter 6 (this volume) on abuse of a dominant position.

and is not considered neutral. Moreover, the procedure normally takes longer than the EU hearing procedure.[23] In response to criticism, a bill of amendments to AMA to abolish the hearing procedure was adopted by the Cabinet in May 2013 and the diet is supposed to discuss it soon.[24] Accordingly, the hearing procedure may soon be abolished and without passing a hearing process the parties may be allowed to challenge a JFTC decision before the Tokyo District Court instead of the Tokyo High Court.

In the EU there have been calls for the establishment of a specialised competition court with fewer judges. Some even argue that the European Courts should employ dedicated economists to facilitate understanding of complex economic evidence. In Japan, there is no competition court with specialists; nor does the public seem to be clamouring for such a court, for the time being. In Japan, the *shinpan* procedure, which is a quasi-judicial proceeding, is presided over by a hearing officer who often has specialised knowledge in competition law. The need for such expertise cannot always be met, since human resources are limited; this limits the number of investigations that the JFTC can pursue in an effective manner. As noted above, under the 2013 amendments, a party may appeal the JFTC decision before the Tokyo District Court where a panel of three or five judges will hear a case, which is thus expected to ensure the expertise of the court.[25]

TRANSPARENCY AND SPEEDY PROCEDURES IN JAPAN AND THE EU

In the EU, Article 15 TFEU provides that any citizen of the EU has a right of access to the Commission's documents.[26] The right of access is greater in the EU than in Japan, and so is the scope of information that should be disclosed by the authority to the parties. In the EU, for instance, detailed information should be disclosed to the parties in the

---

23 The rules on hearings provide that it is preferable to complete a hearing procedure within two years. See the Rules on Hearing by the Fair Trade Commission, Rule No. 8 of 2005, available at http://www.jftc.go.jp/en/legislation_gls/antimonopoly_rules.files/hearing.pdf.

24 JFTC press release of 24 May 2013.

25 See JFTC supra note 24.

26 For transparency of information in EU competition procedures, see Ivo Van Bael, *Due Process in EU Competition Proceedings* (Kluwer Law International, 2011) pp. 14–15.

Statement of Objections. In Japan, a draft cease and desist order is sent to the addressee but it is less detailed than a Statement of Objections. Furthermore, the parties have no right to receive a copy of the investigation report prepared by the case-handler when an official investigation is launched.[27] Furthermore although the parties have access to a non-confidential version of the documents concerning other companies in the same case that the Commission possesses in the EU investigations, in Japan the parties may be allowed access to the files that the authority possesses concerning them but not concerning other parties such as evidence submitted by other companies in the same case. Thus, the issue of confidentiality in relation to access to the files during investigations is not as important in Japan as it is in the EU.

Over time, greater efforts have been made in Japan to ameliorate the traditional transparency deficit. For instance, as noted in the previous chapter, the JFTC has adopted merger control reforms aimed at enhancing transparency, and parties are now entitled to receive written notice when the JFTC terminates its investigation.[28] Similarly, decisions approving a merger, which previously were not announced in written form, are now provided to the parties in writing.[29] Yet another helpful feature, found in the revised Guidelines,[30] is a description of cases falling outside the jurisdiction of the JFTC. The traditional prior consultation system has also been formally abolished. As a result of this reform, the JFTC will likely have fewer opportunities to engage in informal, possibly opaque manoeuvring. Moreover, by bringing the procedure squarely within a formal framework, the JFTC may be obliged more often to introduce detailed economic analysis when presenting its concerns to the parties. The requirement of a formal document will also be useful not only to make the outcome of the investigation clear to the parties but also to serve as authentic proof of the JFTC's investigation. More generally, it will facilitate public awareness about the decision.

As in the EU, civil damages actions are becoming increasingly common in Japan. In this regard, the right of third parties to obtain

---

27 Yasumi Ochi, 'Proposal on Revised AMA "To Clarify Hearing Procedure" instead of "To Abolish *Shinpan*": Back to Basics of Proposal of Revised AMA Procedure', *Kosei Torihiki*, **726** (April 2011) 44.

28 In a press release of 14 December 2011, NSC indicated that the parties had received written notice from the JFTC to the effect that it would not issue a cease and desist order. See http://www.nsc.co.jp/CGI/news/whatsnew_detail.cgi?section=0&seq=00021108 (in Japanese).

29 Notification Rules, Article 9; Procedural Guidelines, Sections 3, 5 and 6.

30 Revised Guidelines, Section 1.1(1).

access to the JFTC's case files is an important issue. Article 69 AMA provides that an interested party has a right of access to the file, and a right to receive a copy of, as the case may be, a cease and desist order, a surcharge order, a decision to initiate a *shinpan* and a *shinketsu*. According to the relevant case law, an interested party includes not only the parties of the case but also victims of the infringement, and plaintiffs in civil damages actions have often used this provision to obtain evidence.[31,32] Since the JFTC redacts sensitive information from documents before making them available, requesting parties sometimes find disclosures to be unsatisfactory.[33] In this regard, the Tokyo High Court has held that it was inappropriate for the content and extent of disclosures to be assessed by the administrative organ responding to the request, and consequently an amendment of the law was required.[34] In the reform of 2009, Articles 70-15(1) and 70-15(2) were added to the AMA. These provide that the JFTC cannot refuse a request for access to the file unless disclosure may damage a third party's interests or unless the refusal is justified. The information that the JFTC may refuse to disclose includes information regarding an individual employee, production costs, secret know-how and the source from which the JFTC obtained the information.[35]

The process of agreeing on confidentiality generally does not take a long time in Japan. In EU proceedings, if the parties and the Commission cannot agree on which information is confidential and must be redacted prior to disclosure, the Hearing Officer will intervene.[36] In some cases this procedure is so lengthy that a non-confidential version of the decision is published years after the Commission decides the case.

---

31 Wakodo, judgment of Tokyo High Court of 17 July 1971. The appeal was decided by the Supreme Court of Japan on 10 July 1975.

32 See Kenji Kawagoe, 'How to Read Revised Antimonopoly Act' (Mini Legal Analysis No. 172), *Kosei Torihiki Jyoho*, 19 October 2009, p. 8.

33 Ibid. p. 8.

34 *Hakodate Shinbun*, judgment of Tokyo High Court of 27 September 2006.

35 Kawagoe, supra note 32, p. 10. See also JFTC, Investigative standard regarding access and copy of files under Article 70-15 AMA, 30 June 2004.

36 The Commission issued the Informal Guidance Paper on Confidentiality Claims to clarify the procedure in March 2012. Available at http://ec.europa.eu/competition/antitrust/guidance_en.pdf.

THE EU'S COMMITMENT PROCEDURE (ARTICLE 9 OF REGULATION 1/2003)

A system that corresponds to the EU's commitment procedure under Article 9 of Regulation 1/2003 does not presently exist in Japan. However, since a procedure of this kind may expedite cases and appropriate solutions, the prospect of introducing one is currently being discussed. Even in the EU, accepting commitments in order to close an investigation had no formal basis until Regulation 1/2003 was adopted. Until that time, cases were closed once the parties and the Commission agreed informally to undertakings, a prominent example of which was seen in the *IBM* case, settled in 1984. In this case, IBM offered commitments to the Commission after receiving a Statement of Objections, promising to alter its future behaviour. However, with no real enforcement mechanisms the procedure was not considered to be very effective.[37]

Article 9 of Regulation 1/2003 installed a formal system, and enhanced compliance by making sanctions possible in case of breach.[38] In practice, Article 9 is typically used in cases of unilateral conduct, and it is not supposed to be used in cases where the Commission intends to impose a fine, such as where cartels or market-partitioning practices are concerned. The Commission has full discretion as to whether to accept commitments offered by parties under investigation, and occasionally it chooses not to do so, in particular where it takes the view that the commitments are insufficient to remove the Commission's concerns about anticompetitive effects.

In Japan, many consider that there would be significant benefits if an equivalent procedure were introduced, provided it is not abused in order to extract unnecessary concessions. Indeed, in certain cases, fines and a cease and desist order may not be the best remedies for infringement.[39] Commitments could enable more flexible remedies and quick solutions to be agreed through negotiation with the JFTC's case-handlers. On the other hand, Japan will have to give careful thought to some of the lessons from the European experience. First, commitment procedures should not simply become substitutes for normal infringement procedures. This

---

[37] See, e.g., Fin Lomholt, 'Opinion and Comment: The 1984 IBM Undertaking: Commission's Monitoring and Practical Effects', *Competition Policy Newsletter* (European Commission, 3 October 1998), pp. 7–11.

[38] See *Microsoft Browser Choice Screen* COMP/C-3/39.530, Commission decision of 16 December 2009, OJ 2010 C-36/7.

[39] See C-441/07 P *Commission v Alrosa* [2010] ECR I-5949.

would diminish the costs of engaging in anticompetitive behaviour, and hence the overall level of deterrence. Careful case selection would be necessary to mitigate this risk. A second lesson, which again underlines the importance of case selection, is that, where the law is unclear and needs to be developed, commitments might not be an appropriate solution since, given the essentially voluntary nature of commitments, it would likely be futile for the undertakings concerned to appeal the JFTC's decision.

COMPLAINTS

The number of complaints submitted to the JFTC is increasing. Interestingly, 80 per cent of complaints concern predatory pricing. This is partly because there is a relatively high degree of awareness of competition law in the general business community in Japan. Companies faced with aggressive, possibly illegal conduct by other companies normally try to negotiate with those companies in order to solve the problem. But if that does not work, they can seek an injunction under Article 24 AMA. However, since obtaining an injunction can be difficult,[40] it is often more feasible to submit a complaint to the JFTC under Article 45, Section 1 AMA. In contrast to the EU, a refused complainant is not entitled to take legal action to compel the JFTC to take action, or to appeal against the JFTC's decision not to take up the case. A separate administrative organ, which includes members appointed by the JFTC, can review the results of a complaint against anticompetitive conduct, but this system is not frequently used.

In the EU, the European Ombudsman investigates complaints about maladministration of the EU institutions, including the Commission. In 2009, the Ombudsman criticised the Commission for failing to make a proper note of a meeting with computer manufacturer Dell in an investigation of the chip producer Intel. The decision of the Ombudsman is not legally binding but the procedure is generally quicker than appeals lodged before the European Courts.[41] The attention the Ombudsman has given to the Commission's competition law enforcement activities has

---

40 See Chapter 11 (this volume) on private enforcement.

41 Nikiforos Diamandouros, 'The European Ombudsman: Resolving Complaints, Promoting Good Administration', *Mediterranean Competition Bulletin*, 131.

made a significant contribution to the transparency of Commission procedures.[42]

LEGAL PRIVILEGE

In Japan, there is no attorney-client privilege and there is no right to a lawyer's assistance during the AMA investigation, in the same way as in the US and the EU.[43] In the EU, already in 1982 in the *AM & S* case, the Court of Justice recognised a legal professional privilege in EU law, although the scope of the privilege remains controversial.[44]

A primary reason for the controversy is that, insofar as EU law is concerned, communications between companies and their *in-house* counsel are not privileged in the context of EU competition investigations. In most of the EU Member States whose legal systems are based on civil law, in-house counsel are considered employees whose advice is not considered privileged, just like communications between any of the company's other employees would not be privileged. In common law countries such as the UK, the approach is very different, as the same level of privilege that applies to communications with external counsel also extends to in-house lawyers.

On 14 September 2010, the European Court of Justice upheld a General Court judgment finding (in line with the civil law rule) that legal privilege does not apply to communications between a company and its in-house lawyers in the context of EU competition investigations.[45] The case concerned documents seized by the Commission during a dawn raid of the premises of Akzo Nobel Chemicals and Akcros Chemicals. The documents consisted of communications between an Akcros employee

---

42 In March 2012, the Commission published its internal Antitrust Manual of Procedures under Articles 101 and 102 TFEU except for certain parts, such as guidance for dawn raids, in response to the Ombudsman's decision of 3 October 2011, in which the Ombudsman concluded that the Commission had failed to partially disclose the Manual.

43 See e.g., Hiroshi Tega, 'Attorney's Duty of Confidentiality and his Privilege to Refuse to Testify (1)', *Tokyo Metropolitan University Journal of Law and Politics*, **49**(1) (July 2008), 295, at 311–320 (in Japanese).

44 Case C-155/79 *AM & S Europe v Commission* [1982] ECR 1575. For recent discussion, see Jean-François Bellis, 'Legal Professional Privilege: An Overview of EU and National Case Law', *e-Competitions*, **39467** (October 2011).

45 Case C-550/07P, *Akzo Nobel Chemicals and Akcros Chemicals v Commission* ECR I-8301 [2010].

and Akzo's in-house counsel, who was a member of the Dutch Bar Association. The Commission refused to recognise any privilege, relying on *AM & S,* which held that communications are only privileged where (i) the communications are connected with the client's rights of defence, and
(ii) the communications emanate from 'independent lawyers'.[46] In an appeal before the General Court, Akzo and Akcros contested the Commission's interpretation of the scope of legal privilege but their claims were dismissed. They fared no better before the ECJ, which was unconvinced that in-house counsel act independently of their employer in a manner analogous to external lawyers.[47,48]

There are strong reasons why Japanese law should follow the EU approach, as legal privilege encourages candid communications with defence counsel, a necessity from the perspective of effective legal representation. Furthermore, there does not seem to be any compelling reason why communications between a company and its external lawyers, at least, should enjoy less protection in AMA investigations than in EU proceedings.[49]

---

[46] C-155/79 *AM & S Europe v Commission* [1982] ECR 1575, para. 21, supra note 44.

[47] It has been argued that now, since more EU Member States are subjecting in-house lawyers to professional discipline and extending privilege to them, the scope covered by legal privilege under EU competition law should be expanded. See, e.g., Korah, supra note 20, p. 268.

[48] Under the EU Member States rules, correspondence between the company and its in-house lawyer may be protected by legal professional privilege. For instance, the Brussels Court of Appeal held in its judgment of 5 March 2013 that an advice given by an in-house lawyer is protected under certain circumstances. Arret nº 2011/MR/3 de Cour d'appel, Bruxelles, 5 mars 2013.

[49] See, e.g., Japan Federation of Bar Association, Opinion in response to the Report of Round Table Conference regarding Basic Issues of Antimonopoly Act, p. 10. Available at http://www.nichibenren.or.jp/library/ja/opinion/report/data/070823_2.pdf (in Japanese). According to this Opinion, an attorney-client privilege, which is protected in the EU and the US, should cover communications between a company and its lawyer, not least because it is an essential part of a company's rights of defence. Accordingly, although Japan is currently exceptional in considering other jurisdictions' approaches towards this privilege, it should examine the possibility of the future introduction of rules modelled after the US or EU systems.

ADMINISTRATIVE PROCEDURE TO CRIMINAL PROCEDURE

Unlike infringements of EU competition law, serious infringements of the AMA can trigger criminal sanctions. In the EU, the Court of Justice stated that a decision imposing a fine is not of a criminal nature.[50] Moreover, according to Regulation 1/2003, when the Commission imposes fines for competition law breaches, they shall not be of a criminal law nature.[51] In Japan criminal sanctions apply only to certain categories of infringement such as private monopolisation and cartels;[52] in particular, egregious instances of bid rigging or other collusion sometimes lead to a referral of the case from the JFTC to the public prosecutor, who proceeds with a criminal case before the courts. Given the possibility of criminal penalties, one issue that has been debated in Japan is whether imposition of administrative fines followed by criminal prosecution constitutes double jeopardy under Article 39 of the Constitution. However, the case law suggests that, because administrative fines are imposed for administrative purposes while criminal sanctions are imposed to deter antisocial conduct for moral purposes, the two types of punishment are different,[53] and in general the combination of the two is not considered a form of double jeopardy.

In 1990, the JFTC issued its Guidelines on criminal prosecution of AMA infringements, stating that the JFTC prosecutes vicious and important cases and repeated infringements that significantly affect citizens' lives.[54]

As noted above, in such cases JFTC will refer the case to the public prosecutor, and this is the only way to initiate a criminal prosecution. For a long time the JFTC hesitated to make referrals, and criminal enforcement of the AMA essentially lay dormant prior to 1990, apart from the

---

[50] C338/00P *Volkswagen v Commission* [2003] ECR I-9189.

[51] Article 23(5) of Regulation 2003/1.

[52] For instance, unfair trade practices are not subject to criminal sanctions.

[53] For further discussion of this issue, see, e.g., judgment of Supreme Court of 13 October 1998. See also Tadashi Shiraishi, supra note 19, pp. 496–500. As the issue relates to the interpretation of the nature of the fines, the theoretical development of this issue in Japan is rather complicated.

[54] Guidelines on criminal prosecution against AMA infringements, 20 June 1990. The Guidelines were amended in 2005 and 2009. Available at http://www.jftc.go.jp/dk/kokuhatsuhoushin.pdf.

notable exception of the oil cartel case launched in the 1970s.[55] During the SII negotiations, the US, which has devoted significant resources to criminal enforcement since the mid-1970s, called on Japan to make more active use of criminal sanctions in serious competition cases. The JFTC responded positively, if cautiously, and with new impetus carried out a criminal investigation in the 'professional stretch film' case in 1991.[56] In this case, fines ranged from 6 to 8 million yen, and the prosecutor secured prison sentences from six months to a year. In 1993, another cartel was prosecuted, this time for rigging bids for contracts to supply seals ordered for use by a social security office. In this case, surcharges were imposed but no prison sentence was ordered.[57]

In 2005, in response to criticism on the ground that procedural rights were insufficient in administrative procedures that can lead to criminal prosecution, a special procedure was introduced whereby the JFTC examines the necessity of prosecuting a case.[58] Under this system, the investigation can be conducted by the JFTC's dedicated team in close cooperation with the Tokyo High Prosecutor Office.

The first main difference between the criminal and administrative procedures is that, in a criminal procedure, a warrant is required when the authority conducts a compulsory inspection, while under an administrative procedure an inspection may be carried out without a warrant. A second difference is that, under Article 38 of the Constitution the right against self-incrimination is applicable in a criminal procedure, whereas it does not apply in an administrative procedure. However, Article 94-2(2) AMA provides that a refusal to answer a request for information during an administrative investigation conducted by the JFTC is subject to sanction, and the JFTC may indict infringers after the administrative investigation.[59] Thus, in practice, even if a written statement is prepared in the administrative procedure of the JFTC, this should not be used in the JFTC's special procedure for criminal investigation, or in the prosecutor's criminal procedure. Instead, a separate statement should be made in these procedures.[60]

---

55 The sentences imposed on all the guilty defendants were suspended.

56 See JFTC decision of 8 January 1992 and judgment of Tokyo High Court of 21 May 1993.

57 Seal bid rigging case, JFTC decision of 22 April 1993. *Seal bid rigging criminal case*, judgment of Tokyo High Court of 14 December 1993.

58 Makoto Kojyo, 'Investigation under Antimonopoly Act and Procedure for Cease and Desist Order' *Yearbook of Japanese Economic Law Association,* (September 2005) 87.

59 Ibid. pp. 88, 89.

60 See Shiraishi, supra note 19, p. 458.

The particularity of the Japanese competition procedure is the emphasis on a written statement as evidence to establish a wrongdoing. This is a document prepared by a case-handler in the authority's premises based on interviews of the personnel of the company involved. Documentary evidence such as email exchanges or correspondence, which is important in the EU, is in general less important. The reason is that a Japanese judge will attach more importance to statements made to the case-handler than it will to documentary evidence. This is true not just for competition cases but also for administrative litigation in general.

CONCLUSION

Companies are often surprised to know how severe the consequences of infringing EU competition law can be. But the EU grants more procedural rights than Japan, and constantly endeavours to improve procedural problems. The EU has enjoyed more opportunities to consider procedural matters in the context of competition law than Japan. Many companies challenge the Commission before the European Courts, alleging breach of procedural rules, and many clarifications have been provided through this process of litigation. Clarifications also sometimes emerge in the ECJ's preliminary reference procedure, which allows and occasionally requires national judges to ask the Court for authoritative interpretations of EU law. Substantive analytical principles can also be clarified in this way, for example where the Court endorses principles that have been introduced in the Commission's published guidance.[61] In practice, the parties may not know precisely what information the Commission has in its possession or how it assesses the evidence. However, this is inherent in the confidential nature of the competition law procedure. It is difficult to deny that the EU has transparent procedural rules and significant degrees of fundamental rights protection. For its part, Japan is moving towards the EU approach, and weighing the pros and cons of introducing greater procedural rigour. This does not mean that the Japanese procedure will imitate the European system. The appropriate objective is not

---

[61] In some cases, where the published guidance departs from established case law on the ground that a more enlightened approach should guide the Commission's enforcement policy, such endorsement by the Court allows law and policy to 're-converge', which in turn re-establishes legal certainty. See Ekaterina Rousseva and Mel Marquis, 'Hell Freezes Over: A Climate Change for Assessing Exclusionary Conduct under Article 102 TFEU', *Journal of European Competition Law and Practice*, **4** (1) (2013), 32, 50.

rigidity but legitimacy, which may imply a need for flexibility to respond to social and economic reality. What is necessary is a more harmonised system that does not result in unfair treatment in a global context. In general, procedural harmonisation is beneficial for parties under investigation and for authorities conducting parallel investigations. For instance, during an inspection carried out at a company's premises, the JFTC may seize a large number of original documents. Under the applicable Japanese regulation, a company does not have an explicit right to request copies of these documents, or a right to request that the JFTC leave the original documents. Accordingly, it will be difficult for the company to check whether any of the seized documents contain information that may be relevant to any authorities that are investigating the same case in other jurisdictions, or to consider a leniency application in another jurisdiction using the seized document as evidence.

9. Fining policy

HISTORY OF FINING POLICIES IN JAPAN AND IN THE EU

Traditionally, as a form of administrative sanction, the imposition of a pecuniary sanction such as a fine was quite rare in Japan. Furthermore, policy mechanisms having the character of a leniency policy were almost unprecedented.[1] The Japanese 'surcharge' system was introduced in 1977 for the first time to promote more effective enforcement. In 1991, under pressure from the US in the context of the SII talks, in order to enhance its deterrent effects the fixed rate for surcharges was increased from 1.5 per cent to 6 per cent.[2] However, the maximum period for which surcharges could be imposed was limited to the three-year period leading up to the date of the JFTC's infringement decision. In 2005, the fining policy was radically amended and the nature of the fines started to shift from mere 'disgorgement' of illegal profits to something more akin to a sanction. The fixed rate was further increased to 10 per cent and the range of conduct triggering the surcharge was extended. Moreover, the 2005 amendment added both aggravating circumstances, such as repeated illegal conduct, and mitigating circumstances, such as withdrawal from a cartel. However, the most important evolution was the introduction of a leniency policy, which entered into force in January 2006. Further reforms in 2009 increased the number of possible leniency applicants from three to five companies and introduced the possibility of submitting a single application for a group of companies. The 2009 amendments also provided for an additional 50 per cent penalty to be imposed on companies shown to have played the role of cartel ringleader. With regard to the extension of the types of conduct that can be subject to surcharges,

---

1 On the system of 'fines' (surcharges) in Japan, see Daitaro Kishii, 'Developments and Structure of Fining Policy in AMA', *Criminal Law Journal*, **25** (2010) 25 et seq. (in Japanese).

2 See, e.g., Akira Negishi and Masayuki Funada, *Japanese Antitrust Law* (4th edn, Yuhikaku, 2010) p. 15. With regard to the SII talks, see the historical background in Chapter 2 (this volume).

as a result of this reform, exclusionary private monopolisation and certain conducts characterised as unfair trade practices are now covered. In response to criticism that the term 'exclusionary private monopolisation' is unclear, the JFTC issued Guidelines on exclusionary monopolisation on 28 October 2009.[3]

As in the EU, discussions as to how to improve the JFTC's fining policy are still ongoing. Under the AMA, particularly serious cases triggering surcharges may also be investigated under a 'criminal' procedure, while less serious infringements are subject only to a surcharge or just a warning without any surcharge. In Japan, not unlike the situation in the EU, the tendency to increase the amount of the surcharge under the AMA has come about largely as a means of overcoming previously weak levels of deterrence owing to an under-employed criminal procedure (whereas in EU competition law there is no such procedure at all) and, traditionally, to the paucity of civil damages actions.

As for Europe, the Commission adopted its first Leniency Notice in 1996.[4] Subsequently it published guidelines on its method of setting fines in 1998.[5] Since the Commission already enjoyed wide discretion in determining the level of fines, clarification as to its method of calculation was necessary for reasons of transparency and impartiality.[6] From around the year 2000, fines imposed by the Commission were directly linked to the idea that the EU's competition law system had thus far been insufficiently dissuasive. Regulation No. 1/2003 was adopted on 16 December 2002, confirming the Commission's power to impose fines and establishing the scope of that power. Also in 2002 the Leniency Notice was replaced.[7] In 2006, the Commission renewed the Notice on the method of calculating fines and the Leniency Notice. The latter introduced the marker system for immunity applicants and protection of corporate statements against disclosure to claimants in civil damages

---

[3] JFTC Guidelines for Exclusionary Private Monopolization under the Antimonopoly Act, available at http://www.jftc.go.jp/en/legislation_guidelines/ama/pdf/guidelines_exclusionary.pdf.

[4] 1996 Commission Notice on the non-imposition or reduction of fines in cartel cases, OJ C207, 18 July 1996, pp. 4–6.

[5] Guidelines on the method of setting fines imposed pursuant to Article 15(2) of Regulation No. 17 and Article 65(5) of the ECSC Treaty, OJ C9 of 1 January 1998, pp. 3–5.

[6] Richard Whish and David Bailey, *Competition Law* (7th edn, Oxford University Press, 2012) p. 276.

[7] 2002 Commission Notice on immunity from fines and reduction of fines in cartel cases, OJ C45, 19 February 2002, pp. 3–5.

actions.[8,9] The level of the fines imposed continues to increase. For instance, in the cathode ray tubes cartel case, two companies were fined 313.4 million euros and 295.6 million euros, respectively. Further, the same two companies have been ordered to pay additional fines of 391.9 million euros for the same cartel owing to the participation in the cartel of a joint venture they operated.[10]

LEGAL STRUCTURE OF FINING POLICY IN JAPAN AND IN THE EU

In Japan and the EU, the fines imposed by the competition authorities are not criminal in nature but administrative.[11] Article 7-2 AMA provides that a person involved in an infringement should pay a surcharge equal to sales turnover of the relevant goods multiplied by a certain rate. According to a Supreme Court judgment, a surcharge imposed for cartel conduct is the administrative means to ensure the effective enforcement of the AMA to facilitate the prevention of a cartel, in addition to criminal sanctions under Article 89 AMA and damages actions under Article 25 AMA.[12] Although a surcharge under the AMA is an administrative sanction, which may apply in addition to a criminal sanction, an administrative fine is different in its purpose and procedure from a criminal sanction, which is intended to punish anti-sociality and immorality.[13] This judgment thus seeks to navigate around the claim that the constitutional protection against double jeopardy should preclude the

---

[8] 2006 Commission Notice on immunity from fines and reduction of fines in cartel cases, OJ C298, 8 December 2006, p. 17.

[9] See the Commission's press release of 7 December 2006, IP/06/1705.

[10] Cathode ray tube COMP/39437. See the Commission's press release of 5 December 2012, IP/12/1317. The decisions have been appealed to the General Court. LG Electronics, T-91/13 and Philips, T-92/13.

[11] Article 23(5) of Regulation 1/2003 provides that infringement decisions are not of a criminal law nature. With regard to Japan, Article 47 (4) AMA provides that the JFTC's investigative powers should not be interpreted in such a way as to be used for criminal investigations. Nevertheless, Articles 89 to 91 AMA set forth provisions governing investigations where a criminal case is pursued. [The ambiguity here is how Articles 89 to 91 interact with the referral mechanism to the public prosecutor].

[12] *Union of Machinery Insurers of Japan*, judgment of the Supreme Court of 13 September 2005.

[13] Professional stretch film, judgment of the Tokyo High Court of 21 May 1993.

possibility of cumulative administrative and criminal sanctions.[14] Whereas the European Commission issues a decision that includes a fining order at the end of an official investigation, in Japan, fining provisions are not included in the cease and desist decision that declares the parties' conduct to be illegal; rather, they appear in a separate fining decision. Furthermore, addressees of a cease and desist order and a fining order are not always identical. For instance, in Japan a party that participates in a cartel conspiracy but that does not execute the agreed misconduct cannot be subject to fines. More specifically, in a bid rigging case, a party who joins a bid following the cartel meeting but never wins the bid himself during the investigation period will not be subject to fines. By contrast, in the EU in similar circumstances the co-conspirator is likely to be fined together with the other participants.

In the EU, the rationale of fines is to ensure the implementation of EU competition policy. As already mentioned, the Commission is not empowered to impose criminal or custodial sanctions.[15] Articles 23 and 24 of Regulation 1/2003 provide for the imposition of fines and periodic payments.[16] Fines can be imposed on companies for procedural as well as substantive infringements. The current regime for the calculation of a fine is established by the Commission's 2006 Guidelines on the Method of Setting Fines and the 2006 Leniency Notice. In some cases, the Commission's Cartel Settlement Notice of 2008 may also be relevant.[17, 18]

On appeal, the General Court has unlimited jurisdiction to fix the level of fines, and has the ability to cancel or decrease the amount of fines imposed on the Commission, and it can even increase the fine, though that is rare.[19] Unlimited jurisdiction over fines does not amount to a

14 Article 39 of the Constitution.

15 See, e.g., Mark Jephcott, *Law of Cartels* (2nd edn, Jordan Publishing, 2011) p. 217. See Article 23(5) of Regulation 1/2003.

16 For more on the EU fining system, see, e.g., Whish and Bailey, supra note 6, pp. 275–82.

17 Guidelines on the method of setting fines imposed pursuant to Article 15(2) of Regulation No. 17 and Article 65(5) of the ECSC Treaty fines. Official Journal C9, 14 January 1998, pp. 3–5.

18 Guidelines on the method of setting fines imposed pursuant to Article 23(2)(a) of Regulation No. 1/2003, OJ C210, 1 September 2006, pp. 2–5. Commission Notice on immunity from fines and reduction of fines in cartel cases, OJ C298, 8 December 2006, p. 17.

19 As a typical example of a decrease in the fine, in the *Deltafina* case, the General Court reduced the fine imposed by the Commission from 11.8 million

review of the General Court's own motion.[20] The applicant must therefore raise pleas in law against the Commission's decision imposing fines and adduce evidence in support of its pleas. In Japan, the Courts examine and may cancel the JFTC's fining decision. For instance, in February 2012, the Supreme Court overturned the judgment of Tokyo High Court, which annulled the JFTC's fining decision.[21] In this case, the parties alleged that there was not an agreement among them that substantially restricted competition.

As regards the nature of fines imposed by the Commission, Regulation 1/2003 itself characterises them as administrative. However, in the *Menarini* case, the European Court of Human Rights in Strasbourg (the 'ECtHR') stated that the relevant factors to determine whether proceedings are criminal are: (1) domestic classification of the offence although it is not determinative; (2) the nature of the offence; and (3) the nature and severity of the penalty.[22] According to this test, although fines imposed by the Commission in competition proceedings are of an administrative nature, they may be regarded as criminal in this sense because of their high level and their purpose, which is punishment and deterrence. In *Menarini*, the ECtHR held that it is compatible with Article 6 ECHR for administrative authorities to sanction competition law infringements as long as the company has the opportunity to challenge the decision before a judicial body with 'full jurisdiction' that can examine all factual and legal questions in relation to the dispute, and can quash the contested decision.

The issues of equal treatment and proportionality as well as predictability have been addressed by the European Courts, and they have confirmed that the Commission cannot treat comparable situations differently or different situations in the same way unless such treatment is objectively justified.[23]

---

euros to 6.12 million euros owing to insufficient evidence. Case T-29/05. *Deltafina SpA v Commission* [2010] ECR II-4077.

[20] See Cases C-272/09, C-386/10 and C-389/10, *Chalkor v Commission* and *KME v Commission*, not yet published.

[21] Construction bid rigging case, judgment of Tokyo High Court of 19 March 2010 and judgment of Supreme Court of 20 February 2012.

[22] See judgment of the ECtHR of 27 September 2011.

[23] See, e.g., Case T-43/02, *Jungbunzlauer AG v Commission* [2006] ECR II-3435. See also Linda Arcelin, *Droit de la Concurrence: Les pratiques anticoncurrentielles en droit interne et communautaire* (Presses Universitaires de Rennes, 2009) 218 and 219.

FINE CALCULATION

In calculating the level of fines under its Fining Guidelines, the European Commission sets a basic amount for the fines based on, among other things, the value of sales directly or indirectly affected by the cartel, and the gravity and duration of the infringement.[24] In general, the proportion of the value of sales taken into account in order to set the basic amount will be at a level of up to 30 per cent.[25] In cartel cases, the figure will generally be set at the high end of that scale.[26] The determination of the value of affected sales is sometimes difficult. In general, the Commission uses as a reference the last full business year of the undertaking's participation in the infringement, although it can also be more appropriate to use different figures if the last full business year would not be sufficiently representative. In cartel cases the Commission then adds a sum of between 15 per cent and 25 per cent of the value of affected sales as an 'entry fee'; this is a policy choice to attain robust levels of deterrence. The amount derived may be adjusted by other elements such as aggravating and mitigating circumstances and the companies' ability to pay, or by adjustments resulting from the leniency programme or the cartel settlements procedure. Under EU law, a fine may be up to a maximum of 10 per cent of the annual worldwide turnover of a group company.[27] The Commission sometimes accepts a reduction of a fine under 'inability to pay' provisions to prevent companies from going out of business and leaving employees out of work. In the turbulent economic conditions of recent years the Commission developed a refined methodology for calculating the amount of the penalty to be imposed. Where a company violated EU competition law before it was acquired by another undertaking, the fine is calculated on the basis of the turnover and sales figures of the acquired company. However, when companies are jointly and severally liable, the Commission has discretion to claim the total payment of the fine from either of the companies and the Commission does not intervene in subsequent litigation between the companies for compensation.

In the EU, Article 25 of Regulation No. 1/2003 on Procedure provides a limitation period of five years, which restricts the Commission's ability to fine for historic offences. However, this does not prevent the Commission from making a finding of infringement in relation to conduct that

---

24 Fining Guidelines, para. 19.
25 Ibid., para. 21.
26 Ibid., para. 23.
27 Article 23(2) of Regulation 1/2003.

benefits from the application of the time bar. Further, the limitation period is interrupted by any action taken by the Commission or a Member State competition authority. In the case of substantive infringements, the limitation period will expire where more than ten years have elapsed since the end of the infringement without the imposition of a fine.

In this context, the calculation of pecuniary sanctions imposed on cartelists is simpler in Japan. The Japanese method of calculating surcharges is to multiply turnover from relevant products or services during the infringing period with a certain rate fixed according to industry as shown in Table 9.1.

Table 9.1 Japanese surcharge calculation by industry

	Manufacturer	Wholesaler	Retailer
Unreasonable restraint of trade	10% (big company) 4% (small and medium sized company)	3% (big company) 1.2% (small and medium sized company)	2% (big company) 1% (small and medium sized company)
Private monopolisation by control	10%	3%	2%
Exclusive private monopolisation	6%	2%	1%
Joint refusal to deal Discriminatory pricing Unjust low pricing RPM	3%	2%	1%
Abuse of superior position	1%	1%	1%

Source: JFTC

The discretion on the part of the JFTC in calculating surcharges is very narrow. Rigid calculation methods are in fact convenient for the JFTC, which is spared the burden of arduous computations. The advantage is that a clear calculation does not put the JFTC to much trouble in terms of burden of proof of complicated issues. Although discretionary surcharges can be another method of calculation of surcharges in Japan, the policy of the Ministry of Justice and the legislation bureau of the government's Cabinet is that discretionary pecuniary sanctions can be imposed only by a judge. The possibility of authorising the JFTC to start imposing discretionary sanctions as in the EU currently seems remote due to several reasons.[28] The statute of limitations starts to run from the date of the end of the infringement, and the JFTC cannot issue a surcharge order after five years from this date.

Unlike in the EU, there is no 'entry fee' for deterrence purposes and there is a limitation on the period of infringement that can be taken into account when calculating the surcharge, namely, three years. It is submitted that, given this short period, not to mention the other differences described above, the level of deterrence achieved by the fining system in the EU cannot be expected in Japan.[29] The gap may not be quite as wide as it seems, once exposure to private actions and, in egregious cases, the possibility of criminal penalties are taken into account. Nevertheless, since criminal actions in Japan (particularly outside the context of bid rigging) are still of limited frequency and since private actions though increasingly common still fall short of public enforcement activity, deterrence levels in Japan remain behind the curve.[30]

Although, compared to the EU's fining system, the Japanese method of calculating surcharges is more predictable, this does not mean that disputes concerning the amount do not arise. Surcharges imposed in cases of exclusionary private monopolisation can be complicated because calculation based on sales turnover corresponding to the infringement is not possible.[31] Even in a cartel case, the calculation can be unclear. The *Freight Forwarder* cartel case in Japan indicates the types of problem that can arise in calculating fines, and in particular it illustrates the problem of whether a price-fixing agreement regarding a part of products or

[28] See, e.g., Shuya Hayashi, 'Analysis of Discretionary Funding System', Nagoya. *University Hosei-Ronsyu*, **248**, (2013) 178. Also see Takahide Matsuyama, 'Overview of Antimonopoly Policy in 2011', *Kosei Torihiki*, No. 723 (January 2011) p. 5.

[29] See, e.g., Hiroko Yamane, 'Inability to Pay: The European Commission's Fining Philosophy and Practice', *Journal of the Japanese Institute of International Business Law*, **41** (2) (2013) 170 (in Japanese). In the EU, there is no fixed maximum duration of an infringement period. However, as noted above, the Commission cannot impose fines beyond the five-year limitation period.

[30] See Chapter 11 (this volume) on private enforcement.

[31] For a detailed explanation, see, e.g., Akinori Uesugi, *Handbook on Antimonopoly Act International Practices* (Shojihomu, 2012) pp. 295–300 (in Japanese).

services could substantially restrict competition. In this case the JFTC issued a cease and desist order against 12 companies for alleged price fixing of four kinds of charge, including fuel surcharges.[32] These four charges accounted for approximately 12 per cent of the forwarders' total price for their international forwarding service. The JFTC's decision took 12 per cent of the price to be sufficient to constitute a substantial restriction of competition. The fines were calculated based on the companies' turnover from the four agreed categories of charge. However, as long as the relevant product market is defined as an international freight forwarders' transport service, the fines should have been calculated based on the turnover from the entire international forwarding services. As a result, the fines imposed in this case resulted in approximately 88 per cent of reductions of the fines compared to what the fines would have been if calculated based on the turnover of the infringers from the entire international forwarding services.[33] As another example of a company's challenge against the JFTC's calculation, in the *Optical Fiber* cartel case, the company requested a hearing against the JFTC's fining order, alleging that the JFTC's calculation of surcharge was wrong.[34]

It bears noting that the turnover that is taken as the basis of the calculation of surcharges in Japan is turnover from domestic consumers. Thus, for instance, in the *Marine Hoses* cartel case, although it was the first case in which the JFTC issued a cease and desist order on a foreign undertaking whose presence was not in Japan, no surcharge was imposed on that undertaking because it had no domestic turnover.[35] By contrast, when sanctioning the same cartel the European Commission calculated the fines based on a proxy figure.[36] According to the 2006 Fining Guidelines, the Commission is allowed to calculate a proxy that 'reflects both the aggregate size of the relevant sales within the EEA and the relative weight of each undertaking in the infringement'.[37] As a result, while the JFTC imposed a surcharge of 2 380 000 yen (approximately 18 600 euros) on Bridgestone, the Commission imposed a surcharge of

---

[32] *Freight Forwarder*, JFTC decision of 18 March 2009.

[33] See, e.g., Tadashi Shiraishi, 'Antimonopoly Law Case Flash Report', *Jurist*, **1436** (January 2012) 4–5.

[34] *Optical Fiber*, JFTC decision of 15 December 2011.

[35] *Marine Hoses*, JFTC decision of 2 February 2008.

[36] *Marine Hoses*, Case COMP/39406.

[37] Fining Guidelines, para. 18. See also Jephcott, supra note 15, p. 223.

58 500 000 euros on the same company. The Commission considered Bridgestone to be the leader of the illegal conduct, together with Parker ITR.[38]

Another difference between Japan and the EU is that surcharges on certain categories of conduct in Japan, including unfair trade practices, are imposed only if the infringement was repeated within a ten-year period. For instance, if resale price maintenance is detected on only one occasion it is not subject to a surcharge. A repeat offence would then trigger the monetary penalty.[39]

DETERRENT EFFECTS OF FINES

Though they have not quite yet reached EU levels, surcharges are becoming more serious in Japan. A fine of 12.9 billion yen (approximately 97 million euros) was imposed in the *Wire Harness* cartel case in January 2012,[40] while the JFTC imposed about 13 billion yen (approximately 98 million euros) on three companies in the *Bearing* cartel case in 2013.[41] Sanctions of this scale attract media attention and encourage firms to prepare or upgrade AMA compliance and training programmes. Criminal sanctions, which lay dormant until the 1990s, have begun to pick up and have become increasingly severe as a result of legislative reforms. To some difficult-to-measure, these have to be taken into account by would-be cartelists and to that extent make a significant contribution to deterrence.

In Japan, since 1977 when they were first introduced, surcharges were merely considered a means of reducing or eliminating infringers' ill-gotten gains; they were not regarded as a sanction against antisocial and immoral conduct. However, it became difficult to explain recent increases of the surcharge and the adoption of a leniency programme without admitting that the surcharge bears the pecuniary characteristics of what other jurisdictions would call a fine.[42] Now that the perception of surcharges has evolved, irrespective of the turnover in relation to the products or services affected by a cartel, an infringing party can be

---

38 Ibid. See also the Commission's press release of 29 January 2009, IP/09/137.

39 See Chapter 5 (this volume) on vertical restraints.

40 *Wire Harness*, JFTC decision of 19 January 2012.

41 *Bearing*, JFTC decision of 29 March 2013.

42 See, e.g., Toshiaki Tada, 'Various Amendments Regarding Surcharges' Unreasonable Restraint of Trade', *Jurist*, **1385** (15 September 2009) 26 note 5.

subject to fines. Thus, even if the turnover was zero, the JFTC can impose a surcharge.[43] In this sense, Japan is following the EU approach. However, the difference is that the surcharge is calculated based on non-discretionary methods based on the pattern of illegal conduct and size of the company.

Although the EU's fining policy and its enforcement have been carefully examined by Japan, Japan's fining policy (although in the 1970s influenced by the German system) is fairly original and differs from that of the EU. The Japanese policy puts particular emphasis on clear and transparent calculation. This is because, for deterrent effects to be assured, a potential infringer should be able to easily understand how the calculation would be carried out. A clear calculation is desirable in terms of the JFTC's burden of proof as well. The downside of increasing surcharges in order to strengthen deterrent effects will be the imposition, in certain cases, of disproportionate fines. Where this happens, a fine may create more harm than deterrence and may lose expected functionality. A hypothetical alternative approach, where reliance is placed exclusively on criminal sanctions, seems inadequate, as criminal procedures are generally burdensome and the authority cannot open many investigations owing to a lack of sufficient workforce. In any case, extremely high fines for AMA infringements are unlikely to be supported in Japan.[44] In particular, in relation to the cases that are not hard core cartels, it is argued that a cease and desist order is sufficient.[45]

In Europe, since criminal sanctions are not provided for at EU level, deterrence is seen as depending on the high level of fines imposed on

---

[43] See, e.g., judgment of the Tokyo High Court of 24 February 2012; Takayuki Suzuki, 'Dokusen Kinsihou Jirei Sokuho', *Jurist*, **1443** (July 2012) 5 (in Japanese).

[44] Even in the EU Member States, there has been reticence with regard to increasing fines. For instance, in France, the Sénat did not want to increase the ceiling of the fines from 5 per cent to 10 per cent of the company's turnover. See Arcelin, supra note 23, at 216.

[45] See, e.g., Toshiaki Takigawa, 'Stricter Sanctions under Competition Law in the World Deprive Companies of Competitiveness', *Economist* (23 June 2009) 94–5. Professor Takigawa explains that, although it is US policy not to impose fines to punish dominant companies for monopolisation offences under Section 2 of the Sherman Act, the US rules are effective because the decision of the authorities can change the company's strategy and victims can bring a civil damages action with treble damages. Furthermore, according to Takigawa, fines can discourage large companies' competitive activities, and accordingly can harm consumers.

undertakings.[46] Unlike in Japan, the companies are also likely to have high fines imposed for non-compliance of commitments and high periodic penalties even for procedural infringements.[47]

Ideally, the Commission does not need to adopt a large number of decisions if a few well selected precedents make firms aware that compliance is the only way to avoid serious consequences. This approach seems to be driven in part by the need to efficiently manage the Commission's limited resources.

Another consideration may relate to the fact that, in Japan, most of the companies subject to fines imposed by the JFTC are Japanese, while in EU cases, infringing parties are not always European but are often companies based in other countries. In Japan, the publication of the results of the JFTC's investigation tends to seriously damage the company's reputation and affects its business. This kind of reputational sanction has a deterrent effect for a Japanese company.[48] But in Europe it is not clear whether the same applies to a company that does not operate in an environment comparable to the *keiretsu* system. In this respect, the high level of fines routinely imposed by the Commission effectively

---

[46] The 2006 revision of its Fining Guidelines enabled the Commission to increase the level of its fines substantially. For instance, the Commission imposed a fine of 1.5 million euros on Group Danon/Brasseries Kronenbourg in 2004 under its 1998 Fining Guidelines and fined Saint Gobain 896 million euros under its 2006 Fining Guidelines. See the Commission's press releases of 29 September 2004, IP/04/1153 and of 12 November 2008, IP/08/1685. Both Group Danon/Brasseries Kronenbourg and Saint Gobain were recidivists. Brasseries Kronenberg, Brasseries Heineken COMP/C/37.750/B2 and Car glass COMP/39.125.

[47] For instance, the Commission imposed a 561 million euro fine on Microsoft for failure to comply with its commitments. See the Commission's press release of 6 March 2013, IP/13/196. The 'gun jumping' that can trigger a high fine under the EU merger control may be subject to a limited pecuniary sanction that does not exceed 2 million yen. In the *Electrabel* case, the Commission fined Electrabel 20 million euros for implementing its acquisition of Compagnie Nationale du Rhône prior to the Commission's approval. See the Commission's press release of 10 June 2009, IP/09/895. Microsoft (tying) COMP/37792 and Electrabel/Compagnie Nationale du Rhône COMP/M.4994.

[48] In Japan, a company that is sanctioned owing to its illegal conduct under law, including the AMA, sometimes publicly announces that its board members have decided to voluntarily forgo part of their remuneration for a certain fixed period to express their regret and extend their apologies to the public, almost at the same time as the publication of the sanction by the authority. This is a practice called '*misogi*', a clolloquial expression that originally means a ritual purification in Shintoism and atonement for wrong conduct.

obviates the question of whether, in relation to undertakings from this or that country, reputational effects contribute to the encouragement of compliant commercial behaviour.

Under the current regime in Japan, it seems clear that the combination of administrative fines and criminal sanctions, as they have co-evolved over time, achieves a significant degree of deterrence. With respect to hard core cartels, Japan has not only increased the level of its surcharges; it has also lengthened the maximum duration of imprisonment from three to five years. Other measures taken to raise levels of deterrence are sanctions such as: a ban on future participation in bids by companies found to have engaged in bid rigging; measures under company law such as the liability of board members who should have known about and stopped collusive conduct (risk of shareholder suits); and private damages actions. In respect of the latter, Japan and the EU both lag far behind the US, and public action remains the primary source of law enforcement.[49]

LENIENCY PROGRAMME

Although historical backgrounds are different, the tools pioneered in other jurisdictions have proved to be efficient in Japan as well. Notably, the leniency programme, which drew criticism and scepticism before its introduction in Japan, has turned out to be very successful. Leniency techniques and their underlying assumptions were new to Japan, and they did not seem to be compatible with the Japanese culture, which emphasises harmony and order: after all, a defecting informant might risk becoming a commercial pariah once the JFTC's investigation is concluded and the market concerned resumes its activities.[50,51] Accordingly, the pros and cons of introducing a leniency policy were actively discussed,[52] but the pros prevailed and Japan adopted the first version of its leniency programme in January of 2006. On the very day this programme entered into force, the JFTC started to receive applications. The willingness of firms to take advantage of the programme is reflected

---

49 See Chapter 11 (this volume) on private enforcement.

50 See Kishii, supra note 1, at 25 et seq. (in Japanese).

51 See the introduction in Chapter 1 (this volume).

52 For an explanation of EU fining policy and for discussion of the prospects of introducing a leniency policy in Japan, see, Etsuko Kameoka, 'EU Cartel Control and International Cooperation' (in Japanese), in Akira Ishikawa (ed.), *International Economic Law and Regional Cooperation* (Shinzan-sha, 2004) pp. 515–37.

by the fact that, by 2010, the number of annual applications made to the JFTC had reached 131, more than twice the number of applications (60) received that year by the European Commission.[53] Although the leniency programme in Japan differs from that of the EU on several important points, it certainly facilitates the JFTC's factual investigations and, crucially, leads to the detection of cartels that might otherwise remain invisible. In particular, leniency applications made to the JFTC tend to reveal the existence of price-fixing cartels, rather than just bid rigging schemes, which traditionally have been viewed as the principal pattern of collusion in Japan.[54]

As a matter of fact, in the EU, where the leniency programme was introduced a decade earlier, Japanese companies had already started to resort to the EU leniency policy with the hope of reducing or avoiding their expected fines. These firms, and others learning from their experience, had thus already internalised the 'carrot and stick' logic of leniency. Indeed, sensitivity to the benefits of leniency grew in proportion to the exponential rise of fine levels in the EU in the early part of the last decade.

Under the European Commission's leniency programme, the first applicant may obtain full immunity from an administrative fine, which means a 100 per cent reduction. The second and third applicants' fines reductions will be between 30 per cent and 50 per cent, and between 20 per cent and 30 per cent, respectively. Any subsequent applicants have the possibility of a fine reduction up to 20 per cent. In order to obtain immunity or a reduction of fines, a leniency applicant will have to meet a number of conditions. In particular, they will have to provide genuine, full and continuous cooperation throughout the Commission's investigation. Under the Japanese system, the provision setting forth the duty to cooperate with the JFTC after applying for leniency is not as clear as its counterpart in the EU Leniency Notice. In the EU, the duty to cooperate with the Commission encourages the applicant to conduct an internal search of all the evidence it has. This allows the Commission to reconstruct a picture of the cartel. In Japan, meanwhile, the JFTC relies on Article 7-2(16) AMA, which provides for an additional reporting duty

---

53 See JFTC, 'The Situation of Enforcement of the Antimonopoly Act in FY 2011', p. 4, available at http://www.jftc.go.jp/pressrelease/12.june/120606.pdf (in Japanese). For 2011, the number of applications to the JFTC even increased to 143. See also, e.g., Kazuhiko Takeshima, 'Top Runner No. 5', *Jurist*, **1441** (2012), p. 3 (in Japanese).

54 See JFTC Guidelines on Criminal Prosecution and Investigation of Criminal Case, 7 October 2005, Point 1(2).

that the JFTC may impose to obtain the necessary information from a leniency applicant.

In contrast with the EU, in Japan there is a maximum number of companies that potentially can benefit from a fine reduction under the leniency programme.[55] Under the latest version of Japan's leniency programme, a maximum of five companies may be eligible before an investigation is launched, and a maximum of three firms may be eligible after the investigation starts. The first successful applicant benefits from immunity and the second one can obtain a 50 per cent surcharge reduction while the third to fifth applicants are entitled to obtain 30 per cent reductions. After an inspection is launched, only three companies are eligible to obtain a 30 per cent reduction. The biggest difference between the EU leniency programme and the leniency programme in Japan is the fact that, in practice, the first company that applies to the JFTC before an inspection starts is exempted from criminal prosecution.[56]

Unlike in the EU, where the principal criterion is whether evidence submitted has furnished the enforcer with substantially added value, in Japan the applicant may obtain leniency even if the submitted information overlaps with information already provided by another applicant.

Further, in the EU, the practice can be much more complex owing to possible leniency applications submitted to the competition authorities of the Member States. The complexity of such situations, which may cause potential applicants to think twice before becoming informants, is being addressed through initiatives of the European Competition Network (ECN). Notably, most EU Member States have leniency programmes that converge upon the Model Leniency Programme and, typically, provisional short-form procedures are available that function in a manner similar to leniency markers.[57]

---

[55] Following reforms made to the Leniency Program in 2009, a company group can make a single application, and the group is treated as a single applicant.

[56] See 'Surcharges Imposed on Three Companies: JFTC Order in the Bearing Cartel', *Nihon Keizai Shinbun*, 29 March 2013.

[57] ECN Model Leniency Programme. Available at http://ec.europa.eu/competition/ecn/mlp_revised_2012_en.pdf. It aims at ensuring that potential leniency applicants are not discouraged from applying as a result of the discrepancies between the existing leniency programmes within the ECN and the introduced model for a uniform summary application system.

CARTEL SETTLEMENT PROCEDURE

Although leniency programmes in the EU and Japan have thrived, American-style guilty pleas ('plea bargaining') have not been considered feasible in either of these jurisdictions. In July of 2008, the EU introduced a somewhat different kind of procedure to settle cartel cases.[58] The procedure involves bilateral discussions between the Commission and a company under investigation. If settlement discussions lead to a common view between the parties and the Commission, a streamlined Statement of Objections is issued and, provided the parties consider that the SO is an accurate reflection of the settlement, the Commission adopts a short-form decision. The Commission's first settlement decision was adopted in May 2010, following an immunity application made by Micron in August 2002.[59] By February 2013, the Commission had settled six cases under the settlement procedure. One of these was a so-called 'hybrid' case, in which not all parties agreed to pursue a settlement procedure; one company decided, at a rather late stage, to revert to the normal (longer, more litigious) procedure.[60]

Despite the outcome of this case, the majority of settlements have led to overall satisfactory results. The main advantage of the procedure for a company is a reduction of its fine by 10 per cent, which applies in addition to any leniency reduction. To some extent, a settlement may also appear attractive insofar as it might reduce the number of follow-on damage actions owing to the more limited scope of information available in the public version of the Commission's decision. The procedure can also be advantageous for the Commission, as a shorter and simplified procedure reduces the burden of investigation and allows more dispersed resources to deal with more (presumably serious) cases. A great part of the 'procedural savings' yielded by the procedure is that, since settling companies have confessed to their participation in and responsibility for

---

58 Article 10a of Regulation 773/2004 [2004] OJ L123/18. For the procedure, see the Commission's Notice on the conduct of settlement procedures in view of the adoption of decisions pursuant to Article 7 and Article 23 of Council Regulation (EC) No. 1/2003 in cartel cases, OJ C167, 2 July 2008, pp. 1–6.

59 DRAMs COMP/38511. For the non-confidential version of the decision, see http://ec.europa.eu/competition/antitrust/cases/dec_docs/38511/38511_1813_5.pdf. The Commission's press release is available at http://europa.eu/rapid/press-release_IP-10-586_en.htm. See also Jean-François Bellis, Kris Van Hove and Etsuko Kameoka, 'Latest Developments in EU Cartel Enforcement: The First Commission Settlement Decision', *Journal of the Japanese Institute of International Business Law*, **38** (12) (December 2010) 1641–9 (in Japanese).

60 Animal Feed Phosphates COMP/38.866, decision of 20 July 2010.

the cartel, an appeal against the Commission's decision is normally not undertaken.

The possibility of introducing a settlement procedure is currently being examined in Japan. However, since fines in Japan are not as high as in the EU, and since the duration of cartel investigations is relatively shorter (that is, generally less than one year), it is not entirely clear whether it would be worth adopting this system in Japan. Furthermore, the EU settlement framework is based on the current EU cartel control system and it could provide an opportunity for the case-team but may obscure some aspects of investigation, in exchange for efficient and speedy procedure. Furthermore, in the EU, the Commission is granted a broad margin of discretion as to whether to use the settlement procedure.[61] It is not clear that this discretion is compatible with the Japanese fining policy, under which the JFTC is not granted broad discretion and the procedure is not as flexible as it is in the EU. For these reasons, Japan is well advised to insist on a strong case in favour of such a procedure before taking steps to introduce it in the context of JFTC enforcement. There may be a risk, in light of Japan's continuing efforts to improve procedural transparency in Japanese competition law enforcement, that a new procedure with an element of opacity and shielded communications may be something of a step backwards.[62]

Nevertheless, shorter procedures, early resolution, reduced incidence of appeals and a reduced burden of drafting decisions will undoubtedly appear attractive in Japan, too.[63] As the magnitude of fines grows higher, the benefits of further surcharge reductions complementary to leniency

---

[61] See Jephcott, supra note 15, p. 327.

[62] In practice, the EU's settlement procedure sacrifices some of the procedural guarantees with the parties in exchange for a 10 per cent fine reduction and streamlined procedure. Although the parties are allowed to discuss the content of the envisaged decision with the Commission's team, the scope and the extent of the discussions vary from case to case. Professor Marquis characterises the settlement procedure as 'bounded black box bargaining', which means that the EU regime to some extent obscures some parts of the communications between the Commission and the parties concerned, and that this is a key tool for both sides. See Mel Marquis, 'Settling Cartel Investigations in the EU and Its Member States' (2012), pp. 9–10, available at http://ssrn.com/abstract=2070190. The paper is also available at http://dx.doi.org/10.2139/ssrn.2070190 ('Cartel Settlements: An Overview of EU and National Case Law', e-Competitions N°46057 (2012)), pp. 1–14.

[63] Kazuyoshi Suzuki, 'On Cartel Settlements in the US and the EU', *Hikakuho Zasshi* (Comparative Law Review), **45** (2) (The Institute of Comparative Law in Japan, 2011) 184–5 (in Japanese).

discounts may add to the procedure's appeal. Finally, the openness elsewhere in Asia, notably in South Korea, to settlement-type procedures has not gone unnoticed in Japan.[64]

CONCLUSION

The most important divergence between the EU and Japan in relation to fining policy is the discretion granted to the authority. The JFTC does not have broad discretion to decide the amount of its surcharge, but must follow rigid calculation methods. Since the Commission has considerable discretion to determine the level of fines on a case-by-case basis, subject normally to the indications given in its Guidelines (unless it justifies deviations), a procedure such as cartel settlement becomes meaningful for the parties to obtain further reduction of fines.

The question of how to deter a potential infringer efficiently is, of course, an important issue in both jurisdictions. The EU has pursued efficient deterrence mainly by increasing the amount of the fines it imposes on cartelists. Media attention naturally focuses on the impressive figures, and companies are trying to develop compliance and training programmes. Further procedural transparency is encouraged to justify these extraordinarily heavy sanctions. If the fines imposed by the Commission had not been so high, the visibility of EU competition law among the Japanese business community would not be as high as it is today. In this way, the 'shock value' of the EU's fining policy plays an important role in EU competition policy. Japan, for its part, takes a rather different approach. A fine is one of the elements that contribute to creating deterrent effects, but excessive fines beyond the discretion allowed to 'benevolent government' will not be supported by the public. Japan's policy with regard to surcharges is based on the country's culture and philosophy. The ideology of Confucianism underpinning the moral and philosophical fabric of Japanese society seems to discourage resort to extremely high fines for the purpose of achieving deterrence.[65] According

64 For instance, following the conclusion of the Korea-US Free Trade Agreement, whose content includes the introduction of consent decrees in Korea, the Republic of Korea adopted a bill in November 2011 to amend the Monopoly Regulation and Fair Trade Act to allow the Korean Fair Trade Commission to issue consent decrees.

65 Confucius, who believed that morality and punishment are two instruments that can be used to manage a country, took the view that if the people are guided by edicts and if they are kept orderly through punishment, they will stay out of

to Confucianism, it is not severe punishment or its *in terrorem* effects but rather consciousness that will deter infringement. Further, a moderate way of life and a harmonious State that avoids going to extremes was preached by Confucius under the Doctrine of the Mean. This doctrine advocates harmonious human relations and the moderate management of the State.[66] Further, the downside of increasing administrative fines to strengthen deterrent effects can lead to the creation of more legal impediments, such as disproportionate fines. As a result, an ill-conceived fining policy may do more harm than good, and lose its expected functions. With regard to criminal sanctions, they do not seem the best choice as a primary enforcement mechanism either: criminal procedures are generally burdensome and the authorities cannot open many investigations but are forced to focus on a few serious cases. From the point of view of deterrent effects, undue reliance on criminal law would likewise be ill-advised.

Thus, instead of relying on high fines, Japan may have to explore other means to prevent infringements. For instance, a targeted sanction imposed on an infringer involved in the rigging of a public bid, such as a ban on future participation in tender procedures, can be an important tool to prevent collusive tendering. Such measures are also in place under the national law of various EU Member States.

Ultimately, the EU and Japan remain distinct because of the EU's quasi-federal structure. In a federal context, it is not EU policy alone that must be taken into account by potential infringers but the interaction of EU-level and national-level laws. For instance, criminal sanctions are provided for in some EU Member States, including but not limited to the UK. In many cases, these sanctions constitute part of an overall mix of variable deterrence effects. Furthermore, after a slow start, private damage actions at the national level are also on the rise. By virtue of its constitutional system of 'parallel competences', the EU system is thus closely related to the systems in place at national level. The Japanese system of sanctions, notwithstanding a trend towards more frequent private actions, remains largely isolated.

---

trouble but will have no sense of shame. On the other hand, if the people are guided by virtue, and if they are kept in line with rites and social norms, they will not only have a sense of shame but will also reform themselves. Confucius, *The Analects*, 2011; Kong Xianglin *Confucius*, (Foreign Languages Press, 2010) p. 68.

[66] Ibid. p. 132.

10. IP and competition

HISTORY AND LEGAL FRAMEWORK REGARDING IP AND COMPETITION IN JAPAN AND THE EU

In the EU, the history of complex interaction among IP law, antitrust law and unfair competition law stems from the establishment of the European Community.[1] When the Court of Justice asserted its doctrine of primacy of Community law, it implicitly raised the problem of how to reconcile intellectual property rights granted under national law with the concept of a Common Market with free cross-border trade. When addressing this problem the Court developed a distinction between the existence of intellectual property rights and the exercise of those rights.[2] In the early 1960s, the Commission took the view that most provisions in patent licensing agreements did not breach Article 101(1) TFEU because restrictions of intra-brand competition were thought to emanate from the exclusive nature of the patent right. This approach was articulated in the Commission's Notice on Patent Licensing Agreements, issued in late 1962.[3] However, the Court of Justice overruled this approach in *Consten and Grundig v Commission*, where the assignment of trademark was at issue. In its famous judgment, the Court confirmed that vertical agreements can in some circumstances fall within the scope of Article 101(1) TFEU, and it made clear that the use of a trademark in order to prevent parallel imports flowing from one Member State into another can be incompatible with that provision.[4] The issue of compulsory licensing has been discussed for a long time in the EU, mainly in the context of competition law but also in relation to the free movement of goods within

[1] For details see, e.g., Gustavo Ghidini, *Intellectual Property and Competition Law: The Innovation Nexus* (Edward Elgar Publishing, 2006) p. 99.

[2] See, e.g., Valentine Korah, *An Introductory Guide to EC Competition Law and Practice* (9th edn, Hart Publishing, 2007) p. 337.

[3] See Richard Whish and David Bailey, *Competition Law* (7th edn, Oxford University Press, 2012) p. 773. See also Commission, Communication relative aux accords de licence de brevets, JC (1962) 2922.

[4] Whish and Bailey, ibid. p. 773; Cases 56 & 58/64 *Consten and Grundig v Commission* [1966] ECR 299.

the Common Market.[5] The related high-profile issue of essential facilities has been the subject of controversy since 1992.[6] In 2004, the Commission updated the rules on the licensing of patents and technical know-how, adopting a Block Exemption Regulation for Technology Transfer Agreements and accompanying Guidelines.[7] The Block Exemption Regulation for Technology Transfer Agreements and accompanying Guidelines will be soon reviewed again as the current rules expire in April 2014.

Although Japan does not face problems associated with the construction and maintenance of a Common Market, the possible conflict between IP law and competition law was nevertheless already contemplated in Article 21 of the AMA of 1947. Article 21 AMA provided an exemption from the competition rules for 'conduct which is considered to be the exercise of intellectual property rights'.[8] The occupying forces determining policy in the immediate post-war Japan (GHQ) considered that business arrangements with foreign companies in the form of cartels and patent agreements might have contributed to Japan's imperialist and militarist tendencies.[9] GHQ therefore could not completely ignore the IP considerations in the process of drafting the AMA in Japan. Although the potential conflict between IP protection and competition law was predicted from the outset in Japan, the question of what constitutes 'conduct which is considered the exercise of intellectual property rights' has not been completely settled.

The history of Japanese IP law started more than 100 years ago. The Patent Law, Trademark Law and Copyright Law were all adopted at the end of the nineteenth century. IP law in Japan was strongly influenced by European traditions. For instance, the Utility Model Act of 1905 was

---

[5] See, e.g., Case 19/84 *Pharmon B. v Hoechst AG* [1985] ECR 2281.

[6] *Sealink/B&I-Holyhead*, Case IV/34.689 Commission decision of 11 June 1992.

[7] Commission Regulation 772/2004, OJ L123 of 27 April 2004, pp. 11–17. Commission Notice: Guidelines on the Application of Article 81 of the EC Treaty to Technology Transfer Agreements, OJ C101 of 27 April 2004 pp. 2–42.

[8] Article 21 AMA provides that the provisions of the Act do not apply to such acts as are recognisable as the exercise of rights under the Copyright Law, the Patent Law, the Utility Model Law, the Design Law or the Trademark Law.

[9] The GHQ, which adopted similar programmes for democratisation in both Germany and Japan, found that, in Germany, private business arrangements with overseas companies in the form of patent licensing agreements had been to the advantage of the Third Reich. For further discussion see, e.g., Eleanor M. Hadley, *Antitrust in Japan* (Princeton University Press, 1970) p. 5.

adopted under German influence.[10,11] More recently, the IP Guidelines adopted by the JFTC have followed the European Commission's guidelines, a sign that Japan is carefully observing European trends, as we will confirm below.

Article 10 of the Intellectual Property Basic Act of 2002 is entitled 'consideration for promotion of competition'. It provides that, when certain measures for the protection and exploitation of intellectual property are taken, fair exploitation of intellectual property and the public interest as well as the promotion of fair and free competition must be taken into consideration.[12] Accordingly, even conduct that may appear to constitute the exercise of IP law may not in fact be considered as such, if it would be contrary to the policies underlying the AMA.[13]

Compared to the US, the EU and Japan currently tend to protect licensees more than licensors, a difference that can be explained by the desire to promote the diffusion of innovation. This tendency arose earlier in Japan. From a strategic perspective, the EU's concern for licensees has likely been motivated by the fact that US companies rather than European undertakings hold technically advanced important patents in various sectors and license them to, among others, European companies. Similarly, after World War II, Japan needed access to advanced Western technology, and took steps to remove 'unfair' restrictions imposed by foreign licensors in order to encourage innovation by Japanese licensees. Since Western companies were viewed as dominant and superior to Japanese firms, the imposition of unfair terms and conditions on Japanese licensees was considered an abuse of a superior bargaining position. The kinds of case involving IP rights in this context included refusals to license, unfair licence terms, tying obligations, excessive royalties and grants of exclusivity.

Before Japan's entry in 1964 into the OECD, which promoted capital liberalisation, the Japanese Foreign Investment Law provided for a prior check on International Technology Agreements. When the JFTC found any problematic clause in a notified agreement, it encouraged the parties

---

10 See, e.g., Yosuke Okada, 'Law and financial studies of patent system', Financial Review, Research Centre, Ministry of Finance, p. 4, available at http://www.mof.go.jp/pri/publication/financial_review/fr_list3/r46/r_46_110_137.pdf (in Japanese).

11 The current Act is Utility Model Act No. 123 of 1959.

12 Intellectual Property Basic Act of 2002, available at http://www.kantei.go.jp/jp/singi/titeki/dai8/8siryou1.pdf.

13 See, e.g., Akira Negishi and Masayuki Funada, *Japanese Antitrust Law* (4th edn, Yuhikaku, 2010) p. 417.

to modify it. This was changed in 1968 by the Guidelines on the International Technology Transfer Agreement, under which the JFTC made international technology agreements subject to *ex post* examination. The Guidelines issued in 1968 indicated which licensing terms were to be regarded as 'black' clauses (and hence unfair trade terms) and which 'white' clauses (and hence the legitimate exercise of IP rights), and they specified that international agreements had to be notified to the JFTC under former Article 6, Section 2.

However, since the Guidelines were applicable only to technology transfers from foreign to domestic firms, they were naturally criticised for being protectionist. Towards the end of the 1980s, both the EU and Japan were influenced by thinking in the US, according to which IP rights and antitrust principles are not at odds but rather complement each other, since each ideally promotes welfare and innovation. For both the EU and Japan, technology transfer became a subject discussed in the regular meetings between the JFTC and the European Commission, and, for instance, on 9 November 1988 in Brussels the subject of the meeting was 'technology transfer and competition law'.[14] In the following year, the JFTC issued its Guidelines on Patent Know-How Licensing Agreements, which applied to both foreign and domestic parties equally, and which brought the JFTC's approach closer to the 'Rule of Reason'. The Guidelines were subsequently further revised in 1999 and 2007. In the meantime, the notification requirement for international agreements was abolished in 1997.[15] Taking account of Japan's rate of economic growth, the JFTC's rules developed step-by-step towards the approach taken by the EU and the US.[16] Currently, the JFTC is less interventionist with regard to licensing agreements than it once was.

Restrictions on improvements by licensees to licensed technology have been an important issue in Japan since the period when the International Technology Agreement was notified to the authority, because the strategy

---

[14] JFTC, *History of Antimonopoly Policy Fifty Years*, Volume 2 (Kosei Torihiki Kyokai, 1997) p. 583.

[15] Ibid. pp. 440–41. In 1970, among the notified international agreements to the JFTC, the number of the technology agreements to introduce foreign technology was 1179 while there were 78 technology agreements to invest in foreign countries. In 1996, the number of the technology agreements to introduce foreign technology was 36 while there were 69 technology agreements to invest in foreign countries.

[16] In particular, the current IP Guidelines and Guidelines on Private Monopolisation of 2009 essentially follow the EU approach. See, e.g., Fumio Sensui, 'Intellectual Property Law and Competition Law', *Kosei Torihiki*, **731** (September 2011) 4.

of Japanese companies normally consisted of not merely the exercise of the rights to advanced Western technology but also the improvement of this technology by the Japanese companies and licence fringe or peripheral technology rather than core technologies. Accordingly, the JFTC's Technology Transfer Guidelines provide that restrictions on R&D and the exclusive grant-back are in principle unfair trade practices and are excluded from the safe harbour, which is fixed as a product market share of the company that conducts the business using this technology below 20 per cent.[17]

As at the time of writing the current regime in force in the EU for technology transfer agreements consists of Regulation 772/2004 and the accompanying Technology Transfer Guidelines.[18] In licences between competitors, restrictions on the R&D activities of one of the parties is considered a hard core restriction under Article 4(1) of the Technology Transfer Block Exemption Regulation while in a licence between non-competitors it may be exempted provided certain conditions are met (Article 5(2)). Although compulsory grant-back and assign-back of severable improvements are not exempted under Article (1)(a) and (b), the block exemption is lenient with regard to other kinds of restriction.[19] Further, the R&D Block Exemption Regulation also sets down some conditions regarding exploitation of IPR.[20]

In the EU, the Commission has completed its public consultation on the application of the EU competition rules for the assessment of technology transfer agreements in anticipation of the expiry of the current Technology Transfer Block Exemption Regulation on 30 April 2014. There are some pending issues concerning IP and competition that are likely to have a direct effect on certain industries, such as patent settlement agreements among pharmaceutical companies. For these and other practices, the European Commission has been pursuing several cases in the pharmaceutical industry, in particular following the completion of a sector inquiry in this field. In Europe, the competitive

---

17 See IP Guideilnes, Chapter 4.5(8).

18 Regulation 772/2004 on the application of Article 81(3) EC to technology transfer agreement (2004) OJ L123/11.

19 See, e.g., Makoto Kurita, 'Intellectual Property Right and Anti-Monopoly Law (19): Licensing Agreement and Antimonopoly Act (6)', *The Invention*, **7** (2012), 50–51.

20 Regulation 1217/2010 on the application of Article 101(3) TFEU to research and development agreements (2010) OJ L335/36.

Table 10.1 Development of the competition law treatment of IP in the EU and Japan

EU		Japan	
1962	Notice on Patent Licensing Agreements	1947	Article 21 AMA
1984	Patent Licensing Block Exemption Regulation 2349/84	1968	Guidelines on International Technology Transfer Agreements
1989	Know-How Licensing Block Exemption Regulation No 556/89	1989	Guidelines on Patent Know-How Licensing Agreements
		1999	Guidelines on Patent Know-How Licensing Agreements
1996	Technology Transfer Block Exemption No 204/96	2005	Guidelines on Establishment of Patent Pools
2004	Technology Transfer Block Exemption Regulation No 772/2004 Technology Transfer Guidelines	2007	Guidelines on IP Licensing

consequences of licensing practices in the pharmaceutical sector may implicate not only the competition rules but also the rules on the free movement of goods.[21]

EXAMPLES OF BALANCING IP LAW AND COMPETITION LAW IN JAPAN AND THE EU

As seen above, the complex issue of the interactions between IP law and competition law is an issue in both Japan and the EU (see Table 10.1). IP law grants an inventor exclusive rights in return for his invention to allow him to recover his investments and to secure a fair reward. Excessive protection of IP rights is likely to discourage dissemination of technology

[21] For details regarding IP rights and the free movement of goods, see, e.g., Frank L. Fine, *The EC Competition Law on Technology Licensing* (Sweet & Maxwell, 2006) pp. 3–6.

and prevent further development of the technology, amounting to distorted competition. The goals of IP law and competition law, which are not always compatible, have to be carefully balanced. Further, enforcers (and scholars) have been facing the challenges created by rapid technological evolution.[22]

Although Article 21 AMA provides that the AMA provisions do not apply to acts recognisable as the exercise of rights under the Copyright Act, the Patent Act, the Utility Model Act, the Design Act or the Trademark Act, it does not clearly refer to the issue of the interactions between IPR and competition law. In 1985, owing to the yen's high exchange rate and an increase of Japanese consumers' purchase power, imports of foreign-branded products increased and parallel imports surged. A series of judgments examined claims of parallel imports banned based on IPR infringements. Later, the JFTC Guidelines of 1999 made it clear that the abusive exercise of IPRs is considered an infringement of the AMA.

The exclusive nature of IP rights does not necessarily mean that they create a stronger position in the market, since substitutable technology might be available.[23] Moreover, the protection of IP rights aims at promotion of competition, because by protecting incentives to innovate, it encourages further innovation in the market and efforts to create better products and services for consumers.[24] One example of the occasional tensions between competition law and IP law concerns quantitative restrictions contained in a licensing agreement. In such a scenario, the licensor limits the volume or number of licensed products made with the licensed technology. In the JFTC Guidelines of 1999, minimum and maximum volume restrictions were treated separately. The core divergence between IP scholars and antimonopoly law scholars is on the question of whether volume restrictions should be considered the exercise of IP rights (in which case, the AMA exemption applies). IP scholars generally consider that such a restriction does not concern the content of the right and thus cannot be considered an exercise of the right. For their part, antitrust scholars tend to support the idea that restricting the

---

[22] See, e.g., Hiroyuki Odagiri, 'A Few Comments on Subtle Relations between Patent Law and Competition Law', *Yearbook of Japanese Economic Law Association*, (2011) 76. It is suggested that, to balance between patent law and competition law, the competition authority should order more actively compulsory licensing as a remedy in merger control.

[23] See Masako Wakui, *Antimonopoly Law: Competition Law and Policy in Japan* (Arima Publishing. 2008) p. 251.

[24] Ibid. p. 251.

production volume of a licensee constitutes the exercise of an IP right, and the JFTC supports the latter position.[25] However, if volume is restricted jointly by several parties, in particular under patent pool arrangements or multiple licensing, and if this is considered to substantially restrict competition, the conduct cannot be considered an exercise of IP rights but rather amounts to a production cartel.[26,27] In contrast to output restrictions, territorial and customer restrictions as well as restrictions on the scope of exploitation of IP rights are commonly considered to be the exercise of IP rights.

The EU is particularly wary of situations in which dominant players in high-tech sectors use their strong position to gain leverage in neighbouring markets.[28] As discussed below, the tension between IP rights (seeking to reward investment in innovation by protecting IP holders from competition) and competition law (seeking to ensure that dominant companies do not abuse their privileged position) is well illustrated in recent cases of the Commission looking into alleged misuse of market power by companies whose dominance is linked to the fact that their patented technology has been incorporated into an industry standard.

In the EU, technology transfer can be treated in parallel with the way vertical restraints are treated. For instance, the Technology Transfer Block Exemption does not apply to an agreement between non-competitors that restricts the territory into which, or the customer group to whom, the licensee may passively sell the contract goods.[29]

The EU's objective of creating and maintaining a single integrated market is also relevant to the interaction between IP right and competition law. For instance, in order to create a single European digital market, a draft Directive on collective rights management and online multi-territory licensing of musical rights was published on 11 July 2012; it is currently under discussion. The proposal aims at improving the governance and transparency standards of collecting societies, facilitating

---

25 See the English translation of the IP Guidelines, in particular Part 2(5) and Part 4(3).

26 Makoto Kurita, 'Intellectual Property Rights and Antimonopoly Law (15): Licensing Agreement and Antimonopoly Law (2)', *The Invention*, **3** (2012) 46.

27 IP Guidelines, Chapter 3.2(1)(2).

28 See Alexander Italianer, 'Prepared Remarks On: Level-Playing Field and Innovation in Technology Markets', Conference on Antitrust in Technology, 28 January 2013. Available at http://ec.europa.eu/competition/speeches/text/sp2013_01_en.pdf.

29 See Whish and Bailey, supra note 3, at 789.

the licensing of online music across the EU market and promoting the diversity of EU culture.

'NON-ASSERTION OF PATENT' CLAUSE

In Japan, a reference to a Non-Assertion of Patent ('NAP') clause first appeared in the 1999 Patent Know-How Licensing Guidelines. It is also referred to in the 2007 IP Guidelines, which indicate that a NAP is viewed as an illegal trading condition if it damages fair competition. Furthermore, it may be subject to the prohibition of an abuse of a superior bargaining position under Article 2(9) AMA.[30] In the JFTC's *Microsoft* case, on 13 July 2004 Microsoft received a recommendation from the JFTC finding that provisions in its agreements with computer manufacturers, which precluded the assertion of patents against Microsoft and its customers ('NAP' clauses), were inconsistent with the AMA and contrary to the prohibition against dealing on restrictive terms and General Designation 13.[31] In particular, the JFTC considered that the NAP clause discouraged innovation while strengthening Microsoft's position in technology. In the JFTC's final decision of 16 September 2008, the JFTC ordered Microsoft to confirm that it had ceased imposing such provisions on domestic importers.[32]

Microsoft did not accept the conclusions reached by the JFTC in this case because the company believed that the provision at issue fairly balanced IP protection and the need to create a stable environment for the development of the IT industry by avoiding disruptive IP disputes. Microsoft considered that industry and consumers have benefited from this stability, and that IP owners always have the ability to exercise their rights if necessary.

Microsoft alleged that the provision in question was intended to balance respect for intellectual property rights with the avoidance of IP disputes, ensuring that computer manufacturers did not ship a new version of Windows only to raise an IP concern later. Further, Microsoft alleged that, as it would remove the NAP provision from agreements with

---

30 Makoto Kurita, 'Intellectual Property and AMA (21): Licensing Agreement and AMA (8)', *The Invention*, **9** (2012) 46–7.

31 Recommendation of JFTC of 13 July 2002. See http://www.jftc.go.jp/e-page/pressreleases/ 2004/July/040713.pdf. See also press release, JFTC (13 July 2004) available at http://www.jftc.go.jp/en/pressreleases/uploads/2004-July-13.pdf.

32 JFTC decision of 16 September 2008.

computer makers in new contracts to reflect a gradual evolution in the information technology market, the provision contained in old agreements would have limited ongoing effects. In the JFTC decision, no statements were to be found admitting that NAP clauses could have positive effects.

The *Microsoft* case just described is one of the few examples of cases in Japan regarding IP and competition. It is still not entirely clear how the JFTC will approach future cases where the use of IP raises competition concerns. It is considered that the evaluation of unfair trade practices and private monopolisation under the AMA is more difficult than the evaluation of unreasonable restraints of trade, as the line between fair competitive conduct and illegal conduct is not clear. This distinction is important in particular for companies whose business activities are exposed to rapid evolution and innovation. In order to encourage innovation and its benefits, the JFTC may tread more cautiously here than in other sectors.

It should be added that, in Japan, conduct falling under this category is not subject to fines. It has been argued that, in the *Microsoft* case, the deterrent effect of the JFTC's action was insufficient. A European case in another high-tech sector may be illustrative. In 2002, the Commission imposed significant fines on Nintendo and on seven of its distributors for infringing Article 101 TFEU by colluding to prevent parallel trade.[33] In Japan, the JFTC would only have issued a cease and desist order against Nintendo, without imposing a surcharge. On the other hand, the fines in Nintendo would have been less severe if the parties had not taken action to limit trade between Member States, a risky move in light of the EU's clear policy against interference with the free movement of goods across borders.

With regard to NAP clauses in the EU, no-challenge provisions in technology licensing agreements are excluded from the safe harbour under Article 5(1)(c) of the Technology Transfer Block Exemption Regulation. However, there is no Commission decision declaring that a NAP is anticompetitive, although it has investigated NAPs in the past.[34,35] A NAP may be viewed, rather, as a useful tool that avoids

---

33 PO/Nintendo distribution COMP/35706, Commission decision of 30 October 2002.

34 See, e.g., Fine, supra note 21, at 105.

35 See, e.g., Case 65/86 *Bayer AG and Maschinenfabrik Hennecke GmbH v Heinz SuÈllhoÈfer*, [1988] ECR I-5249. See also Kevin Coates, Lars Kjølbye and Luc Peeperkorn, 'Intellectual property', in Jonathan Faull and Ali Nikpay (eds), *The EC Law of Competition* (2nd edn, Oxford University Press) p. 1279.

patent litigation, keeps transaction costs down and promotes competition. Thus, in the context of patent settlement agreements, NAPs are in general thought not to breach Article 101(1) TFEU. The envisaged new rules will clarify that the NAP is likely to be anticompetitive if the licensor knows or could reasonably be expected to know that the licensed technology does not meet the respective legal criteria to receive IP protection.[36]

In sum, according to the Japanese IP Guidelines, a NAP may be regarded as an unfair trade practice, that is, as a 'grey clause'. Compared to the EU, where NAP clauses have not figured prominently as a main issue in a particular case, in Japan there have been a few cases concerning such clauses.[37]

PATENT POOLS

The pooling of patented technologies is not inherently restrictive of competition. To the contrary, the combination of complementary technologies may facilitate their efficient use and exploitation. In other cases, however, the pool may eliminate competition between members of the pool. In Japan there are not many judicial or JFTC precedents relating to patent pools, but the JFTC issued guidelines on patent pools in 2005 and on the use of intellectual property in 2007 to facilitate the competitive assessment of patent pool activities. According to these instruments, patent pools can be problematic under the AMA if commonly determined licensing conditions restrict competition (unreasonable restraint of trade), or if the patent pool prevents a new firm from entering into the market or refuses to license the technology (private monopolisation), or if licensing conditions prevent fair competition in the market (unfair trade practices).[38]

In the *Pachinko* case, a patent management company composed of 19 companies, most of which were manufacturers of Pachinko machines,

---

[36] See Luc Peeperkorn and Anna Vernet and Tobias P. Maass, 'Review of the Rules for the Assessment of Licensing Agreements for the Transfer of Technology under EU Competition Law', seminar presentation for The TTBER Review#2: Increasing Scrutiny to Protect Innovation (Brussels Matters) in Brussels on 13 March 2013. See also Fine, supra note 21, at 105.

[37] See Makoto Kurita. 'Intellectual Property Rights and Antimonopoly Law (19): Licensing Agreement and Antimonopoly Law (6)', *The Invention*, **3** (2012) 51.

[38] See, e.g., Yosuke Okada and Shuya Hayashi, *Economics of the Antimonopoly Law: Case Study of Trial Decisions* (University of Tokyo Press, 2009) p. 252.

had been, since 1961, in charge of licensing of essential patents to produce Pachinko machines.[39] Because the activities in the market looked increasingly lucrative, more and more companies that had been manufacturing other kinds of game machine became interested in producing Pachinko machines. The patent management company and its member companies sought to maintain their market shares and decided not to license non-members. The JFTC considered that the collusive refusal to license to prevent other companies from starting to produce the machines was against the public interest, and that the challenged conduct could not be considered an exercise of rights under Patent Law and the Utility Model Act. The JFTC thus concluded that the collective refusal constituted private monopolisation in breach of Article 2(5) AMA and Article 3 AMA. In relation to the applicability of the exemption Article 21 AMA, although patent pools generally enable efficiencies such as saved management fees that would otherwise be incurred through licensing on an individual basis, the JFTC was more concerned with the pool's exclusionary effects.[40]

In another case relating to patented slot machines, a patent management company was set up to resolve a dispute between manufacturers regarding patent licensing.[41] The slot machine sold by patent pool members occupied almost 100 per cent of the market. But then one member company, disappointed with the royalty fees it had been collecting, decided not to renew its agreement with the patent pool company. Subsequently, the former patent pool member brought an action before the Tokyo District Court against a licensee that had obtained a licence through the patent pool company, claiming that the grant from the patent pool was invalid because the patent pool itself violated the AMA. Since the Tokyo District Court did not accept the claim that the patent pool agreement had expired, the former member company appealed the District Court's judgment before the Tokyo High Court. According to the Tokyo High Court, the patent pool had been established to prevent disputes between a licensor and a licensee, and to facilitate the sound development of the slot machine production market. Furthermore, there was no policy to prevent newcomers or internal control of production and sale prices. The court also held that the management of the patent pool was not outside the scope of technology protection conferred by Patent Law and did not substantially restrict competition in the product and

39 JFTC decision of 6 August 1997.

40 See Okada and Hayashi, supra note 38, p. 254.

41 Judgment of Tokyo High Court of 4 June 2003.

technology markets. Consequently, the former member company's claim against the licensing agreement was rejected.

In the EU, the Technology Transfer Block Exemption is not applicable to 'technology' pools (including patent pools), even when there are only two contributors to the pool. A technology pool is thus assessed case by case for its compatibility with Article 101 and 102 TFEU. According to the Commission's Guidelines, patent pools are akin to joint selling agreements.[42] In November 2002 the Commission cleared an agreement regarding five 3G technology-specific patents in the context of the 3G Patent Platform Partnership in order to create cost-effective licensing of essential patents. As the arrangements were similar to a patent pool, they were reviewed under the criteria governing such pools.[43]

TYING

The JFTC issued a decision on 14 December 1998 against Microsoft whose product 'Microsoft Excel' was the leading product in the spreadsheet market but was not dominant in Japan. However, 'Ichitaro', manufactured by Just Systems, and 'Lotus Organizer' were more popular than Microsoft's 'Word' and 'Outlook' in the markets for, respectively, word-processors and scheduling management programs.

Accordingly, Microsoft Japan adopted a policy of not licensing Excel alone to PC manufacturers but rather bundled its licence of Excel with licences of Word and Outlook. The JFTC considered this to be a breach of the prohibition of unfair trade practices under Article 19 AMA and ordered that Microsoft Japan should cease its bundling policy and accept requests from existing licensees if they sought amendments to the licence agreements so that they could have a licence for only Excel, or Excel and Word (with corresponding royalty reductions).

In the EU, the Commission issued a well-known decision in 2004 against Microsoft for abuse of its dominant position in the market for PC operating systems in breach of Article 102 TFEU.[44] As regards the tying

---

42 See Regulation 772/2004, recital 7. Commission Notice Guidelines on the applicability of Article 81 of the EC Treaty to horizontal cooperation agreements (2001) OJ C3/2, paras 132 et seq. See also Fine, supra note 21, at 109–10.

43 See, e.g., Dessy Choumelova, 'Competition Law Analysis of Patent Licensing Arrangements: The Particular Case of 3G3P', *Competition Policy Newsletter*, **1** (Spring 2003) 41. Available at http://ec.europa.eu/competition/publications/cpn/2003_1_41.pdf.

44 COMP/C-3/37.792 Microsoft.

issue that arose in this case, the Commission considered that the bundling into the Windows operating system of media player software otherwise available on a stand-alone basis had the effect of excluding competitors and amounted to reduced consumer choice and access to innovative products. Independently of the tying side of the case, the Commission also found that it was abuse for Microsoft to refuse to provide work group server interoperability information to competitors. For these offences the Commission fined Microsoft around 497 million euros.

Microsoft appealed the Commission's decision but on 17 September 2007 the Court of First Instance ('CFI' – now the General Court) essentially dismissed the appeal.[45] In relation to the tying, of 'Windows Media Player' with the 'Windows' PC operating system, the Court upheld the Commission's decision as it sufficiently examined the conditions for the tying. The conditions are that: first, the undertaking concerned must have a dominant position on the market for the tying product; second, the tying product and the tied product must be two separate products; third, consumers must not have a choice to obtain the tying product without the tied product; and, fourth, the practice must foreclose competition. Further, it found that Microsoft did not demonstrate the existence of objective justification for the tying and the remedy imposed by the Commission was proportionate.

In relation to Microsoft's refusal to provide interoperability information, the CFI confirmed that the extent of interoperability required by the Commission was well grounded. According to the court, a refusal by a dominant proprietor of such information to provide it to a third party can only be characterised as an abuse if three conditions are met: (1) the refusal must relate to a product or service indispensable to the exercise of a particular activity on a neighbouring market; (2) the refusal must be of such a kind as to exclude any effective competition on the neighbouring market; and (3) the refusal must prevent the appearance of a new product for which potential consumer demand can be found, or alternatively it must prevent technical development contrary to Article 102(b) TFEU. According to the Court, where these criteria are satisfied, the refusal to grant a licence will be held abusive unless it is objectively justified.

The Commission considers that the decision upheld by the CFI focuses on the promotion of interoperability, which contributes strongly to innovation and competition in the software industry while also fully

---

45 Case T-201/04 *Microsoft v Commission* [2007] ECR II-3601.

recognising the importance of IP rights as incentives for innovation.[46] However, Microsoft's market power in terms of the scope, duration and potential to affect markets was so exceptional that it may be a mistake to transpose the Court's statements more generally to other scenarios, particularly since the judgment was not appealed to the Court of Justice.[47]

In the EU's Microsoft browser case (which was unrelated to the case described above), in January of 2009 the Commission sent a Statement of Objections to Microsoft, accusing the company of abusing its dominant position on the market for client PC operating systems by tying its web browser ('Internet Explorer') to the Windows operating system. In this case, Microsoft required OEMs that pre-installed Windows on their client PCs to pre-install Internet Explorer as well. Although OEMs could in theory also install an alternative web browser, they could do so only in addition to Internet Explorer; it was not possible technically for OEMs or users to 'turn off' Internet Explorer. Allegedly, this conduct allowed Microsoft to have its web browser installed on more than 90 per cent of PCs sold. Further, the Commission considered that the alternative distribution channel available to competitors, that is, the downloading of web browsers by users freely from the Internet, was not sufficiently effective to offset the foreclosure effects resulting from Microsoft's tying practice. Subsequently, Microsoft offered commitments to remedy the Commission's competition concerns, and the amended proposal of commitments was accepted by the Commission in its decision of 16 December 2009. The decision made the commitments legally binding upon Microsoft, and no fine was imposed.[48] Under the binding commitments, Microsoft was obliged to offer a 'Choice Screen' that enables users of Windows to choose which web browser they want to install on their computers. The

---

46 See the Commission's press release MEMO/07/359 of 17 September 2007, available at http://europa.eu/rapid/press-release_MEMO-07-359_en.htm

47 See Nicholas Banasevic and Per Hellström, 'Windows into the World of Abuse of Dominance: An Analysis of the Commission's 2004 Microsoft Decision and the CFI's 2007 Judgment', in Luca Rubini (ed.), *Microsoft on Trial: Legal and Economic Analysis of a Transatlantic Antitrust Case* (Edward Elgar Publishing, 2010) p. 75.

48 If the Commission intends to impose a fine on a defendant, it cannot avail itself of the commitments procedure, which is provided for by Article 9 of Regulation 1/2003. This approach makes sense because, if Article 9 is used, the Commission cannot make a finding of infringement; rather, it finds that the commitments are such as to remove its grounds for action.

commitments further precluded Microsoft from retaliating against computer manufacturers that install competing web browsers as default browsers.

STANDARD SETTING

In the EU, in July 2007, the Commission sent a Statement of Objections to Rambus alleging that the company had abused its dominant position in the context of standard setting for Dynamic Random Access Memory chips (DRAMs). According to the Commission the abuse took the form of a 'patent ambush'. Further, Qualcomm was investigated because of allegedly exploitative licensing. Although both cases were subsequently terminated without a formal finding of abuse, they establish important principles about how the Commission applies EU competition law in the context of standard setting.

Rambus carried out its 'patent ambush' first of all by failing to disclose its ownership of patents covering DRAM technology during the standard-setting procedure at JEDEC (an industry-wide standard-setting organisation). Rambus later claimed that these patents were essential to the adopted standard and thus any producers who intended to manufacture DRAM products compliant with JEDEC's standards had to obtain a royalty-bearing licence from Rambus. In its investigation, Rambus proposed commitments to address the Commission's concerns, promising to establish a worldwide cap on its royalty rates for JEDEC-compliant DRAMs for five years. The Commission accepted this commitment and terminated the case without finding an abuse.[49]

In September 2009, for the first time, the JFTC issued an order to a foreign undertaking in the mobile phone technology field.[50] Qualcomm concluded an agreement with Japanese producers of domestic computer terminals, which included a NAP clause (see above) from March 2000 to March 2001. The JFTC considered that Qualcomm had breached the AMA, in particular by engaging in an unfair trade practice (former General Designation 13).

---

[49] COMP/38.636, *Rambus*. As explained above (note 48), in an Article 9 case the Commission does not make any finding of infringement.

[50] *Qualcomm*, JTFC decision of 30 September 2009.

In the meantime, in Europe, on 24 November 2009, the European Commission decided to close its formal proceedings against Qualcomm.[51] As all the complaints had already been withdrawn or were soon to be withdrawn, the Commission did not wish to invest further resources in this case. Since the Commission's decision to drop the investigation does not necessarily mean that it considered Qualcomm's licensing practices to be compliant with the competition rules, the interpretation of the Commission's treatment of the case is not clear. In October 2007, the Commission sent a Statement of Objections to Qualcomm that accused the company of abusing its dominant position when licensing its patented technology included in the WCDMA (Wideband Code Division Multiple Access) standard, which forms part of the 3G standard for European mobile phone technology.[52] According to the SO, Qualcomm had imposed licensing terms and royalties that were not fair, reasonable or non-discriminatory (FRAND) and was thus exploiting its dominant position in the WCDMA licensing market contrary to Article 102 TFEU. Qualcomm was not accused of failing to disclose its essential patents when the WCDMA/3G standard was set (a patent ambush scenario); rather, it had allegedly licensed its technology in breach of its FRAND commitment.

The Commission's view expressed in Rambus and Qualcomm cases is that dominant firms may abuse their dominant position either by failing to disclose the existence of essential patents or by failing to respect FRAND terms when licensing their patents. The Commission did not offer specific views as to what constitutes a reasonable royalty.

According to the Commission, an effective standard-setting process should take place in a non-discriminatory, open and transparent way in order to ensure competition on the merits and allow consumers to benefit from technological development and innovation. In this context, the importance of open standards was also highlighted. However, the question of what terms are considered unfair and/or discriminatory remains unresolved.

Part 4(2)(ii) of the Japanese IP Guidelines recognises that a refusal to license IP rights by a participant in a standard-setting procedure may constitute an unfair trade practice if the participant promised to grant a license on favourable terms, if it is difficult for a licensee to switch to another technology. However, the Japanese IP Guidelines do not mention the criteria that the EU has adopted to limit the applicability of

---

51 COMP/39247 Texas Instruments/Qualcomm. The Commission's press release of 24 November 2009, MEMO/09/516.

52 See the Commission's press release of 1 October 2007, MEMO/07/389.

competition law in cases of refusal to license IP rights. These supposedly strict criteria are intended to ensure that a duty to license is imposed only in 'exceptional circumstances'.[53]

Technical standards are often voluntary and organised by trade associations such as the ISO or the IEEE, or a patent pool. Generally, standards do not cover all products in an industry. Some products may be covered by a standard and others may not be. Therefore, it may be necessary to examine not only the products covered under the standard but also other products with respect to which the parties may be competing.[54]

In Samsung's patent cases, on 31 January 2012, the Commission opened a formal investigation to assess whether Samsung had breached a commitment it gave to a standard-setting organisation to license any standard-essential patents (SEPs) relating to European mobile telephony standards on fair, reasonable and non-discriminatory (FRAND) terms in breach of Article 102 TFEU.[55] A dominant company can infringe Article 102 TFEU by misusing the patent system to block or delay market entry by competing products.[56] Similarly, a dominant company can infringe Article 102 TFEU by bringing legal proceedings as part of a plan to eliminate competition.[57] The Commission considered that, in line with the position the Commission already expressed in its *Google/Motorola* merger decision, actions demanding an injunction to stop exploitation of SEPs against a willing licensee can be anticompetitive.[58]

---

53 See H. Stephen Harris and Hiroshi Ohashi, 'Japan', in R. Ian McEwin (ed.), *Intellectual Property, Competition Law and Economics in Asia* (Hart Publishing, 2011) p. 207. These critieria include the indispensability of access to the allegedly essential IP, the general criterion that the party seeking access use the IP to create a new product, that without acess effective competition will be excluded and that there are no objective grounds for refusal. See also Case C-418/01 *IMS Health GmbH & Co OHG v NDC Health GmbH & Co KG* [2004] ECR I-5039.

54 See Noriyuki Doi, 'Long Lecture: Theory of Industrial Organisation and Competition Policy: No 3. Competition and Concert' *Kosei Torihiki*, **726** (April 2011) 67.

55 The Commission's press release of 31 January 2013, IP/12/89.

56 See the *AstraZeneca* Case COMP/A. 37.507/F3.

57 See case T-111/96, *ITT Promedia v Commission* [1998] ECR II-2937.

58 See Alexander Italianer, 'Prepared Remarks on Level-Playing Field and Innovation in Technology Markets', Conference on Antitrust in Technology, 28 January 2013, available at http://ec.europa.eu/competition/speeches/text/sp2013_01_en.pdf.

Patent litigation regarding the *Apple/Samsung* case continues in several jurisdictions, including Europe and Japan. However, no official AMA investigation is currently underway in Japan.

CONCLUSION

The EU and Japan have been developing an interface between IP rights and competition law in a relatively harmonious way. IP law and competition law both aim at promoting innovation and consumer interests, and in the EU and Japan there has been growing use of antitrust and merger remedies that require interoperability and fair, reasonable and non-discriminatory (FRAND) licensing commitments.

With regard to intellectual property, the legal frameworks in Japan and Europe share some common ground. For example, Japan is a signatory of most of the main international treaties in relation to intellectual property rights, including the Paris Convention for the Protection of Industrial Property and the Berne Convention for the Protection of Literary and Artistic Works.

Recent challenges in competition policy concern IP 'wars' in the technology sector and various practices in the pharmaceutical sector. Japan aims to be better equipped to tackle international IP litigation, and it has amended its Law of Civil Procedure to clarify when Japanese courts have jurisdiction in IP cases in an international context.[59]

However, precedents in Japan regarding competition and IP are still scarce, whereas in the EU a growing number of antitrust and merger cases concern interoperability and FRAND licensing commitments. In order to further develop its law and policy with regard to such issues, Japan first requires more practical experience.

---

[59] Act Partially Amending Law of Civil Procedure and Civil Provisional Remedies Act, Act No. 36 of 2011.

11. Private enforcement

HISTORY AND LEGAL STRUCTURE FOR PRIVATE DAMAGES ACTIONS IN JAPAN

During the first 20 years following the introduction of the AMA in 1947, the number of private lawsuits based on that legislation was small, and no judgment awarding damages was rendered until 1993, although the original AMA that was adopted in 1947 already contained Article 25 AMA, which provides a private damage action.[1] During the SII negotiations, the US urged Japan to facilitate a more active use of private damages actions for AMA infringements, above all those involving exclusionary conduct.[2] The number of private actions for damages then substantially increased in 1996. Since then, at least seven cases each year have been brought, with the figure occasionally exceeding 20 cases.[3] The tendency is for more and more plaintiffs to win in damages actions, or at least to obtain a favourable settlement.

In Japan, there are two systems of private damages action for AMA infringements. One is established by Articles 25 and 26 AMA, and the other is based on Article 709 of Japan's Civil Code.[4] Litigation under Articles 25/26 AMA and Article 709 Civil Code can be brought simultaneously by the same plaintiff, if so desired.[5] However, a plaintiff can only initiate an action under Articles 25/26 AMA if the JFTC has taken a final decision finding that the defendant's conduct was in breach of the AMA. Specifically, under Article 25(1) AMA, an injured party may bring such

---

[1] See, e.g., Miyuki Takazawa, 'Antimonopoly Act and Collective Actions', *Issue Brief*, **576** (28 March 2007) 1 (in Japanese). Available at http://www.ndl.go.jp/jp/data/publication/issue/0576.pdf.

[2] JFTC, *AMA Policy Fifty Years History*, Volume 1 (Kosei Torihiki Kyokai, 1997) p. 487.

[3] See Simon Vande Walle, 'Private Enforcement of Antitrust Law in Japan: An Empirical Analysis', *The Competition Law Review*, **8** (1) (December 2011) 16, available at http://www.clasf.org/CompLRev/Issues/Vol8Issue1Art1Walle.pdf.

[4] Law No. 89 of 1896.

[5] Cumulative actions would be advantageous in terms of the selection of the court (the Tokyo High Court has exclusive jurisdiction to hear Art. 25 matters).

an action before a 'special panel' designated to hear AMA cases at the Tokyo High Court. Under Article 25(2) AMA, strict liability applies and there is no need for the plaintiff to demonstrate negligence or wilfulness on the part of the defendant. Generally, this system has not been used frequently owing to its corresponding requirements such as the prior adoption of a JFTC decision (which may never happen, particularly if the JFTC resolves a matter informally) and the exclusive jurisdiction at first instance of the Tokyo High Court, which is not conveniently located for many would-be litigants. Accordingly, it is not rare for a case to be settled before judgment.[6] As a recent example, in the *Japanese Highway Public Corporation* case, a plaintiff who took over the claims of the Japanese Highway Public Corporation against certain construction firms brought an action under Article 25 AMA. The construction companies were held to be jointly and severally liable for the damages. The damages were calculated based on a comparison of average prices for similar tenders.[7]

The limitations of Articles 25 and 26 AMA are not decisive, however, because instead of waiting for a JFTC decision a complainant may seek general tort damages under the Civil Code before local courts irrespective of the adoption of a decision by the JFTC. Unlike the system under Article 25 AMA, jurisdiction in tort cases is not limited to the Tokyo High Court but may be brought before any District Court in Japan. In civil litigation, a JFTC decision, if any, is filed with the court but is only used to provide information. One of the advantages of seeking damages under the Civil Code is that the plaintiff is not obliged to limit the scope of infringement to the infringement period or the precise conduct covered in a JFTC decision. As the basic structure of the Civil Code is rather similar to those of Continental European countries, it is for the claimant to prove causation and damages, which in some cases may be a formidable task. US-style discovery, punitive damages (including treble damages) and class actions are not allowed in Japan.

In some cases plaintiffs have faced difficulties in calculating the damages caused by an infringement, particularly where, as in a cartel

---

[6] At the beginning of 2010, 19 cases under Article 25 AMA were pending before the court, while during the same year 12 more cases were brought. One case was settled, while the court rendered a judgment in favour of a plaintiff in another case. At the end of 2010, the number of pending cases under Article 25 was 30. See the JFTC's Annual Report of 2010, http://www.jftc.go.jp/info/nenpou/h22/index.html (in Japanese).

[7] The Japanese Public Highway Corporation case, judgment of Tokyo High Court of 30 August 2011.

case, estimations must be made. In view of this difficulty, the Civil Law of Procedure was amended to introduce a new provision – Article 248 – that allows the judge to determine a reasonable amount of damages.[8] With regard to standing, in Japan not only the direct purchasers but also indirect purchasers may seek to recover damages before the courts in the actions under both the AMA and the Civil Code.[9]

On 1 April 2001, it also became possible under Article 24 AMA for private plaintiffs to seek an injunction to stop conduct that is considered unfair trade practice contrary to the AMA. Article 24 AMA provides that a plaintiff must prove that he suffers or is likely to suffer extreme damages by the conduct. Further, a preliminary injunction under the Civil Provisional Remedies Act can be granted where it is necessary to avoid any substantial detriment of imminent danger.[10] This mechanism is supposed to complement the enforcement activities of the JFTC. Although injunction cases under Article 24 have been limited, a few recent cases have been brought. Notably, Softbank BB and Softbank Telecom sought an injunction against NTT East and NTT West in October 2011, alleging that both companies unilaterally refused to deal with them. According to the plaintiffs, this amounted to an abuse of a superior bargaining position and thus an unfair trade practice under Article 19 AMA.

Under the Local Autonomy Law,[11] Japan experienced a trend of increasing numbers of direct damages actions (local resident lawsuits) in the 1990s, a trend that came to an end when the direct cause of action was eliminated by amendment. However, these actions related specifically to bid rigging, whereas damages actions based on other categories of infringements have not been prevalent in Japan.[12] Damages actions based on bid rigging have different characteristics than other kinds of claims because in such cases the direct victims of the misconduct are public authorities. The system of litigation established by the Local Autonomy

---

8 See, e.g., Hiromitsu Miyakawa, 'Japan', in Albert A. Foer and Jonathan W. Cuneo (eds), *The International Handbook on Private Enforcement of Competition Law* (Edward Elgar, 2010) p. 535.

9 Judgment of Supreme Court of 8 December 1989. See also Tadashi Shiraishi, *Competition Law of Japan* (2nd edn, Yuhikaku, 2009) p. 676.

10 Civil Provisional Remedies Act, Act No. 91 of 1989. See Mitsuo Matsushita and Kazunori Furuya, 'Private Antitrust Actions in Japan', *CPI Antitrust Chronicle*, **1** (April 2013) 6.

11 Law No. 67 of 17 April 1947.

12 Article 242.2 Local Autonomy Law. For discussion, see Simon Vande Walle, supra note 3.

Law was rather popular. Under this system, an action against colluding bidders was brought directly by local residents on behalf of their local government, but the entire recovery went to the local government. As noted above, this system was amended in 2002 and now residents can only request their local government to take action, an essentially discretionary choice.

Public organisations have standing to bring a suit under either Articles 25/26 AMA or Article 709 of the Civil Code, the general tort provision described above.[13] Under Article 709 and the State Redress Act, a complainant alleging that the JFTC's decision did not correctly establish an illegal conduct under the AMA could bring a suit against the State for recovery of damages incurred.[14]

Shareholder derivative actions also play a significant role in private enforcement in Japan.[15] One such suit was brought against managers in the context of the *Optical Fiber* cartel following the adoption by the JFTC of a cease and desist order in May 2010 and the imposition of a surcharge. According to the shareholders, the managers breached their duty to the company concerned by failing to make a leniency application. The action was brought by an association of lawyers and public accountants representing shareholders' interests.[16]

An OECD report of 1999 recommended that, in order to expand the scope of AMA enforcement and to strengthen private rights of action, the

---

13 It seems difficult to find reasons why damages actions in collusion cases other than bid rigging cases are relatively scarce in Japan. On the other hand, shareholders' derivative actions have been used and might become more common in the future, provided they can allow a company to recover a substantial amount. See Akinori Uesugi, *Handbook on International Competition Practices* (Shojihomu, 2012) p. 141 (in Japanese).

14 Act No. 125 of 27 October 1947.

15 See also the cartels and bid rigging in Chapter 4 (this volume). In the *Saitama Saturday Association* case, following the arrests of numerous politicians and the senior managers of construction companies owing to the discovery of corruption in relation to bid rigging in the construction sector, the shareholders brought derivative actions. The Tokyo High Court ordered the defendants to pay damages, stating that even if a director considered that corruption was beneficial for the company's interests, it was outside the scope of its legitimate authority. Judgment of Tokyo District Court of 22 December 1994. Local resident suits brought under the Local Autonomy Law in relation to the Saitama bid rigging scandal are discussed by Vande Walle, supra note 3.

16 The association, called Lawyers for Shareholders' Rights, was established in 2010. See *Nihon Keizai Shimbun*, 15 June 2010. See also Yasuo Daito, 'Advanced AMA Audit to Detect a Cartel: To Win "Leniency Race"', *Business Law Journal*, **57** (December 2012).

quota limiting the number of practising lawyers in Japan should be abolished.[17] Considering the fact that more and more Japan-qualified lawyers are experiencing difficulties finding work in the country and in light of the fact that the Japanese legal market is relatively small, increasing the number of lawyers in Japan hardly appears to be a perfect solution; on the other hand, increasing the number of practitioners in the specific field of Japanese competition law does seem to contribute to a more positive use of the AMA by private parties.[18]

The objective of achieving more effective damages actions has also been a topic in trade negotiations between Japan and foreign parties, including the EU. Negotiators from the EU and from the US have urged that Japanese law and procedure be amended to make it easier for alleged victims to challenge anticompetitive conduct in court.[19]

HISTORY AND LEGAL STRUCTURE OF PRIVATE DAMAGES ACTIONS IN THE EU

In the EU, the Treaty of Rome did not provide specific provisions regarding actions for damages. Such litigation has been, rather, principally an issue regulated under the laws of the EU Member States, subject at the margins to certain principles of EU law. At the EU level, the European Commission is developing policy initiatives that, inter alia, are aimed at ensuring that victims of infringements of EU antitrust law receive compensation for the harm they suffer, a possibility that must be guaranteed according to the case law of the Court of Justice. The Commission also provides general and case-related support to national judges as they apply the EU competition rules. In terms of legislative measures, the Commission has for years envisaged a Directive on private damages actions, and to build momentum towards legislation it issued a

---

17 See OECD, 'Country Studies: Japan – The Role of Competition Policy in Regulatory Reform 1999' (1999) pp. 27–8.

18 See, e.g., Tadashi Shiraishi, 'Choice of Bringing Damages Suffered by a Company under AMA before a Court', *Business Law Journal* (February 2012) 56.

19 See OECD, 'The Role of Competition Policy in Regulatory Reform 1999' (1999), p. 27. This report mentions that EU and US negotiators concentrated on opening the door to injunctions under the AMA and facilitating damages actions for plaintiffs by easing plaintiffs' burden of proof of damages.

Green Paper in 2005 and then a White Paper in 2008.[20] Although the Commission has been considering the issue of collective redress (a variation on class actions) for several years, a definitive legislative framework on private damages actions has not been adopted at the time of this writing. After the Commission had discussed, internally and with the Member States and the European Parliament, the shape of a possible legislative instrument or instruments that would regulate collective redress and the quantification of damages,[21] in June 2013, it adopted a proposal for a Directive on antitrust damages actions as well as a Communication on quantifying antitrust harm to provide guidance determining the exact amount of damages.[22]

As widely reported, some in Europe have been concerned that expanding private damages actions under EU law would open the lawsuit floodgates and create a US-style litigation culture. Furthermore, increased exposure to class actions may discourage potential leniency applicants from approaching competition authorities.[23] However, with regard to private actions, partly because of the common law system in the UK, private damages actions have become more common than they were a decade ago, although most cases so far have been settled out of court. Important developments have also been underway in Member States other than the UK, such as Germany. One of the initiatives that has allowed damages actions to go forward where cartel victims suffer damages too dispersed to give individuals an incentive to litigate is the aggregation of claims by private companies.

Overall, since the state of affairs differs widely in the Member States, with some systems exhibiting more 'litigation-friendly' features than others, forum shopping has become a common part of legal strategy in

---

[20] Green Paper: Damages actions for breach of the EC antitrust rules, COM (2005) 672, 19.12.2005; White Paper: Damages actions for breach of the EC antitrust rules, COM (2008) 165, 2.4.2008.

[21] See the Commission's explanation for action for damages on its website, available at http://ec.europa.eu/competition/antitrust/actionsdamages/index.html.

[22] Proposal for a Directive of the European Parliament and of the Council on certain rules governing actions for damages under national law for infringements of the competition law provisions of the Member States and of the European Union, COM(2013) 404, 11.6.2013 and Communication from the Commission on quantifying harm in actions for damages based on breaches of Article 101 or 102 of the Treaty on the Functioning of the European Union, C(2013) 3440, 11.6.2013.

[23] See, e.g., Linda Arcelin, *Droit de la concurrence: Les pratiques anticoncurrentielles en droit interne et communautaire* (Presses Universitaires de Rennes, 2009) p. 162.

the EU. It should be pointed out that in Europe, on the public enforcement side, companies that have been found by the Commission to infringe the competition rules bring appeals before the General Court, and even immunity applicants may bring appeals.[24] This may delay the proceedings of damages actions before a national court because, under EU law, a national court is precluded from taking a decision that runs counter to a decision of the Commission (even one that is being challenged before the EU Courts). The General Court examines both the legal and factual analysis of the Commission decision. Thus, the essential analysis of the Commission, including the scope of the product concerned, the infringement period and the matter of whether the undertaking concerned participated in an infringement may change as a result of an appeal. This may substantially affect the amount of damages claimed. The judgment of the General Court is subject to appeal to the ECJ, and it often takes several years to obtain a final judgment. The delay at the level of national proceedings may thus last for a long time. In some cases the national court may expedite the process by submitting a preliminary reference to the Court of Justice under Article 267 TFEU.

DISCLOSURE OF EVIDENCE

This is the one of the areas in which the EU is more advanced than Japan, although given the lack of pre-trial discovery system, both jurisdictions share the same problem. According to the ECJ, the right to claim private damages must be guaranteed in order to ensure the full effectiveness of competition law, and the procedures for recovering damages caused by competition infringements must be effective.[25] To be effective, disclosure of evidence held by the Commission may be necessary.

Currently in the EU there is a discussion regarding the balance between, first, the need to encourage private damages claims, which may depend on disclosure of information possessed by the competition agencies, and second, the public interest in preserving the effectiveness of leniency programmes, which are in turn crucial for effective cartel

---

[24] In the *Air Cargo* cartel case, Lufthansa appealed to the Court of First Instance even though it had been granted immunity from fines by the Commission. Airfreight COMP/39258 of 9 November 2010.

[25] In *Manfredi*, Case C-295/04-298/04, the ECJ reiterated this principle, which it had already established in *Courage v Crehan*, Case C-453/99.

enforcement.[26] In particular, cartel participants oppose the disclosure of confidential versions of the Commission's decision and of documents submitted to the Commission, including leniency documents. The Commission considers that companies that voluntarily cooperate with the Commission in revealing cartels should not be put in a worse position in relation to damages actions than other cartel participants that did not cooperate with the Commission. However, without any disclosure, a claimant may have difficulties in establishing a claim or quantifying loss.

In *CDC v Commission* the General Court annulled the Commission's order to refuse access to the document in question, which was the statement of contents of the case file in the hydrogen peroxide cartel, because the Commission had not established that disclosure of the statement of contents would specifically and effectively undermine the purpose of the investigation.[27,28] Subsequently, in March 2012 the Commission published an informal Guidance Paper on confidentiality claims to clarify how parties may claim confidentiality contained in submissions.[29] In *Pfleiderer*, ECJ stated that where a national court seeks to determine the discoverability of leniency documents in the possession of a national competition authority, a case-by-case balancing of the need to protect leniency documents and the legitimate interest of plaintiffs in access to evidence must be carried out.[30] Transparency Regulation 1049/2001 provides for the right of access of any citizen of the EU and any natural or legal person residing or having their company's registered office in a Member State to documents of the EU institutions, with certain exceptions such as where commercial interests must be protected, or where the purpose of inspections and investigations is at risk.[31] Furthermore, disclosure of the contents of case files of the Commission and of the national competition authorities by order of the EU courts, Member State courts or the courts outside the EU may be possible. In

---

[26] In practice, the leniency/marker application is done by the lawyer for the applicant in person and the application is read out by him at the Commission's office in order to limit the risk of creating a non-privileged document vulnerable to discovery in any damages action brought in the national courts.

[27] *Hydrogen Peroxide and Perborate* COMP/F/38.620.

[28] Case T-437/08, *CDC Hydrogen Peroxide Cartel Damage Claims (CDC Hydrogen Peroxide) v Commission*, Judgment of the General Court of 15 December 2011, not yet published.

[29] See http://ec.europa.eu/competition/antitrust/guidance_en.pdf.

[30] C-360/09 *Pfleiderer AG v Bundeskartellamt*, not yet published.

[31] Regulation (EC) No. 1049/02001 of the European Parliament and of the Council of 30 May 2001 regarding public access to European Parliament, Council and Commission documents, OJ L145/43-48 of 31 May 2001.

fact, access to the files possessed by the national competition agencies has been examined before the national courts and the judgments are not always consistent.[32] In this regard, the proposal for a Directive includes provisions to ensure sufficient access to evidence to obtain compensation together with sanctions for non-compliance, failure to protect confidential information and abuse.[33]

The possible negative effect of a lack of appropriate protection of confidentiality would be that potential defendants may be discouraged from coming forward under the leniency programme for fear that the information submitted to the authority would later be subject to a disclosure order, thus exposing them to liability before the courts. This concern can be shared by the Commission and by the JFTC in Japan. However, one of the differences between the EU and Japan would be the quantity of the information disclosed under the normal competition procedure. For instance, the Commission's non-confidential decision is generally more detailed and voluminous than the JFTC's published decisions. To rectify this situation, in the reform of 2009 a special rule under Article 83-4 AMA was introduced. This provision allows the court to order the production of documents for an injunction in order to facilitate antitrust actions. In this regard, in the context of private damage actions, disclosure of information can be more efficient because the procedure is based on the Code of Civil Procedure.[34]

Japan has not adopted a US-style system of mandatory pre-trial discovery. However, an order to submit documents can be issued.[35] Under the Law of Civil Procedure, some documents, including information that a lawyer has obtained during his professional performance, should not be disclosed and are excluded from the order to submit documents, except in certain circumstances.[36] It is not clear how this works in practice owing to a lack of detailed provisions and practical cases. In the US, defendants that might otherwise have to pay treble

[32] In January 2012, the Amtsgericht Bonn in the *Pfleiderer* case stated that the Bundeskartellamt was obliged to release a non-confidential version of its decision and any seized documents, but that leniency submissions were not to be disclosed. Beschluss des Amtsgericht Bonn vom 18. January 2012 (Az. 51 Gs 53/09).

[33] See the Commission, supra note 22, Article 8 of a proposal for a Directive.

[34] Law No. 109 of 1996. See Akira Inoue, 'Japan', in Renato Nazzini and Gordon Blanke (eds), *International Competition Litigation: A Multijurisdictional Handbook* (Kluwer Law International, 2012) p. 449.

[35] Articles 220 and 221 of the Code of Civil Procedure.

[36] Article 220 of the Code of Civil Procedure.

damages under the Sherman Act and would in any case face the heavy burden of mandatory discovery often settle cases out of court. By contrast, in the EU and Japan, companies potentially subject to damages actions do not have the same strong incentives to adopt this strategy. Instead, firms sometimes try to delay proceedings, hoping that a claim for damages will be withdrawn. Comparatively, the self-inflicted costs of delay are not as expensive as the discovery procedure in general.

ARBITRABILITY OF COMPETITION LAW

Considerations of balance between the autonomy of arbitration and the effective enforcement of competition rules are common in both the EU and Japan. In Japan, there is no precedent regarding the arbitrability of competition law issues, and discussion of this issue has not been very active, in particular, in relation to the international arbitrability of domestic and foreign competition laws.[37] According to Article 13 (1) of Japan's Arbitration Law, in order for an arbitration to be valid the subject matter should be a civil dispute that may be resolved by a settlement between the parties.[38] Furthermore, the courts which have examined the relationship between infringements under the AMA and the 'public interest' within the meaning of Article 90 of the Civil Code have not rendered clear judgments on this issue. However, since Article 90 of the Civil Code makes conduct contrary to the public interest invalid, and since, generally, an infringement of the AMA should be regarded as being contrary to the public interest, the infringing conduct should be void under Article 90 of the Civil Code. Thus an arbitration award cannot settle a dispute over an infringement of the AMA. Although the Supreme Court has held that contracts in breach of the AMA are not automatically considered void, it is submitted that this judgment does not contradict a general tendency among lower courts to state that AMA infringement is normally contrary to the public interest and therefore void under Article 90 of the Civil Code.[39,40]

[37] See, e.g., Kazuo Tosa, 'Arbitrability of Disputes Concerning the Anti-monopoly Law: Conflict between Regulation on Public Interest and Private Dispute', *Kagawa Hogaku*, **13** (1) (1993) 139.

[38] Arbitration Law, Law 138 of 1 August 2003.

[39] Judgment of the Supreme Court of 20 June 1977.

[40] Tadashi Shiraishi, *Competition Law of Japan* (2nd edn, Yuhikaku, 2009) pp. 650–51.

Overall, the judgments are not clear, and they do not consider AMA infringements automatically to offend the public interest.[41] In the *Toshiba Elevator Technics* case, Toshiba Elevator Technics refused to supply parts necessary for the maintenance of elevators because the plaintiff did not have a service contract for maintenance.[42] Toshiba Elevator Technics, which had a market share of around 90 per cent in the market for the maintenance of Toshiba elevators, was sued by its customers before the Osaka District Court and, having lost at trial, appealed before the Osaka High Court. The appeals court agreed with the lower court that Toshiba Elevator's conduct was illegal under Article 19 AMA. In particular, the Osaka High Court found that the contested behaviour (a refusal to supply as opposed to tying) was causally linked to the claimed damages under Article 709 of Civil Code and consequently rejected the appeal.

In the EU, the arbitrability of EU competition law has been discussed at the level of both the EU and the Member States.[43] In the EU, Article 101 TFEU (and by extension its counterpart, Article 102) is a matter of public policy. Therefore, even if none of the parties in a pending national procedure relies on the EU competition rules, a national judge is obliged to apply those provisions on his own motion if, under national law, he is obliged or allowed *ex proprio motu* to apply *domestic* public policy rules.[44] However, whether this actually occurs in arbitration proceedings is not always clear. In 1982, the Court of Justice held that arbitral tribunals were not courts or tribunals within the meaning of Article 267 TFEU, and hence could not refer to the Court questions of EEC (now EU) law.[45] This partly explains why, as in Japan, case law in the EU is relatively scarce.

Although the arbitrability of competition law tends to be accepted in both the EU and Japan, in practice there is some doubt with regard to the capacity of arbitrators to apply competition rules. This is particularly so given the complex economic evidence and analysis on which competition

---

41 See Shiraishi, ibid. p. 652. See also Gifu Credit Association, judgment of Supreme Court of 20 June 1977.

42 *Toshiba Elevator Technics*, judgment of Osaka High Court of 30 July 1993.

43 For further analysis, see, e.g., Etsuko Kameoka, 'The Arbitrability of the EU Competition Law', *Journal of the Japanese Institute of International Business Law*, **28** (11) (November 2000) 1335–6 (in Japanese).

44 See Case C-126/97, Eco Swiss [1999] ECR I-3055, para. 36; Jonathan Faull and Ali Nikpay, *The EC Law of Competition* (Oxford University Press, 2007) p. 168.

45 *Nordsee Deutsche Hochseefischerei GmbH v Reederei Mond Hochseefischerei Nordstern AG & Co KG* C-102/81 [1982] ECR 1095.

cases often turn. On the other hand, one advantage of arbitration is that, as the parties can appoint an arbitrator suitable to decide an individual dispute, they can choose one with competition law expertise.[46] By contrast, national trial judge and appellate judges tend to be generalists lacking a profound knowledge of competition law, at least until they have handled a sufficient number and range of cases.

A binding arbitral award is immune to appeal on the merits, and it may be enforced all over the world by virtue of an international convention (the New York Convention) that has been concluded by around 150 countries, including all EU Member States.[47] Arbitration also generally entails a flexible and relatively short procedure (sometimes just a matter of weeks), and rules on burden of proof and sufficiency of evidence may be somewhat relaxed, although the opacity of arbitration proceedings makes this difficult to evaluate. In light of the foregoing advantages of arbitration proceedings, in the EU the Commission's Revised Notice on Remedies explicitly provides for the use of arbitration, specifically in connection with access commitments made in order to secure clearance for notified mergers and acquisitions.[48]

CONCLUSION

The general cultures of the EU and Japan have traditionally been less litigious compared to the US. However, with more efficient mechanisms facilitating private damage actions in Europe and Japan, different cultural attitudes are apt to emerge. In the EU, the choice among enforcement mechanisms has thus far been left to the Member States, and the development of private damages actions vary from country to country. As noted above, the diversity among Member States has encouraged forum shopping according to, inter alia, the availability of necessary evidence. While regulatory competition is not always bad, uneven playing fields in the domain of justice may result in unequal treatment for both plaintiffs and defendants, and may produce divergent outcomes. This is currently

---

46 See, e.g., Shunichiro Nakano, 'Claims Based on Antimonopoly Law and International Arbitration', *Arbitration and ADR* (Shojihomu), **7** (May 2012) 112.

47 See the website of the 'New York Arbitration Convention', available at http://www.newyorkconvention.org/new-york-convention-countries/contracting-states.

48 See Commission Notice on remedies acceptable under Council Regulation (EC) No. 139 2004 and under Commission Regulation (EC) No. 802/2004, C 267/1 of 22 October 2008.

one of the major challenges for Europe with regard to private enforcement, and it remains to be seen what the EU legislator will attempt and accomplish in this respect. Japan, for its part, has a unitary legal system and thus does not face the same set of issues.

In Europe, private enforcement is seen as having primarily a compensatory function, but insofar as damages actions present a credible risk of exposure to liability, they are also capable of affecting *ex ante* decisions about whether to comply with or transgress the law. To that extent they may also have a deterrent effect. In Japan, although the deterrent effect of private enforcement is still limited except for public bid rigging cases, where private actions played an important role from the 1990s until 2002 (see above) and where, even under the current system, public entities frequently seek damages.[49]

As regards disclosure of evidence in the possession of competition authorities, as the Court of Justice declared in *Pfleiderer*, the disclosure of documents should be proportionate. The appropriate balance depends on the existing rules of each jurisdiction. In Japan, the rules for disclosure, including access to the files of the JFTC, are not as clear as they are in the EU. The information disclosed during and after an investigation is also generally more limited than in the EU procedure. The problem of discovery may prevent the authorities from cooperating efficiently in multijurisdictional investigations. For example, the risk of disclosure of leniency materials in the EU might discourage Japanese companies under parallel investigations in Japan and Europe from providing the JFTC with a waiver regarding confidentiality of information because the companies may be afraid that the information could be used in private damages actions in an EU Member State. This sensitive issue provides some impetus to seek coordinated global solutions to find mutually optimal enforcement procedures.

[49] See Vande Walle, supra note 3 at 8 and 9. Vande Walle's detailed empirical analysis shows that, although local government and public agencies have recovered tens of billions of yen, firms have obtained much less, and consumers have recovered virtually nothing.

12. International aspects of competition law enforcement

HISTORY OF INTERNATIONAL ASPECTS OF COMPETITION LAW AND POLICY IN RELATION TO JAPAN AND THE EU

The importance of international cooperation is made clear by the benefits enjoyed from the harmonisation of competition law and policy in increasing the numbers of parallel investigations in several jurisdictions.[1] Further, the Commission's severe investigation of competition cases and its power to impose huge fines, its extraterritorial application of EU competition law, and more generally the distinctive character of EU competition law, which occasionally leads to outcomes that diverge from those produced under US law, have been drawing attention in many parts of the world, and Japan is no exception. In more and more multi-jurisdictional mergers and international cartel cases, the EU and Japan conduct parallel investigations and cooperate with each other.

For Japan, international aspects of competition law have been related more to pressure from foreign jurisdictions than to cooperation with foreign agencies. Japan has been subject to foreign pressure for at least the last 20 years.[2] The most well-known source of external pressure, often linked to conflicts in the sphere of international trade, has been the

---

[1] See, e.g., OCED, Discussion on Limitations and Constraints to International Co-operation: European Union, 23 October 2012, DAF/COMP/WP3/WD(2012)41, p. 2 (indicating that the number of the cases in which the Commission cooperates with other agencies is increasing and that investments made in cooperation are justified by the benefits such as coordination of dawn raids, access to information, greater coherence in outcomes and more efficient enforcement).

[2] For example, in November 2010 and February 2011, the US announced the US-Japan Economic Harmonization Initiative. In the context of this initiative, the US called for increased efficiency and transparency of merger review in Japan. See http://www.mac.doc.gov/japan-korea/EHI/EHI%20USG%20Agenda%20Items%202-11-11%20FINAL.pdf, in particular p. 7.

US. But the EU has exerted some direct and indirect influence as well, although this influence has been based more on the form of cooperation than on pressure. In the context of competition policy and enforcement, and in addition to contacts between case teams on specific cases, the EU and Japan launched as early as 1980 an ongoing practice of information exchange meetings for the purpose of enhancing cooperation. Their annual meetings normally include the Commissioner in charge of competition policy and a Commissioner of the JFTC.[3] In this forum the two agencies have emphasised the importance of a common framework to enforce competition policy efficiently, and they have expressed their commitment to setting a good example of cooperation and coordination among developed jurisdictions for the potential inspiration of countries (or regional groupings) with emerging competition law systems.[4]

Modern competition law and policy has thus been harmonised progressively in Japan under pressure and influences from the outside world. However, compared to the moment when Japan opened the country after *sakoku* (period of national isolation) and compared to the time when it adopted the Antimonopoly Act under the pressure of GHQ, Japan has more self-confidence and a broader base of experience. Having played the role of debutante and follower, Japan today understands itself as a leader in this field and actively provides training and promotes the development of competition law in emerging economies, above all in Asia.

At the global level, given the absence of a single world antitrust body, conflicts between the various agencies and the rules they apply should be dealt with in the context of international agreements and networks. The EU and Japan have actively contributed to the convergence and harmonisation of competition enforcement. A significant example, perhaps taken for granted now, is that, together with other major jurisdictions, the EU and Japan established the International Competition Network (the 'ICN').

---

[3] The meeting is currently held annually. The latest meeting took place on 4 July 2012. See http://www.jftc.go.jp/pressrelease/12.july/12070301.pdfsee. One of the topics is international cooperation: http://www.jftc.go.jp/pressrelease/11.july/110713.pdf (in Japanese).

[4] See, e.g., Kazuhiko Takeshima, 'Cooperation and Alliance between Japan and EU in Competition Policy', *Europe*, **257** (Spring 2009) 6; Neelie Kroes, 'Competition Policy Bringing Consumers Benefits', *Europe*, **257** (Spring 2009) 7; Delegation of the European Commission to Japan, 'Press, Public and Cultural Affairs' (in Japanese).

For the EU, the international elements of competition law and policy have shifted: no longer is the key question whether the EU can apply its law extraterritorially against a company in another jurisdiction where the company's anticompetitive conduct has adverse effects in the country concerned; the more pressing issue today is how to achieve optimal cooperation between competition authorities when pursuing international competition infringements.[5] The Commission has used competition policy with the aim of fostering social welfare and economic efficiency and protecting small business, thereby promoting an integrated Common Market and sometimes imposing liability on the US multinational corporations.[6] The globalisation of competition cases sometimes led to divergent approaches and prominent conflicts, in particular between the EU and the US competition authorities. Subsequently, the two sides have spared no effort to avoid contrary case outcomes in the context of bilateral and multilateral cooperation. The EU and the US have concluded not only cooperation agreements but also an Administrative Arrangement on Attendance, which is an understanding about the administrative arrangements to be used when applying their agreements.[7] In addition, the EU-US Best Practices on Cooperation in merger investigations was issued in 2002 and updated in 2011.[8] With these instruments and their occasionally intensive joint practice, the bilateral cooperation regime of the EU and the US is rather more advanced than the one between the EU and Japan. The US and Japan also signed a competition agreement to enhance cooperation and build longstanding relationships between the two jurisdictions in October 1999.[9]

---

5 See, e.g., Richard Whish and David Bailey, *Competition Law* (7th edn, Oxford University Press, 2012) p. 489.

6 See, e.g., Tony A. Freyer, *Antitrust and Global Capitalism,1930–2004* (Cambridge University Press, 2006) p. 399.

7 See Report from the Commission to the Council and the European Parliament on the application of the Agreement between the European Communities and the Government of the United States of America regarding the application of their competition laws 1 January 1999 to 31 December 1999, COM/2000/0618 final, para. 3.

8 See EU-US merger working group, Best Practices on Cooperation in Merger Investigations, available at http://ec.europa.eu/competition/mergers/legislation/best_practices_2011_en.pdf.

9 See the press release of the Federal Trade Commission of 7 October 1999. Available at http://www.ftc.gov/opa/1999/10/japandoj.shtm.

MULTILATERAL COOPERATION IN COMPETITION POLICY

As the first main event of multilateral cooperation in the field of competition, the JFTC has referred to the establishment of the Economic Committee in 1921 as a result of the World Economic Conference in the League of Nations. The Economic Committee was supposed to examine harmful restrictions of competition affecting the free economy.[10] Among other important historical events, in 1980 the United Nations Conference on Trade and Development ('UNCTAD') adopted the Set of Multilaterally Agreed Equitable Principles and Rules for the Control of Restrictive Business Practices,[11] and in late 1961 the OECD Council adopted Resolution 1961 concerning Action in the Field of Restrictive Business Practices and the Establishment of a Committee of Experts.[12] The continuous work done by the OECD Committee on Competition Law and Policy contributed to the work in the WTO as well.[13] Although discussions on competition were introduced in the WTO first in 1996 and later in the Doha Round, and although conclusions were reached concerning an envisaged multilateral competition agreement, the WTO's competition policy agenda was jettisoned and it has not been revived.[14] Although the Doha Round has gone nowhere, the EU and Japan shared the idea that negotiations on multilateral antitrust rules should be included on the WTO agenda.[15]

Currently uniting 114 competition authorities including those of the EU and Japan, the International Competition Network has, in its first ten years, contributed significantly to the harmonisation of global antitrust law and policy. In recent years, the JFTC has raised its profile in the ICN, occupying leadership positions and coordinating the work of competition

---

[10] See JFTC, *AMA Policy Fifty Years History*, Volume 2 (Kosei Torihiki Kyokai, 1997) p. 564 (in Japanese).

[11] See UN Doc.TD/RBP/Conf/10/Rev.2 (22 April 1980).

[12] See OECD/C(61)47(Final).

[13] See JFTC, supra note 10, Volume 1 p. 503.

[14] See, e.g., Jonathan Faull and Ali Nikpay, *The EC Law of Competition* (Oxford University Press, 2007) p. 935.

[15] See, e.g., Frédéric Jenny, 'Globalization, Competition and Trade Policy: Convergence, Divergence and Cooperation', in Clifford A. Jones and Mitsuo Matsushita (eds), *Competition Policy in the Global Trading System* (Kluwer Law International, 2002) p. 295; Clifford A. Jones and Mitsuo Matsushita, 'Global Antitrust in the Millennium Round: The Ways Forward', in Jones and Matsushita, ibid.

agencies in various areas of policy.[16] Although the ICN has drawn great attention in the last decade, UNCTAD remains significant as a forum for the exchange of information on competition policy developments, catering especially to developing countries.[17]

BILATERAL COOPERATION IN COMPETITION POLICY

With regard to the investigation of individual cases on the basis of bilateral cooperation, the EU has richer experience not only because it has dealt with some landmark cases under the EU-US cooperation agreement but also because the Commission conducts its investigations in close cooperation with the competition authorities of the EU Member States.[18] The EU has concluded competition cooperation agreements with several other countries, including Japan. Cooperation with the US has become particularly important for the EU since, as noted above, the two jurisdictions have sometimes issued conflicting decisions on several important merger cases.[19] The most prominent examples have been Boeing/McDonnell Douglas and GE/Honeywell; more recently, differences emerged in relation to the proposed merger between Deutsche Börse and NYSE Euronext. By contrast, there is no case that indicates a significant level of divergence between the EU and Japan. The JFTC has hesitated to enforce its competition law in cases arising outside its territory, and it tries to avoid situations in which its decision contradicts those of other jurisdictions. However, the *BHP Billiton/Rio Tinto* case – which involved only non-Japanese companies – signalled a change of the JFTC's attitude. Meanwhile, merger procedures and analysis are being

---

[16] For instance, the ICN held the first Advocacy Working Group in Paris on 26 and 27 October 2012 to develop practical tools and to facilitate sharing of experience among agencies. See, e g., Marianne Faessel-Kahn, 'ICN-Advocacy Working Group – Workshop: Le premier Workshop de l'ICN Advocacy Working Group se tien à Paris à l'initiative de l'autorité de la concurrence', Concurrences n°1-2013, Chroniques Politique internationale, pp. 230–32.

[17] See, e.g., François Souty, CNUCED: Le Groupe intergouvernemental d'experts du droit et de la politique de la Concurrence pousuit le mouvement impulsé à Doha par la Ministérialle en avril 2012 et montre que les organismes de lONU n'ésitent pas à concurrencer d'autres organismes internationaux, Concurrence n°4-2012, Chroniques Politique internationale, pp. 195–200.

[18] See Article 11 of Regulation No. 1/2003.

[19] See, e.g., Van Bael and Bellis, *Competition Law of the European Community* (5th edn, Kluwer Law International, 2010) pp. 773–6.

harmonised in the world's main jurisdictions to avoid divergence to the extent possible. With regard to the JFTC and the European Commission, setting up a collaborative framework for the two agencies is useful, as it facilitates cooperation during their investigations and facilitates compatible decisions.

In addition to multilateral cooperation, Japan concluded competition cooperation agreements with the US in 1999, with the EU in 2003 and with Canada in 2005. The EU concluded its cooperation agreement with the US in 1991 (refined in 1998) and with Canada in 1999. The EU also concluded cooperation agreements with South Korea and Switzerland.[20] These agreements are helpful in particular for international cartel investigations. As a consequence of such cooperation, and largely owing also to JFTC's leniency programme, investigations into international cartel cases have become more frequent.[21] However, the EU-Japan cooperation agreement is not considered a 'second generation agreement' allowing the exchange of confidential information between the agencies; this issue will be subject to further discussions.[22]

As explained above, in addition to contacts between case-teams on specific cases, the European Commission and JFTC have organised regular information exchange meetings since 1980. In the context of these meetings the agencies confirm the importance of a harmonised and fair framework to enforce competition policy efficiently. They also strive to provide an indicative model of cooperation to inspire or be emulated by the authorities of emerging competition law jurisdictions.[23,24]

---

20 Agreement between the European Community and the Government of the Republic of Korea concerning cooperation on anticompetitive activities, OJ L202 of 4 August 2009, pp. 36–41 and Agreement between the European Union and the Swiss Confederation concerning cooperation on the application of their competition laws (2013). The Commission's press release of IP/13/444 of 17/05/2013.

21 In past cases involving Japanese companies, such as the *Vitamins* cartel case, the JFTC was only able to issue a warning without any sanctions. Other jurisdictions investigated the *Vitamins* case under their leniency programmes, and heavy sanctions were doled out.

22 See, e.g., Akira Negishi and Masayuki Funada, *Japanese Antitrust Law* (4th edn, Yuhikaku, 2010) p. 68.

23 See supra note 3.

24 See Takeshima and Kroes, supra note 4.

In 2003, the EU and Japan signed a framework agreement providing for the coordination of enforcement activities and the reciprocal exchange of information.[25,26] Under the EU-Japan agreement, one party can request that the other party initiate enforcement action in a specific case. Each party is required to give careful consideration to the important interests of the other in the course of its enforcement activities. Examples of practical cooperation are numerous. Notably, in the *Panasonic/Sanyo* merger case and in the *BHP Billiton/Rio Tinto* case, the Commission and JFTC actively exchanged information.[27] In *Panasonic/Sanyo*,[28] the Commission's case-team contacted the Japanese and US agencies at a very early stage of the investigation (prior to notification), and during the procedure a great deal of information was exchanged among the three authorities. This was facilitated by their respective bilateral agreements.[29] The parties also granted a waiver to the Commission to enable it to share confidential information with the Japanese and US authorities.

In practice, the exchange of information and cooperation between case-teams of the Commission and JFTC mainly concern cartel cases while the majority of contacts between the Commission and the US agencies are related to merger cases. When BHP Billiton sought to acquire shares in Rio Tinto (both Australian and UK companies), the case-teams of the JFTC and the Commission frequently exchanged information, including by conference calls and by email, in order to discuss procedural progress, analysis of the case and prioritisation of the issues.[30]

---

[25] See JFTC's website at http://www.jftc.go.jp/en/international_relations/agreements/pdf/J-ECagreement.pdf.

[26] For further details regarding the Agreement, see Yves Devellennes and Giorgios Kiriazis, 'Enhanced EU/Japan Cooperation: The Commission Proposes to Conclude an Agreement', *Competition Policy Newsletter* (2002–3), pp. 25–8, available at http://ec.europa.eu/competition/publications/cpn/2002_3_25.pdf.

[27] See JFTC press release of 13 July 2011.

[28] *Panasonic/Sanyo* COMP/M. 5421 and *BHP Billiton/Rio Tinto* COMP/M. 4985.

[29] See, e.g., Rita Devai, Tobias P. Maass, Dimitrios Magos and Robert Thomas, 'Merger Case M.5421 Panasonic/Sanyo: Batteries Included or "Lost in Translation"?', *Competition Policy Newsletter*, **1** (2010) 60. According to the article, cooperation with the Chinese authorities was not possible given the absence of a bilateral agreement between the EU and China. (Subsequently, a Memorandum of Understanding between the Commission and the Chinese authorities was concluded.)

[30] See the presentation entitled 'Cooperation of competition agencies on merger control' by Katsunori Inaguma, the JFTC Merger Unit case-handler in

Moreover, in addition to its competition agreement with the US, Japan has also entered into competition policy arrangements in Economic Partnership Agreements (EPAs) with Singapore, Malaysia and Peru. Another EPA is envisaged with Australia. The EPAs that have been concluded provide not only for general cooperation but also for the notification to the other party of enforcement actions that affect that party's important interests.[31] Further, the current Japanese government (under Abe) currently intends to join negotiations on the Trans-Pacific Partnership ('TPP') with the US, Australia, Singapore and seven other countries. To this end the government has set up 24 working groups to examine a variety of issues relating to the TPP. The market covered by the TPP would occupy approximately 40 per cent of the world market while the EU market covers 26 per cent of the global market.[32] One of the working groups is responsible for competition policy; it is instructed to discuss enforcement issues, improvements in competition policy and cooperation among competition agencies to prevent the benefits from the TPP from being harmed by anticompetitive activities including cartels.[33] The advantages of successful negotiations would include greater cooperation between Japan and countries with whom it does not yet have any competition agreement, and expansion of the activities covered by the EPAs with Singapore and Malaysia. Similarly, if the envisaged EPA between Japan and Australia stops short of providing for detailed competition cooperation between their authorities, the future competition chapter of the TPP can fill the gap.

---

the *BHP Billiton/Rio Tinto* case, International Competition Seminar held by Keidanren, 'Merger Control in a Global Economy', Tokyo, 22 January 2009 (See also Chapter 7 on mergers in this volume). Mr Inaguma also explained the need to avoid incoherent decisions among the agencies and to decrease the burden of companies to encourage cooperation with the JFTC and other agencies.

[31] For the Japan/Singapore EPA, see http://www.mofa.go.jp/region/asia-paci/singapore/jsepa-1.pdf. For the Japan/Malaysia EPA, see http://www.mofa.go.jp/region/asia-paci/malaysia/epa/content.pdf. For the Peru/Japan EPA, see http://www.mofa.go.jp/region/latin/peru/epa201105/pdfs/jpepa_ba_e.pdf.

[32] See 'TPP negotiations: advanced team making steady progress', *Nihonkeizai Shinbun*, (13 March 2013).

[33] For the TPP negotiations, with particular reference to competition policy, see http://www.npu.go.jp/policy/policy08/pdf/20111014/20111021_1-9.pdf.

EXTRATERRITORIAL APPLICATION OF COMPETITION RULES

For a long time, it was assumed that any agreement with anticompetitive effects in the Common Market was to be considered illegal under European competition law even if it was concluded outside the European Community (as it then was) by foreign companies that did not conduct business activities in any of the Member States.[34] However, even today the Court of Justice (ECJ) has not yet specifically recognised the 'effects doctrine'. In the cases decided by the ECJ, it has always been possible to find other grounds on which to base jurisdiction, such as the single economic entity doctrine.[35] According to this doctrine, affiliate companies located abroad may be subject to EU jurisdiction if, for example, their subsidiaries are located within the EU.[36] In the late 1980s, the Court adopted an 'implementation doctrine', which allows the exercise of jurisdiction if an agreement concluded abroad has been implemented within the EU.[37] Further, although there is some debate about whether the Court of First Instance ('CFI' – now the General Court) did apply the effect doctrine, it seemed to confirm in the *Gencor* case that the effects doctrine applies.[38] Thus, in the EU there may be two standards: one under the *Wood Pulp* case for cartels and one under the *Gencor* case for merger control.

Already at a fairly early stage, JFTC was obliged to consider international aspects of competition law enforcement. Beginning in the 1970s, the export of cheap Japanese products created problems and tensions in foreign countries. Car exports to the US were a telling example. As the automobile industry tried to find a way to export cars without causing trade friction, the Ministry for International Trade and Industry (MITI) guided companies to restrict their exports under its 'orderly marketing'

---

[34] See, e.g., Valentine Korah, *An Introductory Guide to EC Competition Law and Practice* (9th edn, Hart Publishing, 2007) p. 35 Wood Pulp VI/29.725.

[35] For its part, the Commission has long taken the view that EU law recognises the effects doctrine in competition cases. See the Commission's XIth report on Competition Policy (1981), points 34–42. See also, e.g., Whish and Bailey, supra note 5, pp. 495–6.

[36] See Cases 48/69 etc., *ICI v Commission (Dyestuffs)* [1972] ECR 619.

[37] Joined Cases C-89, 104, 114, 116, 117 and 125-129/85, *Ahlstrom and Others v E.C. Commission* (Wood Pulp Cartel) [1988] ECR 5193.

[38] T102/96, *Gencor Ltd v Commission* [1999] ECR II-793. See also Patrick Capps, Malcolm Evans and Stratos Konstadindis, *Asserting Jurisdiction: International and European Legal Approaches* (Hart Publishing, 2003) p. 116.

policy. The JFTC considered that an export cartel was an unreasonable restraint of trade, and that Article 6 AMA was applicable to an export cartel fixing quantity, price and region with anticompetitive effects in a foreign market.[39,40,41] Furthermore, there are several cases, including *Nihon Kogaku*, in which JFTC declared that illegal conduct by a foreign company is subject to the AMA if it affects the Japanese market. While the AMA does not refer directly to extraterritorial application, Article 6 AMA prohibits any international agreement that constitutes an unreasonable restraint of trade or unfair trade practices.[42]

In Japan, the issue of *procedural* extraterritorial application of the law is often discussed separately from the issue of *substantive* extraterritorial application of the law. This has led to criticism against JFTC's indirect extraterritorial application of the AMA. As noted above, Article 6 AMA prohibits unfair trade practices and unreasonable restraints of trade that arise from international agreements. However, JFTC issued infringement decisions only against Japanese parties willing to accept them, a reflection of sympathy for Japanese parties who were often perceived as being subject to unfavourable clauses imposed by foreign parties. Thus, without being provided a sufficient opportunity to defend itself, the foreign party simply saw its agreement with the Japanese party declared anticompetitive. According to critics, this 'indirect extraterritorial application' of the AMA was incompatible with the fundamental requirements of due process.

---

39 *Synthetic Fiber* cartel case, JFTC decision of 27 December 1972.

40 An export cartel may be exempted under very strict conditions, following the amendment of the Export and Import Transaction Act in 1997. See also Negishi and Funada, supra note 22, pp. 161–2.

41 Professors Fox and Janow recently analysed an export cartel case involving Chinese companies from a competition and trade perspective. See Eleanor Fox and Merit Janow, 'China, the WTO, and State-Sponsored Export Cartels: Where Trade and Competition Ought to Meet', *e-Competitions*, N° 4-2012, pp. 5–7. Japan takes a stricter approach towards outbound export cartels than the EU does and tries to cover export cartels under the AMA, thus avoiding trade issues.

42 In the field of merger control, taking account of the JFTC's report of 1990 and of the 1998 amendment of Chapter 4 of the AMA it is now established that the AMA interpretation allows extraterritorial application. See JFTC, *Dumping and Competition Policy: Extraterritorial Application of AMA* (1990) p. 67; Mitsuo Matsushita, 'Recent Case on Extraterritorial Application of Japanese Antimonopoly Law', *Journal of the Japanese Institute of International Business Law*, **26** (11) (1998) 1131–8.

For instance, in the *Amano/Novo* case, after receiving a distribution agreement between Japanese and Danish pharmaceutical companies, JFTC issued a decision against only Amano, the Japanese company, for accepting an agreement with anticompetitive clauses such as resale price maintenance.[43] Amano accepted the JFTC decision but then Novo filed an appeal. But the Supreme Court confirmed the JFTC decision, holding, inter alia, that the Danish company (Novo) did not have standing to challenge the JFTC decision, because it was not an addressee of the decision.[44] This ruling was plainly controversial given that JFTC's decision allegedly caused Novo injury in fact and thus it should have been provided with an opportunity to defend itself.[45] In this way, the fact that JFTC had not enforced the AMA 'extraterritorially' (in a procedural sense) ironically turned out to be unfavourable to a company located overseas.

JFTC's reticence to enforce the AMA directly against foreign companies was mirrored by provisions in Japanese procedural law, which were inadequate for investigations against such companies.[46] Occasionally, however, such obstacles were overcome. In the *Nordion* case of 1998, JFTC issued its decision against a multinational company located in Canada that had concluded an illegal exclusive purchasing agreement for the Japanese market with a Japanese distributor in Tokyo.[47] Since Nordion did not have any office in Japan, JFTC sent its objections to an attorney who represented the company in Japan. Subsequently it issued an infringement decision, which the company accepted.[48]

In terms of application of substantive law, JFTC's position seems to be shifting from the implementation doctrine to the effects doctrine, although JFTC has not had the opportunity to announce its position officially. In the *Nordion* case, the agreement affected the Japanese market and was concluded in Japan; it was therefore unclear whether JFTC proceeded on the basis of the effects doctrine or the implementation doctrine.[49] The interpretation of these doctrines is strict, and

---

43 JFTC decision of 12 January 1970.

44 Supreme Court judgment of 28 November 1975.

45 See, e.g., Tadashi Shiraishi, *Competition Law of Japan* (2nd edn, Yuhikaku, 2009) p. 407.

46 Until the 2002 amendment of the AMA, Japanese procedural law did not provide for the delivery of documents such as decisions to persons located overseas.

47 *Nordion*, JFTC decision of 3 September 1998.

48 See, e.g., Freyer, supra note 6, p. 242.

49 See Negishi and Funada, supra note 22, pp. 63–4.

international cartels involving foreign companies or foreign-to-foreign mergers often may not be covered, even though similar conduct by Japanese companies has been caught by other jurisdictions, including notably the EU and the US. In the Boeing/McDonnell Douglas merger of 1997, although Japan's flagship airline company was a major purchaser of passenger aircraft manufactured by the parties, and although Japan was thus considered one of the jurisdictions whose market was substantially affected, the AMA did not allow JFTC to investigate the transaction. Under the AMA, JFTC was entitled to conduct an investigation only if at least one of the parties was Japanese.[50] For instance, although JFTC investigated a merger between foreign companies such as Johnson & Johnson and Guidant Corporation, they had subsidiaries based in Japan.[51] The limitations of JFTC's jurisdiction and of the related procedural/judicial framework (for example with regard to the execution of decisions) drew sharp criticism from the Japanese community, and ultimately the AMA was amended to enable JFTC to investigate foreign-to-foreign mergers affecting the Japanese market;[52] consequently, mergers similar to the Boeing/McDonnell Douglas are today handled differently.[53]

Although the US and other jurisdictions tend to follow the effects doctrine, it is not clear that Japan has embraced this doctrine. The first case in which the JFTC enforced the AMA extraterritorially against foreign companies (with no subsidiaries or agents located in Japan) was

---

[50] As a result of the 1998 reform of the AMA, foreign-to-foreign mergers became subject to Japanese merger control.

[51] JFTC decision of 9 December 2005. Acquisition of Guidant Corporation by Johnson & Johnson (2005). The JFTC exchanged information with other agencies including the European Commission, and approved a transaction between US companies with commitments. Another example is an acquisition of Maxtor Corporation by Seagate Technology, where the geographic market was defined as the world market. As for Maxtor Corporation/Seagate Technology, See JFTC, Major Business Integrations in FY2006, June 19 2007. Available at http://www.jftc.go.jp/en/pressreleases/yearly_2007/jun/2007_june_19.files/2007-June-19.pdf.

[52] See supra note 50. Also see, e.g., Hiroyuki Kita, Chapter 6, 'Application of AMA to Foreign Business: In Particular Articles 6, 19 and 3 First Paragraph', *International Enforcement of Compeittion Law: Extraterritorial Application in Global Era* (in Kazuhiro Tsuchida) (Nihon Hyoron Sya, 2012) p. 127.

[53] See, e.g., Shuya Hayashi, 'The Goals of Japanese Competition Law', in Josef Drexl, Laurence Idot and Joël Monéger (eds), *Economic Theory and Competition Law* (Edward Elgar, 2009) p. 54.

the *Marine Hoses* international cartel case of 2008.[54] In this case, JFTC issued cease and desist orders against several companies including British, French and Italian companies, and one Japanese firm. Although this case was considered to be based on the effects doctrine, the foreign companies, which had not supplied Japanese customers, were not required to pay surcharges. According to the terms of the cartel, the Japanese firm and the non-Japanese companies agreed that the non-Japanese participants would not enter the Japanese market. From a typical antitrust perspective this sort of market division would be seen as having distinct effects on the Japanese market as compared with an appropriate counterfactual scenario. However, since, in Japan, surcharges are calculated on the basis of actual turnover from the domestic market, and since the foreign companies did not generate any turnover in Japan, it was formally impossible for the JFTC to fine them. Specifically, the JFTC calculated surcharges based on turnover related only to sales of hoses actually ordered by Japanese purchasers.

In contrast to the outcome in Japan, the European Commission had no difficulty fining the participants in the *Marine Hoses* case, with the exception of the successful (Japanese) immunity applicant. The Commission mentioned that, in calculating the fines, it took into account the value of the undertakings' sales of the goods or services to which the infringement related in the relevant geographic area within the EEA.[55] In the *Gas Insulated Switchgear* cartel case, several Japanese companies had to pay high fines (in total, the Commission imposed fines of 750 million euros[56]) even though they had agreed under the cartel not to enter the European market.[57] Since the Japanese companies had not actually engaged in any activities in Europe, the Commission's decision generated a feeling of unfairness. The fact that more and more Japanese companies are being fined in other jurisdictions, coupled with the fact that some executives have been convicted in foreign criminal proceedings and are facing prison sentences, has caused some concern. The controversial enforcement approaches of foreign jurisdictions have informed discussions regarding the extraterritorial application of the AMA.[58]

---

54 See *Marine Hoses*, JFTC decision of 20 February 2008.

55 See *Marine Hoses*, COMP/39406.

56 On appeal, the fines were partially reduced.

57 See *Gas Insulated Switchgear*, COMP F/38.899,

58 See, e.g., Masahiko Hoshi, 'Extraterritorial application of AMA: developments of theories on extraterritorial application of competition law in Europe and USA as well as their influence and developments in Japan' (23 March 2011). http://hermes-ir.lib.hit-u.ac.jp/rs/bitstream/10086/19081/2/0201100201.pdf.

It seems that the JFTC now stands increasingly ready to impose fines on foreign companies. In 2009, the JFTC not only issued a cease and desist order against foreign cathode ray tube companies; it also imposed fines based on turnover derived in overseas markets. In the same year, in the *BHP Billiton/Rio Tinto* merger case, JFTC tried to send a request for information to the merger parties concerning their iron ore and material ore businesses.

CONCLUSION

As more and more jurisdictions adopt their own competition laws, anticompetitive conduct may be more likely to be subject to foreign rules including leniency regimes, and companies involved in illegal activity may be exposed to criminal and/or administrative sanctions and private claims for damages actions in different jurisdictions. Moreover, several factors accentuate the importance of competition law in the international arena. These include the overall decline of trade barriers (especially tariffs), the revolution of communications technology, the removal of restrictions on foreign investment, the (now deeply contested) turn toward deregulation and the adoption of generally more market-friendly policies.[59] International cooperation among the competition agencies will thus become even more important, and multilateral fora for cooperation will continue to nurture the development and convergence of competition policies and the exchange of information. In these fora, as the number of countries that adopt competition laws increases, the role of jurisdictions with a long history of enforcement will change. At the same time, inter-agency cooperation will become increasingly common. As regards Japan and the EU, the number of cases pursued by parallel investigation is increasing. Bilateral cooperation between JFTC and the Commission can be expected to result in more efficient procedures and a reduced risk of inconsistent case outcomes. However, in terms of exchange of evidence, it is not certain if Japan will be ready to officially sign an agreement in the near future such as the agreement between the EU and Switzerland that includes provisions on the exchange of evidence obtained by the competition agencies when they investigate the same case.[60]

---

59 See, e.g., Francisco Gonzalez de Cossio, 'International Aspects of Competition Law', available at http://www.unis.edu.gt/ap/fetch/international-competition.pdf.

60 See the Commission's press release supra note 20.

As noted above, cooperation between the Commission and the US antitrust agencies has intensified, in particular in merger control as a result of bitter experiences with divergent outcomes in high-profile merger investigations. Yet despite this increasingly close cooperation, there are still significant differences on important issues between these two leading competition law jurisdictions. Furthermore, other jurisdictions are not necessarily following the convergent path that the EU and US authorities have created, and the attitudes towards some issues, such as the treatment of joint ventures and minority shareholdings, are not aligned even in main jurisdictions. In the field of private practice, more and more Japanese law firms are taking the role of a 'hub' with respect to multi-jurisdictional cases involving Japanese companies. They coordinate the companies' strategies regarding competition investigations in several jurisdictions, including their strategies in relation to marker/leniency applications and merger notifications, so that the companies can be defended efficiently and coherently. The more divergent the enforcement policies of foreign agencies, the more important the coordination function of such firms. Although international cooperation may appear to be a policy issue and may not seem to have direct impact on a specific case, it certainly does affect the practice of competition law and the way companies are obliged to devise their defence strategies.

13. Conclusion

Competition law did not grow organically in Japan but was suddenly implanted. The original economic culture was based on cooperation between public administration and private business, and on the protection and promotion of monopoly. This equilibrium had been in place since the time when Japan opened the country to foreigners – and thereby to capitalism – in the Meiji era. It was not part of Japanese culture to fight against anticompetitive activities through public enforcement. Thus, the success of Japanese competition policy was not guaranteed but was rather risky and challenging.[1]

The gradual and subtle ways in which Japanese antitrust policy has been transformed since the introduction of the AMA is unique; it cannot easily be compared to evolutionary trends seen in other jurisdictions. It is sometimes argued that the regulatory culture in Japan is basically bureaucratic, whereas the AMA presupposes a more legalistic style of enforcement.[2] One reason why the enforcement culture of the JFTC appears to be evolving from bureaucratic to legalistic may be the influence of EU law and procedure. Through a series of reforms in recent years, the procedure governing the application of Japanese competition law has gradually become more adversarial and transparent. Formal decisions rather than oral announcements are now being issued. Although the momentum driving the evolution does not come exclusively from Japan's own initiative but has largely stemmed from exogenous factors (as has often happened in Japanese history), it is also true that Japan has become increasingly motivated to examine foreign models, especially that of the EU, and to incorporate desired elements into the Japanese system.[3]

[1] Toru Miyazaki, 'The Past and Future of Antimonopoly Policy: After Reading "Antimonopoly Policy of Japan and Industrial Organisation" written by Misono et al.', *Keizai Hyoron* (Nihon Hyoronsya), **May 1988**, p. 100.

[2] See, e.g., Harry First, 'Antitrust Enforcement in Japan', *Antitrust Law Journal*, **64** (1995) 137–82 at 173–82.

[3] From a linguistic point of view, a number of the Japanese words that mean internal evolution in the society and mentality from the end of the eighteenth century to the first half of the nineteenth century were generally endogenous.

The evolution of Japanese competition law and policy is based partly on a balance between certain perceptions of the national interest that are supported by Japanese industry and the need for adaptation that is imposed mainly by processes of globalisation. There is also, famously in Japan, a balance between competition policy and industrial policy. At present, industrial policy is pursued so as to favour the development of economic power and Japan's ability to cope with competitive pressures. For this purpose, enforcement of competition policy should be strict and enhance incentives for compliance: if commercial wrongdoing escapes sanctions owing to incomplete enforcement, and if infringers maintain harmful practices, from a medium and long-term perspective this will damage the Japanese economy. Fair competition is a crucial driver of a better functioning economy.[4]

Zen Buddhism was introduced into Japan by Dogen, a priest in the thirteenth century. As opposed to Confucianism, which became known to the Europeans, Zen Buddhism did not have a significant effect on European culture and philosophy, in particular in the early stage of its history.[5] Dogen preached that simple practices bring the supreme law and offer freedom from confusion and concern. Dogen's teachings circulated widely, mainly among the general citizens, and have been incorporated within the current modern philosophy. In his *Treasury of the Eye of the True Dharma*, Dogen explained that we can accept the actual state of affairs with which we are confronted if we are spiritually enlightened through Zazen, a kind of meditation. Although this attitude has often been observed in the daily life of the Japanese people, a temporary passive attitude can be a preparation of creative action in practice. It may

---

These new concepts were translated directly from Western languages into Japanese, in particular during a particular period of 20 years since the end of the eighteenth century. For instance, the word 'evolution', which did not exist in Japan before the nineteenth century, was translated as *kakumei* with the help of a concept originating in a Confucian text. See, e.g., Robert Calvet, 'L'adoption des concepts politiques occidentaux dans le japon de Meiji (1868–1912)', in Martine Raibaurd and François Souty (eds), *Europe-Asie: Echanges, Ethiques et Marchés, XVIIe–XXIe siècles* (Les Indes Savantes, 2004) p. 167 et seq.

4 See, e.g., then JFTC Chairman Kazuhiko Takeshima's answer to the question as to the role of competition policy in an interview. Top Runner No. 5, 1441 *Jurist* 3, 2 (2012) (in Japanese).

5 See the introduction in Chapter 1 (this volume). See also Frédéric Lenoir, *Petit traité d'histoire des religions* (Plon, 2008) p. 204. A Japanese Zen Buddhist teacher founded the Association Zen Internationale in 1970 in order to disseminate the tradition of Zen philosophy in Europe.

be that the calm observation of unfolding events appears tantamount to inaction from a European perspective. However, as we saw, Japanese people do not merely quietly accept the status quo to identify problems; they also ponder solutions and analyse similar problems that arise in other jurisdictions.

Although the majority of Japan's population are considered to be Buddhists, their belief in practice is syncretic and consists of a mixture of Buddhism, Shintoism and Confucianism. Overall, Japanese history is based partly on a gradual incorporation of elements of culture that originated on the European Continent but that were often very different from their original character. However, Japan also sometimes took deliberate steps to isolate itself from outside influence, as it did during the *sakoku* period. In other words, it is a deeply ingrained part of Japan's custom to syncretise influences of foreign origin, although adapting them to its own culture can take time.

Against this background, the EU's influence on Japanese competition policy has been increasingly significant. While Japan has been politically and economically influenced by the US for more than 60 years since the end of World War II, and while American antitrust left a distinct mark on the AMA, Japan has started gradually to accommodate the European competition model as well. At first glance this may seem like a new development but, as seen in the introduction to this book, Japan and Europe have an even longer history of cultural and scientific exchanges than do Japan and the US.

It has also been seen that, as opposed to US antitrust law, where efficiency and net output effects are central, EU competition law emphasises openness and access to markets.[6] This ethic, and the greater level of detail found in European law, may more comfortably fit the Japanese competition enforcement culture. The sympathetic reception of European influence in this regard is likely to be facilitated by the fact that, as we have also seen, the basic Japanese legal system was in the nineteenth century largely modelled on those of the Continent.[7]

---

[6] Eleanor Fox, 'Perspectives on Change: Antitrust in No One's World', *Antitrust*, **27** (1) (Fall 2012). Japan, which under pressure from the US and the EU has been making efforts to open its markets (and which today finds itself with a significant trade deficit), has apparently found the EU model to be more useful in responding to these pressures.

[7] Professor Fox (ibid.) has identified the reasons why younger antitrust jurisdictions are more attracted by the EU model than the US model. One of these reasons is the greater level of detail that appears in the European Treaty and European regulations, as compared with the 'open vessels' of US statutory

A related theme of this book has been Japan's tendency, over time and under the influence of other jurisdictions, to achieve greater levels of transparency and fairness. Processes of convergence in competition – which should not be understood as homogeneity – are seen in terms of not only substance but also enforcement activities and policy. The harmonisation of competition law regimes, to the extent that it is feasible and consistent with local conditions, has advantages for both enforcement agencies and for internationally active companies.

Japan continues to move forward with competition policy reform efforts, just as the EU does. The economic, cultural and legal aspects of globalisation have influenced the process of the reform of Japanese competition law in a positive sense. The role of competition law and policy in Japan and in the EU has never been more important than now.

---

law. Although Japan is not a younger antitrust jurisdiction, the same reasoning may well apply to reforms in Japan as well.

Bibliography

Arcelin, Linda, *Droit de la Concurrence: Les pratiques anticoncurrentielles en droit interne et communautaire* (Presses Universitaires de Rennes, 2009)

Atsuya, Joji, *The Introduction to Antimonopoly Law* (Nihonkeizai Shinbunsya, 2012)

Basedow, Jürgen, Stéphanie Francq and Laurence Idot, *International Antitrust Litigation: Conflict of Laws and Coordination* (Hart Publishing, 2012)

Brunet, François and Guy Canivet, *Le Nouveau Droit Communautaire de la Concurrence* (L.G.D.J., 2008)

Capps, Patrick, Malcolm Evans and Stratos Konstadindis, *Asserting Jurisdiction: International and European Legal Approaches* (Hart Publishing, 2003)

Drexl, Josef, Laurence Idot and Joël Monéger (eds), *Economic Theory and Competition Law* (Edward Elgar, 2009)

Ehlermann, Claus-Dieter and Mel Marquis (eds), *European Competition Law Annual 2009: Evaluation of Evidence and Its Judicial Review* (Hart Publishing, 2011)

Faull, Jonathan and Ali Nikpay (eds), *The EC Law of Competition* (Oxford University Press, 2007)

Fine, Frank L., *The EC Competition Law on Technology Licensing* (Sweet & Maxwell, 2006)

Foer, Albert A. and Jonathan W. Cuneo (eds), *The International Handbook on Private Enforcement of Competition Law* (Edward Elgar, 2010)

Freyer, Tony A., *Antitrust and Global Capitalism 1930–2004* (Cambridge University Press, 2006)

Gerber, David J., *Global Competition: Law, Markets, and Globalization* (Oxford University Press, 2010)

Gerber, David J., *Law and Competition in Twentieth Century Europe: Protecting Prometheus* (Clarendon Press, 1998)

Gohara, Nobuo, *Japanese Structure of Antimonopoly Law* (Seibunsya, 2004)

Hadley, Eleanor M., *Antitrust in Japan* (Princeton University Press, 1970)

Haley, John O., *Antitrust in Germany and Japan: The First Fifty Years, 1947–1998* (University of Washington Press, 2001)

Hildebrand, Doris, *Economic Analysis of Vertical Agreements: A Self-Assessment* (Kluwer Law International, 2005)

Iyori, Hiroshi and Akinori Uesugi, *The Antimonopoly Laws and Policies of Japan* (Federal Legal Publications, 1994)

Jephcott, Mark, *Law of Cartels* (Jordan Publishing, 2011)

JFTC, *AMA Policy Fifty Years History*, Volumes 1 and 2 (Kosei Torihiki Kyokai, 1997)

Kazuhiro, Tsuchida, *International Enforcement of Competition Law: Extraterritorial Application in Global Era* (Nihon Hyoron Sya, 2012)

Korah, Valentine, *An Introductory Guide to EC Competition Law and Practice* (Hart Publishing, 2007)

Lowe, Philip and Mel Marquis (eds), *European Competition Law Annual 2010: Merger Control in European and Global Perspective* (Hart Publishing, 2013)

Matsushita, Mitsuo, *International Trade and Competition Law in Japan* (Oxford University Press, 1993)

Matsushita, Mitsuo (ed.), *EC Economic Law* (Yuhikaku, 1993)

Matsushita, Mitsuo and John D. Davis, *Introduction to Japanese Antimonopoly Law* (Yuhikaku, 1990)

Matsushita, Mitsuo and Clifford Jones (eds), *Competition Policy in the Global Trading System* (Kluwer Law International, 2002)

McEwin, R. Ian, *Intellectual Property, Competition Law and Economics in Asia* (Hart Publishing, 2011)

Monti, Girogio, *EC Competition Law* (Cambridge University Press, 2007)

Murakami, Masahiro, *Antimonopoly Act* (Iwanami Shoten Publishers, 2005)

Nazzini, Renato and Gordon Blanke (eds), *International Competition Litigation: A Multijurisdictional Handbook* (Kluwer Law International, 2012)

Negishi, Akira and Masayuki Funada, *Japanese Antitrust Law* (Yuhikaku, 2010)

Noland, Marcus and Howard Pack, *Industrial Policy in an Era of Globalization: Lessons from Asia* (Institute for International Economics, 2003)

Ochi, Yasumi, *Japan, U.S. and European Competition Law* (Shojihomu, 2005)

Okada, Yosuke and Shuya Hayashi (eds), *Economic Impact of the Antimonopoly Law: Case Studies in Recent Court and Tribunal Decisions* (University of Tokyo Press, 2009)

Raibaurd, Martine and François Souty (eds), *Europe-Asie: Echanges, Ethiques et Marchés, XVIIe–XXIe siècles* (Les Indes Savantes, 2004)

Richardson, J. David and Edward M. Graham (eds), *Global Competition Policy* (Institute for International Economics, 1997)

Roth, Peter and Vivien Rose (eds), *Bellamy & Child's European Community Law of Competition* (Oxford University Press, 2008)

Rubini, Luca (ed.), *Microsoft on Trial: Legal and Economic Analysis of a Transatlantic Antitrust Case* (Edward Elgar, 2010)

Shiraishi, Tadashi, *Competition Law of Japan* (Yuhikaku, 2009)

Souty, François, *Le droit et la politique de la concurrence de l'Union européenne* (Montchrestien, 2013)

Spiritus-Dassesse, Anne, Cyril Nourissat and Robert Wtterwulghe, *Le juge de commerce face au droit communautaire de la concurrence* (Faculté Universitaire Saint-Louis, 2007)

Takeda, Kuninobu, *Merger Control and Efficiency Defense* (Taga Shuppan, 2001)

Takigawa, Toshiaki, *Competition Laws and Policies in Japan, US and EU* (Seirin Shoin, 2010)

Uesugi, Akinori, *Handbook on International Competition Practices* (Shojihomu, 2012)

Van Bael, Ivo, *Due Process in EU Competition Proceedings* (Kluwer Law International, 2011)

Van Bael, Ivo and Jean-François Bellis, *Competition Law of the European Community* (Kluwer Law International, 2010)

Vogel, Louis, *Droit Européen de la Concurrence* (SAS LawLex, 2010)

Wakui, Masako, *Antimonopoly Law: Competition Law and Policy in Japan* (Arima Publishing, 2008)

Whish, Richard and David Bailey, *Competition Law* (Oxford University Press, 2012)

Wils, Wouter P.J., *Principles of European Antitrust Enforcement* (Hart Publishing, 2005)

Zimmer, Daniel (ed.), *The Goals of Competition Law* (Edward Elgar, 2012)

Index